ETHICS

BY THE SAME AUTHOR

Consumers and Wage-Earners:
The Ethics of Buying Cheap

$1.00

The Right to Work:

$1.00

Innocence and Ignorance:
M. S. Gillet, O. P.
J. Elliot Ross

$2.00

Sanctity and Social Service:

$1.00

Indulgences as a Social Factor in The Middle Ages:

$1.00

THE DEVIN-ADAIR COMPANY
23 East 26th Street   New York

ETHICS

From the Standpoint of Scholastic Philosophy

by

J. ELLIOT ROSS, Ph.D.

Formerly Professor and Associate
Administrative Director

SCHOOL OF RELIGION,
UNIVERSITY OF IOWA

NEW YORK
THE DEVIN-ADAIR COMPANY

Printed in the United States of America

*This book is gratefully dedicated to
my good friend*
HENRY GARRITY
*without whose interest and
encouragement it would
not have been*

Nihil obstat

ARTHUR J. SCANLAN, S.T.D.

Censor Librorum

Imprimatur

✠ PATRICK CARDINAL HAYES, D.D.

Archbishop of New York

CONTENTS

PART I. FUNDAMENTAL ETHICS

PART II. INDIVIDUAL ETHICS

PART III. SOCIAL ETHICS

PART I
FUNDAMENTAL ETHICS

ONE: *The Approach to Ethics*[1]

1. There Are Mechanical Laws. We all know that there are certain physical laws governing the operation of machines. If we feed molasses, instead of gasoline, to the carburetor of a Ford car the engine will not function. Or if we say we care nothing for tradition and custom, and are going to use good manila twine for an aerial, we shall never hear anything over our radio. Machines must be operated subject to definite limitations taken into consideration by their designers.

2. There Are Hygienic Laws. Analogous limitations apply to the machine of the human body. There are certain laws of health. If we violate them, if we go against the body's nature, we court disaster. Man's body was designed to function in a certain way, and it must be treated accordingly. The history of medical science has been a progressive understanding of the conditions under which the body effectively operates.

3. There Are Laws of Mental Hygiene. Moreover, it is not only man's body that has laws of right living—there are also laws of his mind. Modern psychologists have been learning more and more about mental hygiene. Bodily ills are frequently the result of wrong mental habits. The mind reacts upon the body as well as the body reacts upon the mind. Man is a unit. Some things are right and some things are wrong from the standpoint of the effective functioning of the whole man.

4. There Are Moral Laws. But man is not simply an animal, and not simply a rational animal—man is a social animal. Each individual man lives in relations with a number of other men. And from the standpoint of such relationships, of his proper functioning as a social animal, some things are right and some things are wrong. Man is more complex than an automobile or a radio set, more complex than an animal body, or even than an individual mind. Perfect physical health might be accom-

[1] A page listing principal works on Ethics will be found at end of book.

plished at the expense of right intellectual development, and keen intellectual development might be accomplished at the expense of right social relations. What is "right" or "wrong" for a man must envisage the whole hierarchy of his needs and purposes.

5. **Meaning of Moral "Right" and "Wrong."** Because man is not merely a machine, governed exclusively by mechanical laws, not merely an animal body governed by physiological laws, but a rational being endowed with some power of determining his own actions irrespective of mechanics and physiology, the words "right" and "wrong" applied to his acts take on an added meaning. And when we ask what acts of a man will fit in with his nature, and with the end his Designer, or Inventor or Creator —the name does not matter—had in view, we are imparting a new content to "right" and "wrong" in this connection. That new content is what we call "moral right" and "moral wrong." There are moral laws as well as mechanical or physiological or mental laws. We must learn as best we can what are these moral laws envisaging the whole of man. That is the task of Ethics.

6. **Moral Laws Guide to Most Efficient Living.** But it should be kept in mind that our investigation of these moral laws is largely from the same viewpoint as our investigation of the laws under which machines or human bodies work. That is, we wish to know how man can function most efficiently. Moral laws are not the whim of an irresponsible Deity, they are not mere prohibitions to take the joy out of living. On the contrary, moral laws are an expression of the way in which we must act if we are to get the most out of living, as mechanical laws are an expression of the way we must treat machines if we are to get the greatest efficiency out of them.

7. **Reason the Means for Learning the Moral Laws.** Ethics prescinds from any supernatural revelation that the Creator may have made, and depends upon reason as the means of finding the laws governing the morally right action of man. The familiar name of conscience is merely another term for reason applied to the determination here and now of what I ought morally to

do. And so Ethics can be defined as the *science of the moral rectitude of human acts as known by the light of reason*. The guide of Ethics is reason, just as much as it is the guide of physics or of astronomy. From an ethical standpoint, reason is to occupy itself in determining what acts are in conformity with man's hierarchical nature—bodily, mental, social—in the light of his relationship with his Designer, Inventor, Creator, and with other human beings who are equally related to this same Designer. Man's nature, therefore, is called the proximate norm of morality, and the nature of the Designer is called the ultimate norm of morality.

8. Moral Conceptions Influenced by Knowledge. Consequently, the more we know of God's nature through philosophy, or of our own nature through any of the sciences, the more accurately we can gauge morality. For instance, let us say that we have a moral obligation to safeguard our health with reasonable care. Obviously, what is considered reasonable care will depend upon the outlook of medical science at the particular time. The discovery of disease producing microbes revolutionized our idea of reasonable care.

9. Why Ethical Codes Differ. Since reason is our guide in Ethics, it is not surprising that different peoples at different times in the world's history have arrived at very different ethical codes, just as they have arrived at different conclusions by exercising their reason in the field of astronomy or physics. In fact, we should expect men widely separated in time and place to differ more in their ethics than in their physics and astronomy. For in the ethical field reason is subject to emotional disturbances having no place in astronomy.

10. Examples of Differences. At one time in India, for instance, it was thought to be the duty of a widow to be burnt with the body of her dead husband. Some tribes have thought it the duty of a son to put his aged father out of his misery. And no one can read the Pentateuch without realizing that human sacrifice was once practiced. It has even been said, if not with complete exactness at least with considerable foundation, that everything we look upon today as morally right was once considered morally wrong, and vice versa.

11. Evolution as Accounting for Differences. Prior to Darwin, these differences in ethical codes had been accounted for, generally speaking, as differences between what was true and what was false. But with the application of the theory of evolution to everything in the universe, many evolutionists began to take a different view of these differences in ethical codes. Such differences, they said, were not differences between true and false, any more than the differences between a dog and a horse were true or false. These ethical differences were merely the result of different evolutionary influences, and marked a different stage in evolution, as the horse marked a different stage in evolution from the dog.

12. Social Evolution. Man, it was claimed, has evolved from the primitive to the savage, the barbarous, and the civilized stages in his social organization. Each one of these stages had its appropriate moral outlook, and could have no other. Differences were not due to any divine Revelation for one group, nor to any greater insight into truth.

13. Moral Evolved from Non-Moral. Moreover, as the living had evolved from the non-living, as the sentient from the non-sentient, the intelligent from the non-intelligent, the human from the non-human, so the moral had evolved from the non-moral. There was a difference in degree but not a difference in kind between the moral and the non-moral.

14. Modicum of Truth in Evolutionary Position. Undoubtedly there was considerable truth in this position of evolutionists. Man's moral outlook is to a large extent conditioned by the point he has reached in social development. We can no more expect a savage to have the same moral code as a civilized Christian Englishman than we can expect him to have the same astronomy, or physics, or medicine. If Thomas Huxley and Herbert Spencer had been brought up among cannibals, they would probably have enjoyed eating human flesh.

15. Extreme Evolutionary Position. The error in the attitude of the extreme evolutionists, however, was in the conclusions they drew from their premises. Because the moral outlook of any group is dependent upon the social stage that group has reached, they concluded that there is no objective morality. Morally right and morally wrong are merely tags to indicate a result of evolutionary forces at a particular time or place. They paraphrased Hamlet, and maintained that nothing's either right or wrong but evolution makes it so. "True" and "false" cannot really be applied to questions of morality, but merely "customary" or "not customary."

16. Fallacy in the Evolutionary Position. On the face of it, there is a certain plausibility attaching to this evolutionary position, and it is small wonder it won numerous adherents. But the fallacy is evident when we apply the same reasoning in other fields. The astronomy of savages is very different from the astronomy of the Royal Astronomical Society. No evolutionist, however, would therefore conclude that astronomy is merely a question of social custom. He would not think of saying: "Because astronomy developed out of astrology, therefore it has no more claim on our credence than astrology. Everything is measured by its origins, not by the terminus of its development, or by any objective standard of true and false."

17. Evolutionists' Reasoning Applied to Medicine. Modern medicine can be traced back to primitive magic. Do evolutionists contend that therefore one might as well consult a witch-doctor or an Indian medicine man, as a member of the Royal Chirurgical Society? Not a bit of it. They admit that medicine has been getting closer and closer to the truth. We do not know everything about the workings of the human body, by any means, but we do believe that there are objective laws governing that body, that some things are helpful and some things are harmful to bodily health in spite of what savages may have thought about the matter.

18. Applied to Physics. Modern physics had its origins in a quaint animism. Everything that modern physics holds has been denied by some savage tribe or other. Is there then no objective physical truth? Is it just as true that thunder is the angry voice of some god, as that it is the result of electrical forces? No physicist judges the achievements of modern science by the science of Terra del Fuegans or Australian Bushmen.

19. Reductio ad absurdum. What is sauce for the goose is sauce for the gander. If all morality is discredited because different people at different times have held different moral codes, then all science is discredited because different people at different times have held different scientific viewpoints. If morality has no claim upon us because it developed from the non-moral, then the rational has no claim upon us because it developed from the non-rational.

20. The Truly Rational Viewpoint. The really reasonable viewpoint is to hold towards morality the same attitude one holds towards physics and astronomy. No matter how many mistakes have been made in the past, there is an objective truth, and reason is the ultimate judge. Are the reasons for holding to a geocentric universe sound or false? Are the reasons for holding that suicide is morally wrong, sound or false?

21. Method of Ethics Only Scientific. It is the purpose of Ethics to ask these questions. What are the reasons for holding that any particular act is morally right or morally wrong? We should come to our conclusions without regard to what primitive man or African savages held. The truly scientific method is to ask for evidence, not to rule evidence out of court to start with on the unscientific assumption that there can be no objective truth in a particular field.

22. Essential Distinction Between Morality and Social Custom. Now even on the basis of evolution, morality is distinguished in some way from social custom. The horse *may* have evolved from the dog, but it is different from a dog, and zoologists can describe the difference. How would the difference between social custom and morality be described? It consists in the fact that morality implies a reference to some Being above men, to whom all men are responsible; whereas social custom is recognized as purely human.

23. This Distinction Universal. All people who have any moral code at all, have distinguished between social custom and morality. We say, for instance, that it is against our present social customs to cut lettuce with a knife. But no one dreams that there is any moral implication in this custom. Even the tenderest conscience can cut the tenderest lettuce with a knife and feel no remorse. But to cut an enemy's throat is against something more than social custom—it is against morality. Why? Because to cut a man's throat brings one into conflict with his rights, and those rights rest ultimately on the conception of some Supreme Being to Whom all men are responsible.

24. Supreme Being Necessary for Morality. Morality, then, includes several elements. First, there is the belief that back of all human beings stands some sort of Supreme Being. The assumption of morality is that a Supreme Being has rights over each human being, and that certain consequences follow therefrom. Sometimes items in a moral code concern only the relations of the individual to the Supreme Being. At other times, morality may concern the relations of one man to another man. But these human relations do not take on the essential element of morality unless they are referred back in some way to a Supreme Being. This reference may imply a specific act of will by the Supreme Being, or it may imply only a general will on His part that each man should respect the rights of all other men.

25. Supreme Being Must Care About Human Acts. Secondly, there is underlying all morality the assumption that the Supreme Being cares about what human beings do. Presumably, we could have a Supreme Being who would care no more about what human beings thought of Him than Mussolini cares what I think or say of the dictator of Italy. Likewise, the Supreme Being might not care any more what one human being does to another than He cares what one amoeba does to another. But if the Supreme Being does not care what human beings do, then there is no morality. No people has ever put any act into the category of morality without believing that the Supreme Being cared about that act.

26. Free Will Necessary for Morality. And finally, there is usually implied in all morality some power of self-determination on the part of the human agent.

27. Morality Consistent with Evolution. These elements of morality—freedom of the will and a Supreme Being who cares how that freedom is exercised—are not affected by the mere fact of particular items in a moral code having been once mere social custom, or by the evolution of the moral from the non-moral. There were men, before evolution was heard of, who denied human freedom and the existence of a Supreme Being; and there are evolutionists who accept human freedom and a Supreme Being. Whether a Supreme Being exists Who cares what the little human ants crawling on this speck of dust do, or whether those ants have a power of doing one thing rather than another, are questions apart from evolution. Those who assume that the study of comparative morality has proved that morality has no more authority than social custom, are indulging in an evident *non-sequitur*. Still more flimsy is the assumption that because "moral" is derived from "mores," meaning custom, therefore "moral" is the same as customary. It would be equally apt to argue that "calculus" is a study of mineralogy, because "calculus" means a little stone. Words can evolve into entirely different meanings much more readily than dogs can evolve into horses. I suppose that our modern word "let" has evolved from the Elizabethan "let." But when Hamlet said, "I'll make a ghost of him that lets me," he was using the word in a very different sense from the present day professor who might say to a pupil, "I'll make a logician of you if you let me."

28. Two Categories: Socially Customary, Morally Obligatory. We have, then, two categories in regard to the actions of human beings—the category of socially customary, and the category of morally obligatory. Undoubtedly men have differed very widely in what they have placed in these two categories. And sometimes men have come to look upon a particular action as morally obligatory because it is a custom of long-standing, or because they were told to do so by some authority. But because some mistakes were made in the long history of mankind, does not mean that therefore we should throw up our hands and say that there is no objective truth in this field of morality, or that human reason is unable to reach the truth.

29. Custom Does Not Create Category of Morally Obligatory. Custom sometimes transfers an act from the category of morally indifferent to the category of morally obligatory; or from the category of morally obligatory to the category of morally indifferent. But that does not mean that custom creates the category of the morally obligatory. The objective existence of the category of morally obligatory acts depends upon whether or not a Supreme Being exists to whom human beings have a certain relationship. The existence of a Supreme Being is a legitimate object for the exercise of human reason, just as the existence of atoms or electrons is a legitimate field for human reason. A Supreme Being's existence is not to be ruled out by the fact that human beings from time to time have differed as to His nature or attributes or the relationship between Him and themselves; any more than the existence of electricity is to be ruled out by the fact that from time to time men have differed as to its nature and attributes.

30. Moral Values Differ from Exchange Values. It is in this idea of the existence of an objective Supreme Being with whom human acts can have some relationship that moral values differ essentially from exchange values. For there cannot be said to be an absolute objective exchange value. By very definition, exchange value implies its creation by social custom or economic conditions. There is no absolute objective standard of exchange value, corresponding to the idea of an objective Supreme Being, so that the closer we approximate to a true understanding of this objective standard, the more correct we are in attributing value to any particular thing.

31. No Objective Exchange Value. For instance, we look upon gold as valuable, and savages look upon glass beads as valuable.

Neither gold nor glass beads have any intrinsic quality making them valuable. Whatever value they have is a question of social custom, or of the economic and industrial stage in which the group happens to be. Where the custom is to attribute value to gold, there gold is valuable; where it is customary to attribute value to glass beads, there glass beads are valuable. There is no objective standard of value by which we can say that Americans are right in attributing value to gold and savages are wrong in attributing value to glass beads. As we pass into some other economic stage, some other medium of exchange may be substituted for gold.

32. False Analogy Between Moral Values and Exchange Values. "By analogy," it is argued, when we look upon polygamy as morally wrong, and many savages look upon polygamy as morally right, our viewpoints are merely different. One viewpoint cannot be said to be truer than the other, but merely to be indicative of a different social organization. Environment, which includes social and economic development, naturally produces a different set of moral values as it produces a different set of exchange values. As one set of exchange values is not truer than another or better than another by any absolute standard, so one set of moral values is not truer or better than another by any absolute standard. It is all a question of relativity, of what is better considering the particular environment and stage of evolution.

33. Evolution Consistent with Objective Morality. But the analogy between moral values and exchange values does not really hold unless it can be shown that there is no objective Supreme Being with Whom human beings have certain relationships. The identification of morality with social custom and the rejection of all objective morality is not a legitimate inference from the theory of evolution as applied to human society. Whatever bearing evolution has on the particular problem of an objective morality is merely indirect, because of its bearing on theism in general. If evolution were inconsistent with a belief in a Supreme Being, then no evolutionist could believe in objective morality. But we have too many first class scientists who are evolutionists and also theists to hold any such essential incompatibility between evolution and theism.

34. Objective Morality Not Entirely Static. However, all objective morality is not necessarily entirely static. There can be a development of morality, an evolution. And scientific studies may indirectly affect moral concepts. Morality can be objective in the sense of depending upon the relationship of men to a Supreme Being, and yet men can have a deepening knowledge of what is implied by this relationship. And it may also happen that social custom or changed environment may influence the application of some principle flowing from the relationship between men and a Supreme Being.

35. Evolution of Morality. For instance, we have the principle that extra-marital sexual satisfaction, or desire therefor, is against the moral code. This is based upon the belief that the Supreme Being intended marriage as the means of propagating the race, and extra-marital satisfaction would endanger marriage. But even in the Bible there is a clear indication of an evolution of what is meant by marriage, in that the polygamous marriages of patriarchal times disappeared. Consequently the range of what was meant by extra-marital satisfaction was increased.

36. How Social Custom May Affect Morality. There is a still clearer illustration of how evolution in social custom may affect morality and transfer an act from the category of morally indifferent to the category of morally wrong. When everyone went naked, all parts of the human body were such a familiar sight that they aroused no special sexual thought. Nakedness was morally indifferent. However, after men had worn clothing for generations, a complete exposure of the body was sufficient to create sexual thoughts and desires. And so the mere evolution of a social custom can take an act from the category "morally indifferent" and transfer it to the category "morally forbidden."

37. Increased Scientific Knowledge May Affect Application of Moral Principles. Similarly, what was "morally obligatory" may become "morally forbidden." For instance, increasing scientific knowledge can give a greater insight into the application of moral principles, and so change the moral character of an act. We have, for example, the moral principle that each one is bound to take reasonable care of his health. This principle is based on the belief that the Creator has given us life, and that He wants us to cherish the gift. In the early nineteenth century, under certain conditions, reasonable care would have been interpreted as implying blood-letting. But with the advance of medical science, those same conditions today might imply blood transfusion. Greater knowledge of the human body has taken the act of blood-letting under certain conditions out of the category of "morally obligatory," and has placed it in the category "morally wrong." For to lose blood would be to endanger life, instead of to save it.

38. Formal Morality of Acts Affected by Knowledge. As far as blood-letting and blood transfusion are concerned, the acts objectively remain the same. Given identical conditions, blood-letting always had the same effect upon the health that it has today. Men were simply mistaken at one time in thinking that it was helpful when it was really harmful. But there are other cases, where a changed environment may make what was at one time indifferent become really a violation of the rights of others.

39. Changed Conditions May Affect Even Objective Morality. This can be shown from the application of the principle that any one individual should not needlessly endanger the lives or safety of others. In the eighteenth century, the imbibing of a small amount of alcohol, let us say a pint of 2.75 strength, was not dangerous to the person drinking nor to those around him. But today when we live in an automobile age and those who are not driving cars are dodging them; when in factories, on railroads, almost every hour of the day the safety of thousands depends on the efficiency of others in handling themselves, drinking may be a different matter. The amount of alcohol that a hundred years ago was a matter of indifference to everyone, may now make an individual a source of danger to others.

40. Reasonable Respect for Lives of Others Affected by Machine Age. Suppose merely for the sake of argument, that science demonstrates that drinking a pint of 2.75 beer will reduce the average individual's sensory and motor responses to such an extent that he becomes dangerous in handling machinery. Then by the moral principle that one should not needlessly endanger the lives of others, he should refrain from drinking—at least when he is to handle machinery within the time that the effect of the alcohol lasts. The moral principle remains the same, but the application of the principle has changed by the evolution of human society into a dominantly machine society.

41. Distinction Between Social Custom and Objective Facts. Similarly, I suppose that it was bad manners—against social custom—to expectorate on the floor of a railroad coach long before Pasteur laid the foundation for a germ theory. Now it is looked upon not only as bad manners but also as contrary to the laws of health. But this does not prove that social custom and the laws of health are one and the same identical thing; and by the same token, social custom is not identical with moral laws. Increasing knowledge of the laws of health has had to combat many a social custom—as common drinking cups. It was once customary for women to have wasp-like waists through corsets, but that was not therefore healthful.

42. Professional Ethics. One thing perhaps, that has led to a confusion of custom with morals, has been the loose use of the word ethics as indicating the custom of certain groups. We speak of the ethics of the legal and medical professions to cover certain rules of professional conduct. Thus it is unethical for physicians to advertise. But it is not *morally* wrong for a physician to violate this rule of his profession, and it would be better if some word were used that did not imply morality.

43. Authority Does Not Create Category of Morality. Nor does the fact that moral attitudes have sometimes been imposed from above by rulers prove that there is no objective morality. The Old Man, or the King, or the Priest, may sometimes have compelled the people to accept their enactments as having a divine sanction. Perhaps the theory of the divine right of kings originated in some such way. But hygienic—or unhygienic—attitudes have also been imposed from above without anybody concluding therefrom that medical science is merely a question of imposition by authority and has no basis in objective fact.

44. But Custom and Authority May Be Right. Whether or not any particular act is morally right or morally wrong is a question of evidence. The conviction that a certain act is morally wrong may have developed out of social custom or may have been imposed by authority, and yet reason may today be able to show that custom or authority had somehow hit on what was a legitimate ethical conclusion. But in considering ethical proofs, it must be borne in mind that moral questions differ from mathematical or physical questions, and that as they are of a different nature, ethical questions are not susceptible of the same kind of proof as are chemical or physical questions.

45. Nature of Ethical Proof. Physical Science, as Eddington pointed out, deals only with pointer readings. Generally speaking, questions of physical science can be isolated and subjected to the laboratory method. But ethical questions cannot be reduced to pointer readings, and as a usual thing they cannot be investigated in a laboratory. Therefore, it is as unreasonable to demand the same kind of proof for ethical questions as for physical questions, as it would be to demand one of our senses to do the work of all the others. Each division of mental efforts has its own field, its own methods, its own kind of proof.

46. Ethical Proof Not Weaker Than Scientific Proof. This is not to say, however, that ethical proof is weaker than much scientific proof. The exactitude of physical science is frequently overrated, as can readily be seen by reading such modern books as *The Mysterious Universe,* by Sir James Jeans, or *The Nature of the Physical World,* by A. S. Eddington. The deeper physicists delve into the nature of matter and of light and of electricity, the more they lose of their mid-Victorian cocksureness. There are many hypotheses in science, resting largely on a *belief* that some day they *may* be proved. But then, again, they may not be proved, for the march of scientific progress is lined with the wrecks of abandoned theories. And surely no scientist would want to say anything stronger about the unsatisfactoriness of any moral principle than what Eddington says about electronic activity—*"Something unknown is doing we know not what."* No one has brought out more clearly than Prof. Robert Millikan the tentative character of any scientific conclusion. Those who are interested should read his *Evolution in Science and Religion,* a series of lectures delivered at Yale. In fact, when a new scientific theory is proposed one is almost reminded of those words of St. Peter in the *Acts,* "The feet of them who are about to bury thee are already at the door"; or of those lines in a once popular song, "one more task for the casket-maker, one more job for the undertaker."

47. Conviction from Ethical Proof May Be Firm. Ethical proof, however, can be just as strong and conclusive as the proofs offered by any of the social sciences—history, political economy, sociology. And although the proof may not in the abstract be as demonstrative as the proof for a proposition in geometry, yet the resulting conviction can be just as firm. In fact, one might almost say that ethical convictions can be stronger than convictions in mathematics. For certainly no one can have stronger conviction than this, that he should lay down his life for his conviction. And there have been innumerable men who have been willing to suffer loss of money, friends, reputation, even life itself, rather than do what they were convinced was ethically wrong. The Anglican Archbishop Whately, in his essay, "Some Historical Doubts Regarding the Existence of Napoleon Bonaparte," clearly reduces to an absurdity the position of those who require physical certainty in the social sciences.

48. Appreciation of Ethical Proof Needs Moral Preparation. Ethical proof differs from scientific proof, too, in that it needs a moral preparation to appreciate its force. In this, Ethics is similar to aesthetics. One must know something about art, he must have taste to start with, if he is to appreciate the reasons why one picture is good and another poor. In one of his discourses before the University of Oxford, Newman brings this out with persuasive clearness. "Is not this the error, the common and fatal error, of the world," says Newman, "to think itself a judge of Religious Truth without preparation of heart? 'I am the Good Shepherd, and know My sheep and am known of Mine.' 'He goeth before them, and the sheep follow Him, for they know His voice.' 'The pure in heart shall see God'; 'to the meek mysteries are revealed'; 'he that is spiritual judgeth all things, the darkness comprehendeth it not.' Gross eyes see not; heavy ears hear not. But in the schools of the world the ways toward Truth are considered high roads open to all men, however disposed, at all times. Truth is to be approached without homage. Everyone is considered on a level with his neighbor; or rather the powers of the intellect, acuteness, sagacity, subtlety, and depth, are thought guides into Truth. Men consider that they have as full a right to discuss religious subjects, as if they were themselves religious. They will enter upon the most sacred points of Faith at the moment, at their pleasure,—if it so happen, in a careless frame of mind, in their hours of recreation, over the winecup. Is it wonderful that they so frequently end in becoming indifferentists, and conclude that Religious Truth is but a name, that all men are right and all wrong, from witnessing externally the multitude of sects and parties and from the clear consciousness they possess within, that their own inquiries end in darkness?"

49. Formal Morality. So far we have been insisting upon the existence of an objective morality, in spite of all the differences between one age and another as to what is thought to be the content of the moral code. This objective morality, apart from the concept of the agent at the time of acting is called *material* morality. What the agent thinks is called *formal* morality. And as far as the relationship of the individual with the Creator is concerned the important thing is formal morality. Paradoxically, we may say that an individual may sometimes have a moral obligation to do something that is objectively wrong.

50. Examples of Formal and Material Morality. The distinction between formal and material morality will be clearer through a few examples. Let us suppose, for instance, that in filling a prescription the drug clerk inadvertently put the wrong label on a bottle. The nurse, following the label, thinks that she is administering the proper medicine, when in reality it is something that under the circumstances will kill the patient. Objectively, the act of the nurse is homicide, the taking of the life of a human being. But formally, her act is good, because she thinks it is good, and she has no way of knowing that an error has been made in filling the prescription.

51. Another Example. Reversing the situation, suppose that a nurse wishes to hasten the death of a rich uncle so that she can come into a legacy. She gives what she thinks is injurious to the man, but which in reality is helpful. Objectively the act of the nurse is good, because the result is good. But formally, her act is bad because she thinks it is bad.

52. Mistake in Regard to Fact. In the cases just suggested, the mistake of the nurse is in regard to fact, rather than in regard to a moral principle. She knows well enough that she should not take the life of the patient, and is mistaken as to the appropriateness of the medicine for taking his life. But the mistake can be about a moral principle, as well as about a fact.

53. Mistake in Regard to Principle. Let us suppose a savage tribe in which the tribal traditions impose on a son the moral obligation of putting his aged and suffering father out of existence. The son growing up in this environment never questions the obligation. As far as his own conscience is concerned, he is morally obliged to take his father's life. Materially it is murder, but formally it is not. And that son if he spared his father would be failing morally. In sparing his father, he would be doing what is materially good, but what is formally wrong.

54. Summary. Ethical systems can be broadly divided into absolute and conditional. Since this text is concerned with an objective, absolute moral system, it is essential to get this idea clearly at the very beginning. For this reason the subject is approached from the analogy of the objective laws in other fields. Then it is shown that although custom, authority, social and economic conditions may often account for particular items in a moral code, they do not create the category of morally right and wrong. This category depends upon the existence of a Supreme Being who cares how human beings use their power of self-determination, free will. The attitude of this Supreme Being towards human conduct is independent of social custom, evolution, authority —hence objective absolute. However, He is concerned with men doing what they conscientiously believe to be right, therefore it is necessary to understand the distinction between *formal* and *material* morality. It is material morality that is objective and absolute. Prescinding from revelation, reason is the means of making formal morality and material morality coincide. And although the scientific method cannot be applied to ethics, nevertheless, with the proper moral preparation, certainty of conviction can be achieved in this field.

SUGGESTED READINGS

1. Read essay by Bishop Whately called "Some Historical Doubts Regarding the Existence of Napoleon Bonaparte." This is an extremely clever *reductio ad absurdum* of the position of those who require physical certainty in moral sciences.
2. Read Newman's *Grammar of Assent* for a thorough analysis of the process by which the mind comes to assent to any proposition.
3. Make a comparison between the articles on Ethics in the *Catholic Encyclopedia* and the *Encyclopaedia Britannica*.

QUESTIONS

1. Is there an analogy between moral laws and mechanical and hygienic laws?
2. Does the observance of moral laws make for efficiency in living, as the observance of mechanical laws makes for mechanical efficiency?
3. In ethics, what means is used to learn moral laws?
4. How do you explain that at different times and places men have arrived at different conceptions of moral laws?
5. Is there an evolution in morals?
6. What is included in idea of morality?
7. Is morality simply social custom?

TWO: *Human Acts*[1]

55. Definition. Ethics is that branch of philosophy which deals with morality, and for that reason it is frequently called "moral philosophy." Sometimes Ethics is defined as the moral rectitude of human acts considered in the light of natural reason. But it seems better to call it a branch of philosophy rather than a science. For although "science" is sometimes used in a broad sense, as merely indicating classified or systematic knowledge, and so is applied to sociology or to history, to many the word "science" connotes the laboratory method. Philosophy as well as science implies systematic knowledge; and philosophy further implies an investigation of causes, whereas the physical sciences are concerned with a description of sequences. Since the distinction between philosophy and theology is that philosophy is restricted to what can be learned by reason alone, as apart from a supernatural revelation, there is no need of adding to the definition, "considered in the light of natural reason." Moreover, Ethics embraces material as well as formal morality, whereas human acts would restrict it to formal morality. For a human act is voluntary, free, and directed to a known end.

56. The Norm of Morality. Naturally, Ethics is closely related to other branches of philosophy. From natural theology it accepts the postulates of a Supreme Being, the Creator of human beings, their complete dependence on Him, and His concern with what men do. With this as a basis, Ethics works out the duties of men to the Creator, and their rights and duties with regard to one another. The nature of God is the *ultimate norm of morality,* and the *proximate norm is man's own nature as a creature.* By conformity or difformity with these norms, acts take on the quality of moral goodness or badness.

57. Ethics Presupposes Free Will. From psychology, Ethics accepts the postulates of intelligence and freedom in men. It is true

[1] For a fuller discussion of human acts, cf. Cronin, *Science of Ethics,* Ch. II.

that some psychologists do not admit free will and intelligence. And on such a basis Ethics is impossible. For if there be no intelligence and no freedom, then a man's acts are as mechanical as those of a Ford car. There is no moral difference between the brakes of an unoccupied car parked on a hill slipping, and as a result the car running over a man; and the act of a man driving a car deliberately—if we can use "deliberately" to describe what by hypothesis is purely mechanical—running over a child playing in a street because he does not take the trouble to stop the car. For any morality there must be some freedom, or power of self-determination, in the agent.

58. Relation of Ethics and Psychology. Ethics and psychology are related, too, because both have for their fields the acts of human beings. But psychology considers all actions of men; whereas Ethics is concerned only with actions having a moral color. Thus psychology may be deeply interested in sleep or in purely reflex actions, but Ethics is not. And even where both disciplines deal with the same act, they do so from different standpoints. Memory, for instance, is for psychology merely a process of recalling ideas or sensible images; for Ethics it is the occasion of calling up desires for conduct either good or bad, as the memory of prayers at a mother's knee may lead to praying, or the memory of alcoholic stimulation may lead to intoxication.

59. Relation of Ethics and Economics. Much of political economy, of course, has no ethical bearing; but some economic questions, such as usury, are also ethical. Many economic relations involve problems of justice, and the principles of justice lie within the field of Ethics. For the correct application of such principles to economic questions political economy must furnish the data. Thus Ethics may establish the right of men to living wages, but in any concrete circumstances it will be for economists to determine the content of a living wage. Consequently, Ethics and political economy should be mutually helpful. Each should cheerfully recognize the province of the other.

60. Relation of Ethics and Sociology. The relation of Ethics to sociology is very similar to the relation between Ethics and political economy. Much of sociology is beyond the scope of Ethics, but much also depends upon ethical principles. This is notably true of marriage, family relations, and the right of the individual against the State. One of the greatest safeguards against an ultimately hurtful sociology is the clear recognition of an objective moral good and bad. On the other hand, sociology may often furnish the factual basis for ethical judgments. The two disciplines should go hand in hand, with appreciation for the fact that what is ethically wrong cannot be sociologically desirable.

61. Relation of Ethics to Civil Law. In these days when the omnipotent and totalitarian State has become an actuality in several countries, the relation between Ethics and civil law is extremely important. Many civil laws have no ethical implications, and others simply put the power of the State behind ethical dictates. But it should be strongly insisted upon, that, in the words of our Declaration of Independence, the individual has certain inalienable rights which the State should not violate. God and the moral law are above the State and above any autocratic ruler. The best safeguard for the individual is a recognition of this fact.

62. Method of Ethics. As we have said, Ethics is a branch of philosophy, rather than a science, and consequently the method of Ethics will be philosophical rather than scientific. Several different methods, however, may be distinguished under the broad designation of philosophical. The *intuitive method* looks upon ethical truths as known directly once the subject and predicate of a proposition are understood. The *inductive method* proceeds from the particular to the general, drawing a moral principle from the examination of a great number of individual cases— for example, the unanimity of individuals holding to the wrongfulness of marriage between brothers and sisters points to a general law underlying this view. The *deductive method* proceeds from the general to the particular.

63. Ethics Mainly Deductive. To use the intuitive or the deductive method exclusively is unreasonable. It would seem perfectly clear that we must start with at least one primary truth that cannot be proved, else we should never get anywhere. Such intuitively known truths, however, are probably very few, perhaps being restricted to the general principle, *do good, avoid evil*. Sometimes it is necessary to draw upon experience to establish a proposition, as that society is natural to man, or in making specific the content of a general principle. Thus medical science, based on experience, will dictate what is necessary for reasonable care of life. However, Scholastic Ethics is mainly deductive.

64. Conscience. It is true that many persons speak of conscience as the "voice of God," or the "still small voice telling us right from wrong," as if we had some faculty for intuitively in all circumstances knowing good from evil. But strictly speaking, conscience is merely reason telling us here and now that an act is good or bad, or that we have an obligation of performing or refraining from particular acts. Reason is under the same limitation in regard to morality as in regard to anything else. We are conditioned by our general knowledge and upbringing. And the facility with which we reason on moral questions can be increased through exercise, just as by practice it can be increased in the field of mathematics. The man who deliberately goes against the dictates of his reason by doing what he knows is morally wrong blunts his faculty of distinguishing between right and wrong. Whereas one who always acts as his reason (that is to say, his conscience) dictates in moral matters acquires a keenness in deciding accurately about moral affairs.

65. Conscience and Emotion. Moreover, moral actions are always mixed with emotion. Reason is apt to be swayed by desire. The power to deceive one's self is almost unlimited. Thus a man under the influence of love may make the most obvious mistake of judgment in marrying a woman. If this be true where no moral question is involved—assuming that both are morally free to marry—it is also true when there is a question of morality. The wise thing, therefore, is to form the judgment before the emotions are aroused, and then to hold fast to this judgment when the emotions begin to tug at the leash of reason.

66. Only Human Acts Are Moral. In so far as formal morality is concerned, an act must be human to be moral. A human act is *voluntary, free and directed towards a known end.* Therefore anything affecting the voluntariness, freedom or knowledge of the agent at the time of acting affects his moral responsibility for the act.

I. VOLUNTARINESS

67. Division of Voluntariness. Voluntariness may be *perfect* or *imperfect; simple* or *conditional; direct* or *indirect; positive* or *negative, virtual* or *interpretative.* Only those divisions between semicolons are necessarily mutually exclusive. For it will be seen from the explanation to follow that one and the same act may possess perfect, simple, direct, positive, and actual voluntariness.

68. Voluntariness is

(1) *perfect,* when we clearly know, and fully intend the act, and its direct consequences—as a man fully awake, shooting a burglar with intent to kill.

imperfect, when we know the act only obscurely, and do it more or less unwillingly:—as a man partially aroused from a sound sleep, and in this condition firing at a burglar.

(2) *simple,* when we will the act merely for itself.

conditional, when we will the act only as a condition necessary to obtain something else:—thus, a ship's captain who throws his cargo overboard to save his ship, directly wills the destruction of the cargo, but not *simply,* as he does it only to gain a different end.

(3) *positive,* when we will to perform the acts necessary to accomplish a certain purpose.

negative, when we will not to take the necessary means:—a man who wills not to study for an examination, *negatively* wills his failure.

(4) *actual,* when we think of and consent to what we do, at the moment of performing the act.

virtual, when the thing done is a result of a former intention which has passed out of the field of consciousness at the time of acting; *e.g.,* one who deliberately lights a cigar and then gives his whole attention to something else, virtually wills his every puff.

interpretative, when, though we have never actually willed a particular action, we would have willed it had it been properly presented to us:—as a man in China, who had never heard of baptism, is said to have baptism of desire provided he would have desired it had he known God wished him to receive it.

(5) *direct,* when we will the thing in itself either as an end or as a means.

indirect, when we will the thing not in itself but only because we have willed another action which caused this one.

69. Indirect Voluntariness. Direct and indirect voluntariness suggests two interesting and important questions. One concerns the imputability of the consequences of an act, the other the imputability of the means used to attain an end, usually put in the form: Does the end justify the means?

70. Imputability of Consequences. If a man intends directly only one action but that action has certain foreseen consequences, which he does not directly intend, and at which he is really displeased, is he responsible for those consequences? Supposing that the act itself is lawful, but some of its consequences are evil, is he bound (anticipating our definition of "evil" and "bound") to refrain from the act?

71. When Consequences Are Not Imputable. [2] The theory is clear, though its application is often extremely difficult and gives occasion for much casuistry. Such an action is unlawful except under the following conditions: "(1) The action, viewed in it-

[2] McDonald, *Principles of Moral Science,* Bk. II, Ch. II.

self, is good or at least indifferent; (2) the agent does not intend the evil effect, but only the good (it is well to add in some cases: and provided there is no danger of subsequent evil consent or intention); (3) the good effect is produced as immediately as— that is, not by means of—the bad; and (4) there is a sufficiently weighty reason for permitting the evil effect." [3]

72. Application of These Principles. Let us suppose that a person whose clothes have caught fire jumps into a lake to extinguish the blaze. The fire is extinguished, but incidentally the person drowns. Is he guilty of suicide? No, because all the conditions we have enumerated are present. The action of jumping into the lake was in itself indifferent; the agent did not intend drowning, but the extinguishing of the fire; the good effect—putting out the fire—is not caused by the drowning; and there was a sufficient reason to justify the action, namely the avoiding of the agony of death by fire.

73. A Graphic Expression of These Principles. A diagram will make these principles clearer. In figure 1 we have the case of direct volition. A represents the act and C the direct and only consequences. If C be evil then A is never allowable. Figure 2 shows both good (Cg) and evil (Cb) consequences following from A. Since the good consequences are caused by the evil, it is not lawful to perform A. Finally we have the case shown in figure 3. Here good consequences and bad flow from A with equal immediacy; that is, the good consequences are not secured through the evil; the good consequences outweigh the bad, as represented by the larger size of Cg as compared with Cb; and Cb is not intended by the agent.

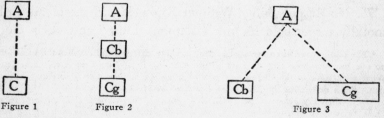

Figure 1   Figure 2   Figure 3

[3] Lehmkuhl, *Theol. Moral.*, I, No. 12.

74. Does the End Ever Justify the Means? [4] When the means are indifferent—*i.e.,* neither good nor bad in themselves—then they may receive a certain extrinsic justification from a good end, and it is perfectly lawful to use them; but when the means are intrinsically evil, no end, no matter how good and how far outweighing the evil, ever justifies them. The nearest approach to what might seem the end's justification of the means is to be found in the case of a man bent on committing a certain crime, when it is allowable to persuade him to commit a lesser crime of *the same genus.* Thus a man who intends to steal from a poor widow and cannot be dissuaded from actual theft, may lawfully be urged to rob a millionaire miser instead. At first sight this may seem evil advice, but a more careful analysis shows that the man has already committed theft in his heart and is obstinately determined to commit it in fact. The advice that he steal from the rich miser, simply keeps him from that aggravation of his guilt which would be added to it by the widow's poverty. Hence the act of persuading him is justifiable.

II. Influences Making Actions Less Human [5]

75. Basis of Moral Responsibility. Man's moral responsibility is based upon the possession and the exercise of two faculties—the cognitive and the volitional. Hence anything which reduces the influence of these faculties upon one's actions reduces one's responsibility. In proportion to the lessening of one's knowledge or freedom one's culpability for one's action is lessened.

76. No Responsibility Without Knowledge. First of all, to be morally responsible for one's acts one must know their moral

---

[4] The Jesuits have often been accused of teaching that the end justifies the means, but no one has ever been able to point to this teaching in any book by a reputable Jesuit. What gives color to the charge is a misunderstanding of these two points under discussion. For a defense of the Jesuits, see *The Catholic Mind.*

[5] Cf. Maher, *Psychology,* Chs. XVIII, XIX; Janet, *L'Automatisme* (Paris, Alcan, 1889); James, *Principles of Psychology,* Ch. on "Habit"; Jules Payot, *Education of the Will;* O'Malley and Walsh, *Essays in Medicine,* Chs. V, IX, X, XVII, XXVII.

character.[6] No matter how serious may be the action objectively, there can be no formal sin unless the agent knows what he is doing. This is perfectly evident in the case of a person walking in his sleep and in that condition of somnolence shooting another. It is likewise true, though perhaps less generally acknowledged, that there is no formal sin if the agent be entirely awake but does not *know* that what he is doing is wrong. And this applies both when he is ignorant of the nature and the consequences of the action, as when a nurse gives a deadly poison fully convinced that it is a curative medicine; and when he knows the character of the action but thinks it is lawful, as in a savage killing his suffering and infirm father, because his tribe's code of morals commands this as a filial duty.

77. Distinction Between Vincible and Invincible Ignorance. In this connection, however, a very important distinction must always be kept in mind,—that between *vincible* and *invincible* ignorance. When the means to remove one's ignorance could not be taken, then the ignorance is invincible, and hence inculpable. Moral impossibility is sufficient here, and the fact that we do not suspect our own ignorance (when this is not due to failure on our part to take any steps we should have taken) constitutes such impossibility. When the ignorance can be removed, it is vincible. One who acts under vincible ignorance is morally responsible for his deeds.

78. Ignorance of Law and Ignorance of Fact. Again, it is important to remember the distinction between *ignorance of fact* and *ignorance of the law,* because it has great bearing upon the system of probabilism. One who is ignorant of the law may understand the objective facts of a case very thoroughly, but does not know that a law forbids or commands certain actions under the circumstances. To take an example from ecclesiastical law, an ignorant Spaniard, who in his own country is not bound to abstain from meat on Friday, may know perfectly well the day of the week when in France, but he is ignorant of the fact that

---

[6] Cf. Cathrein. *Moralphilosophie,* Vol. I, p. 94 ff.

the ecclesiastical law of abstinence binds in that country. One who is ignorant of fact may know the law, but does not realize that a particular fact comes under the law, because he is mistaken about its real nature. Thus a hunter seeing an animal moving in the brush may be thoroughly convinced that the object is a bear, though in reality it is a man. He knows the commandment, Thou shalt not kill; but he does not know that this commandment forbids his killing this particular animal, because he does not know that this animal is a man.

79. No Moral Responsibility Without Freedom. So much, then, for ignorance as reducing man's responsibility. But the cognitive faculty is not the only one conditioning his culpability. To be imputable an act must be free, and any influence lessening freedom just so far lessens the guilt or merit of the deed. The will may be compared to the driver of a chariot. Normally he is in control of his steeds, either consciously or because he has habituated them to certain ways of acting. But it requires constant watchfulness. If they be at all spirited, if they be easily scared, if they have strong impulses of rivalry, the task will sometimes be exceedingly difficult and may even be entirely beyond his powers. The steeds in man are his passions, and unless they are broken as a horse is broken, unless they are trained to obey the touch of the will on the lines, they may bolt and become uncontrollable. The passions or emotions may be defined as movements of the sensuous appetitive faculty which impels towards what is good and averts from what is evil.[7]

80. Division of Emotions. The division of the emotions is not particularly important. No satisfactory division has ever been made.[8] But what is important is to train the emotions to obedience, to watch them closely, to keep one's hand constantly on the reins. And for the purposes of practical living four emotions may be singled out as being especially dangerous—*lust, anger, envy, sadness*. These will be treated in their appropriate places in specific Ethics.

[7] Cf. Mercier, *Manual of Modern Scholastic Philosophy*, Vol. I, p. 221.
[8] Cf. Maher, *Psychology*, 8th ed., p. 446.

81. Degrees of Freedom. In so far as the movement of the emotions precedes the command or consent of the will, it is called *antecedent*. If entirely antecedent it is *motus primo-primus* and lacks guilt; if after semi-full advertence the craving is not repelled it is *motus secundo-primus,* and it is not mortally sinful even regarding matter seriously sinful; full consent is *motus secundus,* and in serious matter is mortal sin provided there was sufficient knowledge. But the knowledge by itself does not make a serious action mortally sinful, because it may happen that for some reason the will does not fully consent to the movement even after complete advertence of the intellect. By the time the intellect takes cognizance of the arousing of the passions, they may have become inflamed beyond the will's control. They may have run away, as it were, to revert to the figure of the driver.[9]

82. Freedom Influenced by Habit. The training of the emotions is nothing more nor less than the acquirement of good habits; letting the passions run loose is simply the acquirement of bad habits. We cannot help forming habits any more than a stream can help following some channel. The course may be straight and true and directed towards some definite end, as in a canal; or it may be crooked and irregular and wandering off into all sorts of byways:—but course there must be. In a similar fashion the stimuli entering the nervous system must follow some course of discharge, and the oftener a particular stimulus follows a particular course, the more likely it is to follow the same channel in the future. The more easily it follows any one course, the less conscious direction it needs from the will. And if its course be very deeply cut, it may happen that it will find its outlet before the intellect notifies the will of any need for action, or it may override the attempt of the will to divert it.

83. Importance of Habits. Habits, therefore, or the acquired facility of acting in a particular way,[10] are especially important in any discussion of the influences making actions less human.

[9] Cf. Noldin, *Theol. Mor.,* Vol. I, No. 46, 52.
[10] W. J. Young has defined habit as "perfected association plus perfected co-ordination." *A Study in Practice and Habit,* p. 46.

For they are so numerous that a prominent modern psychologist has said that "when we look at living creatures from an outward point of view, one of the first things that strikes us is that they are a bundle of habits"; [11] and these habits may become so strong as entirely to destroy moral responsibility in regard to particular actions.[12] Given the primary impulse and a strong habit, the result is almost as mechanical as water flowing through a canal. "In action grown habitual, what instigates each new muscular contraction to take place in its appointed order is not a thought or perception, but the sensation occasioned by the muscular contraction just finished. The strictly voluntary act has to be guided by idea, perception and volition throughout its whole course. In an habitual action mere sensation is a sufficient guide, and the upper regions of the brain and mind are set comparatively free." [13]

84. How Habits Influence Moral Acts. Thus walking, first learned with such difficulty, comes finally to need no attention. After sufficient practice a pianist can play a difficult piece while carrying on an animated conversation. There is such a perfect association between one muscular contraction and another that one naturally follows the other without difficulty. And as this is true in different acts, so it is true in acts which objectively have a moral quality. Acts good or bad in themselves can be made so habitual that they result spontaneously from the appropriate stimuli. A church bell in the morning and the Angelus at noon, which tell only the time of day to one person, may, because of habit, immediately lift another's thoughts to God. To one the swinging doors of a saloon, in the old wide-open days, conveyed no temptation. To another they aroused an irresistible impulse to enter, and having entered to drink, and having tasted liquor to drink to intoxication. This is because the sight of these doors had so often suggested a desire which was gratified, thereby cutting such a deep smooth motivated track in the brain that the

[11] James, *Principles of Psychology*, Vol. I, p. 104.
[12] Noldin, *Theol. Mor.*, Vol. I, No. 60.
[13] James, *op. cit.*, Vol. I, 115.

will could only with extreme difficulty, if at all, prevent the whole series of acts from again taking place.

85. To What Extent Do Habits Destroy Freedom? How far any action is habitual, and therefore sufficiently involuntary to fall below the degree of *motus secundus,* it may be difficult to determine in a concrete case; nor can we judge as to what proportion of the acts of any individual is thus robbed of freedom. But we do know that habits can destroy our control over our actions here and now to such an extent that we are carried along irresistibly to perform vicious and harmful deeds.[14] How far acts due to habit are imputable to the agent depends not only on the strength of the habit, but also on how far the agent foresaw the consequences during the formation of the habit, and could have prevented its formation. Should a man deliberately contract the habit of drinking to excess, he is responsible for all the times he may later become drunk, because he willed them *in causa.* If a patient during a delirious fever has been given a narcotic so frequently that an irresistible habit of drug-taking has been formed before responsibility is recovered, evidently he is not responsible for the gratification later.

86. The Practical Rule to Follow. Practically, however, one should never presume that a habit is irresistible. One should always keep on fighting. We should, therefore, be careful to form good habits and to inhibit bad ones. "The great thing, then, in all [moral] education is to *make our nervous system our ally instead of our enemy.* It is to fund and capitalize our acquisitions, and to live at ease on the interest of the fund. *For this purpose we must make* automatic and habitual, as early as possible, as many useful actions as we can, and guard against growing into ways that are likely to be disadvantageous to us, as we guard against the plague." [15]

87. Habits Should Go to the Root of Goodness. We must be careful, however, that our good habits really go to the root of

[14] Cf. Noldin, *Theol. Mor.,* Vol. I, No. 60.
[15] James, *op. cit.,* p. 122.

goodness. So many apparently good and pious people collapse before a strong temptation just because their habits have not touched the foundations of will-power. They have gone to church; they have said prayers; they have given generously to charity, merely because such things were easy or agreeable or customary. There has been no habit formed in them of giving up their own will to please God. Consequently, when the sharp distinction comes between God's will and theirs, they are herded with the goats.

88. Habits Should Cultivate Submission to God's Will. As the end of man is union with God, all habit-forming should be directed towards gaining the power of submitting readily and easily to God's will. Nothing is more to the point in this connection than Professor James' recommendation: *"Keep the faculty of effort alive in you by a little gratuitous exercise every day. That is, be systematically ascetic or heroic in little unnecessary points; do every day or two something for no other reason than that you would rather not do it; so that when the hour of dire need draws nigh, it may find you not unnerved and untrained to stand the test. Asceticism of this sort is like the insurance which a man pays on his house and goods. The tax does him no good at the time, and possibly may never bring him a return. But if the fire does come, his having paid it will be his salvation from ruin. So with the man who has daily inured himself to habits of concentrated attention, energetic volition, and self-denial in unnecessary things. He will stand like a tower when everything rocks around him, and when his softer fellow-mortals are winnowed like chaff in the blast."* [16]

89. Necessity of Ascetic Habits. Another reason why it is necessary to practice asceticism is because "it is not only particular lines of discharge, but also *general forms* that seem to be grooved out by habit in the brain." [17] Hence the man who gets into the habit of seeking sensuous pleasure in legitimate ways is apt

[16] James, *op. cit.*, Vol. I., 126.
[17] James, *op. cit.*, p. 126.

soon to pass on to sinful actions. He has acquired the general habit of looking for pleasure, and in this pleasure-seeking, the stimuli reaching his nervous system will frequently find wrong motor discharges. On the other hand, the man who has trained himself to resist his impulses, to deny his flesh, will have acquired a power that will keep him steady in situations in which the sensuous man would give way to sinful gratification.

90. Knowledge Not Enough to Insure Right Action. The surest way to avoid bad habits is to form good ones. For, as it has been observed, "habit is its own worst enemy, because old habits oppose the introduction of new ones." [18] Since habits mean simply a tendency for stimuli to discharge along certain fixed channels, when once a set of good channels has been formed it is difficult for immoral motivation to take place. Knowledge of good and evil will never be as efficient a protection against temptation as the formation of good habits. "Self-protection that will strengthen the moral life must come largely through the affections or feelings—using these words in a technical sense—mere knowledge is not sufficient. In fact, mere knowledge is never sufficient. 'Socratic' philosophy to the contrary notwithstanding, all knowledge to be effective must have expression in motor responses, and all the knowledge in the world regarding personal hygiene will serve no protective purpose whatsoever unless it is frequently and regularly and attentively acted upon." [19]

91. Warfare Between Good and Bad Habits. Habits, however, are not necessarily permanent acquisitions. Evil habits can be overcome; good habits can be lost through carelessness or overconfidence. Nothing is surer in psychology than the fact of a constant warfare within us between the good and bad; eternal vigilance is the price of victory. In this connection it is interesting to hear a modern psychologist describing the phenomena in a way very similar to that of St. Paul [20] two thousand years ago. "The peculiarity of the moral habits," writes Professor Bain, "con-

[18] Paul Radestock, *Habit and Its Importance in Education* (Boston, p. 99).
[19] Margaret E. Schallenberger, *Self-Protection thru Knowledge and Habit*.
[20] Romans, vii, 23; Gal., v, 17.

tradistinguishing them from the intellectual acquisitions is the presence of two hostile powers, one to be gradually raised to the ascendant over the other. It is necessary, above all things, in such a situation never to lose a battle. Every gain of the wrong side undoes the effect of many conquests of the right. The essential precaution is so to regulate the two opposing powers that the one may have a series of uninterrupted successes, until repetition has fortified it to such a degree as to enable it to cope with the opposition, under any circumstances." [21]

92. Evil Habits Can Be Conquered. If one has been unfortunate enough, however, to contract evil habits he need not despair. Some of the most intemperate have become sober; some of the most debauched pure; some of the most ungoverned meek and humble. All things are possible to him who tries. But there must be system. And in this matter nothing is more useful, perhaps, than the particular examination of one's life each day, a practice so strongly recommended by that great psychologist, Ignatius Loyola.[22]

93. Particular Examen as Means to Conquering Bad Habits. The particular examen is based upon the well-known proverb: *divide et impera.* Slender threads when bound together make an unbreakable cable; fragile sticks in a bundle will resist the strongest man; and an evil character cannot be changed overnight. To break habits we must divide and subdivide. Each year one vicious habit rooted out, in time might make the worst man good, but we must be content to take them one by one. It is essential that one must not assume too big an undertaking for fear of being discouraged and his last state become worse than his first.

> "How shall I a habit break?"
> As you did that habit make.
> As you gathered, you must lose;
> As you yielded, now refuse.
> Thread by thread the strands we twist
> Till they bind us neck and wrist;

---

[21] Quoted by James, *loc. cit.,* p. 123.
[22] Consult Rodriguez, *Christian Perfection;* Scaramelli, *Directorium Asceticum.*

Thread by thread the patient hand
Must untwine ere free we stand.
As we builded, stone by stone,
We must toil, unhelped, alone,
Till the wall is overthrown.

But remember, as we try,
Lighter every test goes by.
Wading in, the stream grows deep
Toward the center's downward sweep;
Backward turn, each step ashore
Shallower is than that before.

Ah, the precious years we waste
Leveling what we raised in haste;
Doing what must be undone
Ere content or love be won!
First across the gulf we cast
Kite-borne threads, till lines are passed,
And habit builds the bridge at last! [23]

94. Subdivide Even One Particular Habit. For this reason it
is well to divide even one special habit. It is a better augury
of ultimate victory for a drunkard to resolve not to drink on
Mondays, and yet to get drunk six days a week, than for him to
resolve never to drink and to fall the same number of times.
It is better for a person with an ungovernable temper to resolve
not to be impatient with one particular individual, and to keep
the resolution, even though otherwise he is as impatient as ever,
say a thousand times a week, than it is for him to determine
never to be impatient again, and actually to fall to the same level
as by the more specific resolution—*i.e.,* impatience a thousand
times a week. For in one case he has accomplished what he set
out to do—not to drink on Mondays, not to be angry with a certain person; in the other, he has failed to keep his resolution.
Objectively the result may be the same—drunkenness six days
a week, impatience a thousand times a week—but subjectively it
is different. A certain confidence and strength is born of having
actually carried through his determination, and this will make

[23] John Boyle O'Reilly.

it easier for him now to go on to soberness on Tuesdays and self-control with someone else.[24]

95. Select the Most Fundamental Habit. In picking out the habit for first attack it is best to select the most fundamental defect of character. Usually there is one outstanding fault that is responsible for most of our falls. The most diverse sins can frequently be traced to one underlying habit. For instance, a man with an uncontrollable temper may quarrel with his wife; she may leave him; he may try to console himself with drink; this may lead to infidelity, and so on. Had he rooted out this one habit in early life, the others would not have come. To find this basic defect will save time. Instead of removing the edifice of one's evil life brick by brick from the top, as it were, this will dynamite the foundations, and much built upon it will collapse at the same time.

96. Keep a Record of Progress. Earnest introspection; what others have said about one, a nickname, will enable one to select the sin for attack with considerable prudence. And having selected it, one should each day or several times a day, examine himself as to how many times he has fallen. One day's record should be compared with another day's, and one week's with another. In this way progress or retrogression can be quickly observed. We must not expect, however, absolute success in regard to some faults, such as impatience. When a reasonable conquest has been achieved, it is best to pass on to some other evil habit.

97. Influence of Heredity. In regard to heredity and disease, we must distinguish between the intellect and the will. Physicians are agreed that certain mental weaknesses may be due to defective heredity, and it is perfectly evident that they will reduce responsibility in as far as they affect the understanding of the character of one's actions. Insanity, feeble-mindedness, and the like, are probably heritable, and in their graver forms destroy all moral responsibility, since they destroy one of the elements necessary for a truly voluntary act. In many other cases it is

---

[24] James, *Principles of Psychology,* Vol. I, ch. on "Habit."

probable that the habits of life of a father or grandfather may
so weaken the physical constitution of his descendants as to make
them less capable, in the moral order, of withstanding the allur-
ing strength of the nervous excitement to which they may be
subjected.[25]

98. Disease. Neurasthenia, melancholia, insanity, injuries to the
brain, epilepsy and numerous other diseases may affect voluntariness by affecting the mind. And we are awaking to the fact that
derangements of mind are much more frequent than was once
suspected. Considerations of environment, heredity and disease
are more and more influencing our courts in determining the
guilt of the accused person. But we are still far from the ideal,
and a future generation may look upon our criminal procedure
as being just as barbarous as the punishment of the out-and-out
insane.

99. Moral Insanity. But in addition to the effect of disease and
heredity on voluntariness by affecting the mind, some psychologists and criminologists think that there is a sort of moral insanity. That is, while the mind remains clear, the will is warped
in a way that prevents responsibility for one's moral actions.
"Prichard was the first to employ the phrase *moral* insanity[26]
to designate a psychic overthrow falling upon the emotional
sphere, and consisting in the benumbing or the deprivation of the
moral sense. It is the *rational* or *emotional monomania* of Es-
quirol, the *instinctive* or the *impulsive* of Morel, the insanity
of action of Briérre de Boismont, the *mania of character* of Pinel,
the *lucid insanity of* Trélat, and the *insanity with conscience* of
Baillarger. In short, it is a peculiar condition in which the intellectual faculties are not affected, but remain intact; hence the
appellations *lucid, with conscience, without delirium, rational.*"[27]
Maudsley, an English physician, has developed this at considerable length, and he can still be read with profit.[28]

[25] O'Malley and Walsh, *Essays in Medicine,* p. 122; cf. also Chs. V, IX, XXI, XXII;
Garofalo, *Criminology,* pp. 92 ff.
[26] *A Treatise on Insanity,* London, 1835.
[27] *Modern Theories of Criminality,* by C. Bernaldo de Quiros, p. 8. Boston, 1912.
[28] *Mental Responsibility,* London, 1873.

SUGGESTED READINGS

1. James, "Freedom of the Will," in his volume *The Will to Believe*.
2. James, *Principles of Psychology,* chapter on "Habit."
3. T. V. Moore, *Dynamic Psychology,* Ch. VII.
4. J. G. Vance, "Freedom," *Dublin Rev.,* Sept., 1919.

QUESTIONS

1. Define Ethics and explain definition.
2. Explain relation between Ethics and
                (a) philosophy   (c) economics
                (b) psychology   (d) civil law
   Answer either a, b, c or d.
3. What process of reasoning predominates in Ethics?
4. What is a human act?
5. Divide voluntariness and give example of each division.
6. When may an act having evil consequences be performed?
7. Does a good end ever justify evil means?
8. What influences make an action less human?

THREE: *The End of Man*[1]

100. State of Question. In the previous chapter it was said that some knowledge of the end was a necessary element of every human act. It will now be necessary to explain more fully what is meant by the "end," and what is, or should be the final end of all human acts.

101. Definition of End. The ordinary meaning of end is the extremity or terminal part of anything materially extended, as we speak of the end of a boat. By analogy, we apply this idea of extremity to the termination of, or close of any assignable duration, as the "end of a perfect day." From this it is but a step to using end to signify the close or outcome of any continued action, or the result of conative action foreseen before actual accomplishment. Continued refinement at last brings end to mean the *mental representation of the result of an action as desirable,* and as *inducing to action.* "An end . . . is that which is desirable in *itself;* or that on account of which or for the sake of which anything is done." [2]

102. Limitation of Discussion. Though it is proper to speak of the end of man in several of these senses, this chapter will consider man's end only in its last meaning, as the issue intended in man's acts, their aim or design.

103. Division of Ends: Proximate, Intermediate, Ultimate. Though we define *end* as something desirable in itself, this does not prevent its being the means to something more desirable. Hence, we distinguish proximate, intermediate, and ultimate ends. A *proximate end* is what the will seeks *immediately* without the interposition of any other end. The proximate end of a thirsty man lapping a stream is to quench his thirst. An *ultimate end* is one *not subordinated* to any other higher end. This may

---

[1] Brosnahan, *Digest of Lectures on Ethics,* IV; Cathrein, *Moralphilosophie,* Vol. I, Bk. II; Rickaby, *Aquinas Ethicus,* Q. I, II; Johann Ude, *Ethik,* pp. 13-22; Schiffini, *Philosophia Moralis,* Disp. 1a.

[2] Brosnahan, *op. cit.,* p. 23.

be either relatively or absolutely ultimate, according as it is the last and highest in a single series of acts or of all possible series. If a man studies in order to pass an examination to secure a position enabling him to marry so that he may perpetuate his name, his ultimate end, relatively, is to continue his name. To secure the position and to marry would be *intermediate ends* between this ultimate end and the proximate end of studying. Whether there be any absolutely ultimate end is the object of this chapter to discover.

104. Division of Ends: Intrinsic, Extrinsic. We distinguish also between *intrinsic* and *extrinsic ends*. The one is attainable within the being itself by the development of its own powers; the other is attainable only by its perfection being brought into relation with some other being. From cosmology we learn that man's extrinsic end is the extrinsic glory of God. His intrinsic end can only be determined by a further consideration of his nature.

105. End of the Agent and End of the Action. Ethicians frequently distinguish between the *end of the action* (finis operis), or that in which the action naturally results, as in alms-giving the result is the relief of the recipient; and the *end of the agent* (finis operantis), or the intention in the mind of the person acting, as by alms-giving to satisfy for one's sins. But in order to avoid confusion, or the necessity of specifying the end of agent or of act, the term end is often restricted to the end of the agent; and the end of the action is called the object.

I. Blessedness Is Man's End

106. There Is No Resultant of Man's Tendencies. Since the intrinsic end of any being is a result attainable in the being itself, we must discover it by investigation of that being's tendencies. And the ultimate intrinsic end will be learned either by finding a resultant of all the different tendencies or by discovering some one dominant tendency. An inanimate being with a tendency to move in one direction with a force of ten pounds and in a direction at right angles with a force of twenty pounds can by a parallelogram of forces be found to have a certain verifiable and prophesiable resultant tendency to move in a definite direction between the two.

107. Problem Is to Find Man's Dominant Tendency. But no parallelogram of forces can ever show the result of man's tendencies any more than plane geometry can solve all the problems of a three-dimension universe. Man is made up of two heterogeneous parts [3] and you cannot combine soul-tendencies and sense-tendencies, as you cannot combine paregoric pills and Pindaric trochees. The only solution to the problem is to find one dominant tendency, or, since man is a sensitive being, an appetency.

108. Man's Dominant Appetency Cannot Be Sensuous. Man being essentially higher than brute animals, as intellect is higher than instinct and will than sensuous appetite, we need not look among man's bodily tendencies for his dominant appetency. We must turn to his soul.

109. Man's Dominant Tendency Is to Desire. The soul's tendencies may be divided into two classes—*apprehensive* and *appetitive*. By the one man apprehends or knows something, by the other he desires or strives after it. Whenever the object of a faculty is properly presented, the faculty is roused to action. Its tendency from potential becomes actual. Man's mind is no exception. Present an object to the intellect under appropriate conditions, and a relation is at once established. There is receptive reaction as knowledge of the object is taken into the mind. But knowledge itself is barren. It is not its own *raison d'être*. Knowledge always leads to some conative action in regard to the object presented, a striving for possession, a repulsion, a disgusted dropping.

110. Hence Man's End Is an Object Filling His Capacity of Desiring. Now, the first tendency by which the object is known is the measure of the second by which it is sought. But though seeking depends upon knowing, it is the *ratio essendi* of knowing. And though we cannot desire what we do not know, we

---

[3] The existence of the soul and its nature are postulates from psychology. For proof of these, cf. Maher, *Psychology,* and McDougall, *Body and Mind.*

can desire what we do know. Hence, we have found in the will of man his final dominant tendency. *Therefore, man's ultimate end will be the attainment of some object filling the intellect's capacity for conceiving what is desirable.*

111. Blessedness the Object of Man's Dominant Tendency.[4] This attainment we call blessedness. We may amplify and explain the definition already given by describing it as a permanent state of freedom from all evil and the possession of all good conceivable by the intellect. There must be no admixture of evil; there must be the possession of all good conceivable by the intellect; and this condition must be unending. Anything less will not fulfill the definition of being the attainment of the greatest good conceivable by the intellect. For if there were any evil in this object, naturally the intellect could conceive of that evil as removed. If there were lack of any good, that would be to predicate evil, as evil is the negation of good. Similarly, if the possession of this good were limited by time, it would not be the possession of all good conceivable, as we can conceive of *unlimited* good.

112. Blessedness Attainable. The fact of man's ultimate end being the attainment of a state of blessedness is logically separable from the possibility of attaining that end. But predicating from *Natural Theology*[5] that God is infinitely wise and good and truthful, it is easy to prove that man can attain blessedness. For if bliss were always beyond any attainable grade of happiness, then the *divine wisdom* would contradict itself in establishing an end we could never reach; the *divine goodness* would be a mockery, in that the very faculties by which we are raised above the brutes would make us more miserable; the *divine truthfulness* would belie itself because the promises implied in the tendencies would be false.

113. Blessedness Is Not Lack of Activity. The comic supplement jokes about the ennui of heaven with nothing to do, are beside the mark. If we know any one thing about God, it is

---

4 Cf. Cathrein, *op. cit.,* p. III.
5 Cf. Boedder, *Natural Theology.*

His inexhaustible activity; and we may conclude that creatures made in His image can only find their final end in some form of activity. When we speak of the peace of the blessed, we mean the full and complete satisfaction of all of their faculties. This satisfaction comes not from idleness but from *perfect activity;* that is to say, not a journeying towards a good not yet grasped, "but an inward, living comprehension of the present all perfect Good." [6]

II. Object of Blessedness Cannot Be Finite

114. What Is the Object of Blessedness? We define blessedness as the attainment of some object filling the intellect's capacity for conceiving what is desirable. What is this object? Is it the same for all men? Does it in any way depend upon the individual intellect or will, so that one man can deliberately decide to be blessed by the possession of some object that would entirely fail to satisfy another? Can any of the thousand and one things we see around us in the world fill the intellect's capacity of conceiving Good?

115. Men Must Seek Blessedness. The earth is inhabited by some two billion people. They are scurrying about the earth's surface like rabbits, burrowing into its bowels like moles, invading the vast empyrean like eagles, incessantly drawn here and impelled there, frantically busy about many things, and all to what purpose? Why all this hurry and bustle, why this ceaseless noise and feverish activity? What does it all mean? Have they found the ultimate end of their existence, the joy and peace that should come from the attainment of perfect Good?

116. Business Cannot Be the Object of Blessedness. Ask the men engaged in this feverish activity if they have found the secret of happiness, and you shall learn the futility of their ceaseless striving. It makes little or no difference whether you ask the question of the employer or the employed, business people or professional, they all feel the wearisome monotony grinding into their souls, see the emptiness of all such pursuits at the very mo-

[6] Cathrein, *op. cit.,* I, p. 133; cf. St. Thomas, *Summa,* I, II, Q. 31, A. 1 and 2.

ment that they are so thoroughly immersed in them; they are all constantly looking forward to that evening hour when they will be freed for a while from this merciless machinery to seek directly for their own ends. For the business or profession in which a man is doomed to spend the greater part of his waking hours is always merely preparatory to something else. Not even in the most commercialized man does mere production become an end in itself. How weary, stale, flat, and unprofitable it all is! Men seldom like their own occupation. Teachers think the law would be so much more congenial; lawyers want to be judges. It matters little what a man is, there is always that "If I were something else" conditioning his happiness, always the mirage of perfect contentment glimmering just beyond his reach.

117. Social Life Cannot Be the Object of Blessedness. But when men are poured out again from the commercial or professional world are they better off? Are they more content if all their hours are hours of leisure? Do they find complete satisfaction in seeking congenial friends? Do they find in a dance, in a theater, or in going to a dinner with some like-minded acquaintance such happiness that they would be content to do nothing else all their lives? Can we conceive of this as the end and meaning of life? Is the final good of all the feverish hours of activity that are spent in business or profession merely the supplying each night an hour or so of such gratification?

118. Leisure Cannot Be the Object of Blessedness. Assuredly, the shallow seeking after what is called "society," the futile chasing after momentary pleasures, can give no real meaning to human life.

> "If all our days were playing holidays,
> To sport would be as tedious as to work."

Those who have the opportunity always to seek amusement, who are known as persons of leisure, are not the fortunate ones of the earth. Far more insistently than do the workers, they feel this question importunately demanding an answer. Into their sterile and empty hours surges the thought which no man can

evade, "What is the use of it all? To what end do I defer to
this person or that? For what purpose do I smile and bow and
dance like a puppet? What thrift may follow on this fawning
if I crook the pregnant hinges of my knees?"

119. Marriage Cannot Be the Object of Blessedness. Nor is the
situation essentially altered if it be not simply an acquaintance,
but more than a friend we seek. Can any man look forward with
absolute satisfaction to an eternity of courtship or honeymoon?
To give one's self to another, to receive the other in return, to
be blended, as it were, into one being—ecstatic though such bliss
may be—cannot really constitute a satisfactory end for existence.
Each remains himself, and there must inevitably come a time
when selfishness will reassert itself, when each will realize that
even this joy does not answer to the entirety of his vital needs.

120. Children Cannot Be the End of Life. Even to gaze into
the innocent faces formed from one's own flesh and blood, to
anticipate the carrying on and perpetuating of one's own name
and character and work, cannot in ultimate analysis furnish a
meaning to life. There must be something bigger as a foil to this
existence, or life is worthless and meaningless, "A tale told by
an idiot, full of sound and fury, signifying nothing."

**121. Testimony of "Successful" Men as to Vanity of Finite
Objects.** Michael Angelo, who succeeded supremely as sculptor,
painter, and lover, wrote in his old age: "Painting nor sculpture
now can lure to rest my soul." [7] With life and reputation and
fame behind him he could see the futility of such success, the
insufficiency of such fleeting satisfaction to give a real content
and meaning to life. Bismarck, replying in 1895 to some con-
gratulations offered him by friends, said: "In my whole life I
have not been perfectly happy for twenty-four hours. The greatest pleasure I had was when I shot my first rabbit." [8] Goethe
declared: "In my seventy-five years I have not had four weeks
of genuine happiness." [9] Humboldt, by the world's reckoning,

[7] Quoted in *Catholic Mysticism,* by Algar Thorold, p. 17.
[8] Quoted by Cathrein, *op. cit.,* I, p. 129.
[9] *Goethes Gespraeche mit Eckermann,* I, 76, *ap.* Cathrein, *loc. cit.*

lived a useful, glorious life, yet at its end he sorrowfully wrote: "Life is the greatest foolishness. And if a man works and labors for eighty years, he must at the end admit that he has worked and labored in vain. We have no inkling as to why we are on this earth. All is and remains meaningless to the thinker, and the greatest blessing is to be born a simpleton." [10] Count de Maistre, who achieved an enviable reputation as a statesman and philosopher, towards the end of his life exclaimed: "I know not what the life of a blackguard is—I have never been one,— but the life of an honorable man is pitiful." [11]

122. Philanthropy Cannot Furnish Life's End. But some who admit that the selfish seeking of these things—commercial success, reputation, society, love—cannot give a meaning to life, yet think that the giving of one's self to another, the spending of one's life in serving humanity, the being a philanthropist, is an end commensurate with man's dignity, one which will satisfy the noblest aspirations of which the human heart is capable. Yet the answer is obvious. What would they have philanthropists provide? Food and clothing and leisure? The very things that failed to satisfy the philanthropists themselves? And if the possession of these things can afford no vital meaning to life, how can the giving them to others become such an object?

III. God Is Real Object of Blessedness

123. The Object of Blessedness Is God. If a man lives long enough he will come, like Bismarck and Humboldt and Goethe, to see the emptiness of all created things. "Vanity of vanities, all is vanity." And if he be fortunate he will come also to realize the rest of that saying of the wise man—"Except to know and serve God." That is the only end that gives a real meaning to life. That is the only object open to every man—rich and poor, old and young, educated and uneducated. These other objects that men are continually seeking are limited in their application.

---

[10] *Memoiren,* I, 365 ff., *ap.* Cathrein, *loc. cit.*
[11] *Ap.* Cathrein, *loc. cit.*

The vast majority of men must go down to graves unwept, unhonored, and unsung. Hence, reputation cannot be man's end; a society of all poor is possible, but not all rich, and consequently wealth cannot be man's end; human love is fleeting, fragile, and subject to grim death and, therefore, cannot be man's end.

124. God Can and Must Be Sought by All. Only one object is universal enough for humanity's end—the Author of all humanity. God Himself can be sought by all. No accident of birth, no lack of worldly goods, no ignorance of human learning can exclude anyone from this company. By the very fact of being a man each one is admitted. God is so universal, that no one can really escape from seeking Him. No matter to what a man turns, there is God. Nothing exists except in so far as it reflects some perfection of the All-Perfect, and it is this shadow of perfection that attracts. Therefore, men who are continually running after worldly gew-gaws are like those seeking the reflection of the sun in a shallow pool while turning their backs upon the sun itself. They are seeking the infinitely obscure shadow of God when they might directly seek God Himself. They cannot appreciate those verses of Miss Guiney:

> "O close my hand upon Beatitude,
> Not on its toys—" [12]

125. All Else Is Vanity. By way of eminence, the intellect can conceive of infinite Good, and hence only God can completely satisfy the desires of the will. There is but one thing that gives meaning to this mortal life of ours, "this hyphen between two eternities"—that is, the realization that it is simply a preparation for something else. Vanity of vanities, all is vanity—worldly goods, reputation, power, *everything—except* to know and to love God and to make one's self ready for the possession of this infinite beauty for all eternity. That and nothing else is the end of this existence.

126. This Life Is a Preparation for Another. No matter how successful the world may count a man, if his heart be set on

[12] *Deo Optimo Maximo.*

anything less than this, he is foredoomed to failure. "What doth it profit a man if he gain the whole world and suffer the loss of his soul." [13] Indeed the man who gains, or wants to gain the whole world and nothing beyond, has already lost his soul, for he has lost the mastery of himself. He is a slave to his ambitions. He cannot help accumulating wealth or grasping power. If a man is not to be smothered under gold, or flesh, or pedantry, he must earnestly realize that this life is simply the ante-room to another. He must grow the faculties here with which to know and to love God, though it be but in a glass darkly, that some day he may see Him more clearly face to face. Men on earth are like blind larvae—they must develop spiritual eyes to look out upon Reality, must develop vision to see God Himself.

127. The Problem of Pain. Here comes in a partial explanation of the problem of physical evil. Why an all-good God should have ordained suffering as the condition of growth, we do not know. But that being so, we can see how pain is simply the means of spiritual growth. It is the tool that God has chosen to carve the marble of our selfish hearts into His divine image. If a man is to know and to love, to be brave and patient and kind, he must serve his apprenticeship of suffering. He may quarrel with the dispensation, but cannot alter it. King or peasant, clown or scholar, all must suffer.

128. Pain the Condition of Growth. Once having accepted this law of nature, life takes on new colors. It is seen as a process of becoming, of growth into something higher and better than the worldly-minded wot of. Wealth, power, reputation cease to be things desirable in themselves. Life is quieted and simplified. Power, if one have it, becomes a means of exhibiting a Godlike mercy; powerlessness is the tool which chips off the rough angle of pride. A man lacks humility—the great Sculptor of his soul takes up the hammer of injustice and the chisel of calumny. The cocoon of sensuous pleasures and of blind self-seeking is gradually burned away by suffering until some day the man's

[13] Matt. xvi, 26.

soul springs forth a winged seraph with eyes that can gaze un-
blinking upon the very face of God.

129. This Life Is the Garden of Character. Thus at last is the
fundamental question of Ethics answered. This life, instead of
being a race for worldly distinction, is seen to be but the opportunity for developing character. " 'Tis in ourselves that we are
thus, or thus. Our Bodies are our Gardens, to the which, our
Wills are Gardiners. So that if we will plant Nettels, or sowe
Lettice: Set Hisope, and weede up Time: Supplie it with one
gender of Hearbes, or distract it with many: either to have it
sterrill with idleness, or manured with Industry, why the power,
and Corrigeable authoritie of this lies in our Wills." [14]

130. Pain May Become Virtue. Once we get this viewpoint of
life, pain and suffering come to be recognized, yes, come even
to be loved, as the tools of the Master Builder. Borne bravely,
humbly, cheerfully, our trials are transmuted into gems of great
price. As the sharp, irksome grains of sand grinding their way
into the body of the mollusk are gradually changed by uncom-
plaining acceptance into pearls to adorn a princess; so our suf-
ferings, accepted as gifts from God, considered as His instruments for molding us into His image, are sublimated into
courage and patience and humility, jewels fit to adorn the Bride
of Heaven.

131. The Privilege of Suffering. Then is it not a privilege to
suffer? Not everyone is deemed worthy of such an honor. Very
significantly does a priest pray every time he vests for Mass:
"Lord, may I be worthy to bear the maniple of weeping and
sorrow." Eternally true is it that "Whom the Lord loveth, He
chastiseth." [15] "Thy rod and Thy staff, they have comforted me,"
wrote David.[16] Because by some mysterious dispensation pain is
necessary for spiritual growth, men should accept it cheerfully
so that through it they may grow into joy.

132. The One Thing Necessary. So things come to be seen in
better proportion. It will matter little a hundred years hence if

---

[14] *Othello,* I, 3.   [16] Psalm xxii, 4.
[15] Hebrews, xii, 6.

today a man be prime minister or a scullion, if he live in a
palace or a slum, whether or not he have the entrée to the so-
called best society, whether justice was meted to him or he
spends his days in hungering and thirsting for it. But it will
make a difference whether or not he knows the meaning of
life and spends his time in growing Godlike instead of chasing
phantoms. Epictetus the slave is as great a character as Aurelius
the emperor; Job on his dunghill is no less than Job in his
palace; Christ on the cross has sanctified suffering and taught
us the meaning of life. When will men realize this? When will
they have the courage to judge by God's principles in judging
success and measuring the value of life? When will men calling
themselves Christians cease to gild and bejewel their crucifixes
until they are irrecognizable as instruments of torture? *This,
then, is man's great destiny, the end of his existence—to know
God, to love God, to shadow forth God in his actions.*

SUGGESTED READINGS

1. Cronin, *Science of Ethics,* I, Ch. III.
2. Hedley, *A Retreat,* II, IV, V, XXV, XXVIII.
3. Bennett, *The Human Machine,* VII, VIII, XII, XVI.
4. Elliott, *The Spiritual Life,* II, III, VIII, XI.
5. De Sales, *Introduction to a Devout Life,* Pt. I.
6. Ming, *Data of Modern Ethics Examined,* Chs. III, V.
7. Hill, *Moral Philosophy,* Pt. I, Ch. I.

QUESTIONS

1. What is an end?
2. How are ends divided?
3. What is man's ultimate end?
4. Can an individual man fail to reach his ultimate end? If so, how?
5. What solution can be given to the problem of physical evil?

FOUR: *Norm and Criteria of Morality*[1]

I. THE NORM OF MORALITY

133. State of the Question. So far we have considered these elements in our definition of Ethics—that it is a branch of philosophy, distinguished in various ways from other disciplines, and that it deals with acts (of human beings) that are free, voluntary, and directed to a known end. There remains to be developed one other point indicated in the definition. For as we were to treat of human actions under only one aspect—that of their moral rectitude—we must now explain what is meant by moral rectitude or goodness in an action.

134. Good Defined. Good is one of those familiar words constantly upon our lips, which, nevertheless, we find difficult to define. The difficulty is increased by the confusion arising from using the term in several senses, and as an adjective and as a noun. Thus we call a strong and sharp knife good, because it serves the purpose for which knives are intended—it is good as an instrument; and we speak of a good exercise or a good medicine when they are calculated to produce the desired results—they are good as causes; and we speak of a painting as good because it possesses the perfections proper to its nature—it is good in itself. Then there is the farther sense in which we speak of a good man, a good act. It will be seen that there is a common element in all these various meanings—that a thing is good when it is desirable. This will not take us far, however, unless we can determine more clearly what makes an object desirable.

135. The Good as Desirable. The Scholastics, following Aristotle, make goodness and being objectively identical. Goodness is simply being considered as desirable. Everything that exists is,

---

[1] Cf. Rickaby, *Moral Philosophy,* Ch. VI; Cronin, *Science of Ethics,* Chs. IV, V; Cathrein, *Moralphilosophie,* Pt. I, Bk. III; Brosnahan, *Digest of Lectures on Ethics,* p. 29 ff.; Ming, *Data of Modern Ethics,* Chs. VI, VII; Humphrey, *Conscience and Law,* Ch. I.

therefore, (in so far as it possesses being) good. And a thing is desirable only on account of its perfection of being, never because of what it has not. It is in this sense that the will is said to tend always towards good. What the will desires is good, in that it has being. If the seeking of this object be evil for a particular agent, it is because it is relatively to that agent out of order.

136. What Is Good in Itself May Be Relatively Evil. Relative good is any object furthering the natural development of a being. An animal needs food in certain quantities in order that its organs and faculties may grow. But food of such a kind or in such an amount as to derange the organs ceases to be a relative good though it remains good in itself. So, too, in the case of human beings made up of a hierarchy of faculties, that which develops a lower organ to greater perfection is relatively an evil if this development takes place at the expense of a higher faculty. The lavishing of so much care upon the body as to have no time and opportunity to train the mind deordinates what in itself is good and renders it relatively evil.

137. Moral Good Is Not Essentially Distinct From Non-Moral. Ethical good is not in essence distinct from the good that we have been discussing. It is simply an object looked upon as desirable because it furthers the attainment of the ultimate end of man. And since this ultimate end, objectively considered, is the Supreme Nature, we say that the ultimate norm of goodness is God's nature. Whatever conforms to that nature and therefore brings us closer to the full fruition of our faculties in the contemplation and possession of the one Supreme Being is good, whatever takes us away from this full fruition of our faculties is evil. *Norm, then, is defined as that object by conformity with which an action takes on the attribute of goodness.*

138. Difference Between Good and Evil Is Objective. From this it will be seen that the difference between good and evil is *objective,* that is, exists in a relation between the action and the Divine Nature independently of the will and intellect of the agent or of God.[2] Being independent of man's will it follows

---

[2] We speak here of material good and evil. How formal evil depends upon the knowledge and intention of the agent will be treated later in this chapter.

that the distinction between good and evil does not arise from custom or education. No universality of action, no authority of teaching, can ever make what is materially evil become materially good. Nor does the distinction between good and evil depend on God's will. Since His nature is unchangeable, He cannot alter the moral rectitude of any action, because moral rectitude is simply the relation between the action and His nature. God could not now turn the moral order topsy-turvy and make an intrinsically evil action (as, for instance, blasphemy) good. Neither could He have decreed this at the beginning of creation. It is true, of course, that what is indifferent may be forbidden by God, and therefore it will be wrong for a creature to do. But this is because from all eternity God's nature requires that all creatures should obey His slightest behest.

139. Ultimate Norm of Morality Is God's Nature; Proximate Man's. God's nature, we say, is the ultimate norm of morality. But there is also a proximate norm in man's nature. The good of an agent is its orderly and fitting perfection; therefore, the fitting and orderly perfection of man's nature is the proximate norm of morality. This nature properly considered is: (1) *Contingent,* dependent for existence upon the Creator, and, therefore, having certain duties to him; (2) *Composite,* as being a complete being with diverse faculties and functions subordinated to each other; (3) *Social,* as having certain contacts with similar beings, whence arise rights and duties.

140. Summary. Hence we may sum up the Scholastic doctrine in the words of St. Thomas: "The proximate rule of free action is reason; the remote is the eternal law, that is, Divine Nature." [3]

II. Criteria of Morality

141. Distinction Between Norm and Criterion. Some writers [4] do not distinguish between norm and criterion, and go on from

[3] *Summa,* I, II, Q. XXI, A. 1; Q. XIX, A. 4.
[4] *E.g.,* Cronin.

here to treat of certain subsidiary standards of morality. But it would seem to make for clearness to define norm as that object by conformity with which an act is good, by difformity with which an act is bad; and then to consider criteria as the means by which we judge of this conformity or difformity. A criterion stands in about the same relation to the norm as a foot-rule to the original model a carpenter may wish to copy. A criterion is a measure; a norm is the standard itself. And hence a criterion need not in itself be absolutely definite and final. The question of conformity with the ultimate norm may in some cases be so complicated that several criteria or measures must be applied.

142. The Natural and Unnatural Use of a Faculty as Criteria. Foremost among these criteria is the natural and the unnatural use of a faculty, that is, respectively, the use of a faculty in such a way as to realize its own end or to frustrate the attainment of that end. To injure a faculty or to render it useless is not the same thing as to misuse it. Misuse means that the faculty is made to perform its own functions specifically and directly, but in such a way that the purpose for which nature intended it, cannot be fulfilled.

143. This Criterion Applied to Lying and Suicide. Thus, the natural end of the power of speech is sincere association, the expression of inner conviction to another. If speech is made to function as a means of expression, but for the expression of falsehood instead of truth, then it is used against its end, and the act is morally bad. Again, we have the case of suicide. All man's faculties have for their ultimate end, as we have seen, the maintenance and completion of the person. When, therefore, we use any faculty to destroy the person, we are using it unnaturally and wrongfully.

144. Other Applications. And as man is made up of many faculties upon different planes, it is unnatural to use a lower faculty to destroy or cripple (even temporarily) a higher power. Order requires that the lower shall be subordinated to the higher. Hence it is morally wrong to deprive ourselves of reason by using intoxicating liquors for purely sensual gratification.[5] But order requires also that the lower shall not be entirely killed or neglected. It is good to pray, yet it is wrong to spend so much time in prayer that the other needs of the person are neglected or the ordinary duties of life left unfulfilled.

145. General Consequences As a Criterion. Another criterion for judging of the moral quality of acts is General Consequences. An act is morally good or bad which, if it were to become general, would necessarily work out respectively for the good or evil of the race. This criterion is based upon the assumption that nature never tends to its own destruction, and that therefore an act tending to destruction cannot be natural. A single act may tend to destruction on account of accidental circumstances or because the good of the agent is subordinated to a higher good. But no such conditions can be urged when we generalize the action.

146. Conditions for Applying This Criterion. When properly applied this criterion gives true certainty, but it is not always easy to apply. The fundamental principle for right application is that the evil consequences must spring specifically and by necessity from the act itself. To make sure of this the following conditions must be verified:

(1) The evil effects must not depend upon the free will of the agent, but must follow necessarily from the act itself. It may be that, human nature being what it is, a man may be obliged to refrain from a particular act which is practically sure to produce a certain reaction in himself or in others. But this is not because the act in itself is evil, but because it is a proximate occasion of what is wrong.[6]

---

[5] To sleep is not wrong, because nature requires it. The good of the whole agent would suffer from any prolonged attempt to do without sleep, and if carried to excess reason itself would be lost. But excessive sleep is wrong, because it deprives us temporarily of reason for mere sensual pleasure, at the expense of our highest rational life.

[6] An occasion of sin is some external circumstance which leads to or induces sin. Occasions of sin are divided into *absolute* and *relative* according as they *per se* and in respect to all men taken generally, or in respect to a few men, lead to sin; and into *proximate* and *remote,* according as they do or do not furnish a *probable* danger of sinning. One is obliged to avoid what are proximate occasions of sin for him (whether

(2) The evil effects must be the result of the act itself intrinsically considered and not of an excess of the act or of lack of
what the act replaces. Drinking too much alcohol produces
drunkenness, but we can not therefore conclude that to take a
small quantity is wrong. If everybody did nothing but bake
bread, society would soon be starved and smothered under a
plethora of loaves; but this does not prove that a baker is as
bad as a murderer.

147. Universal Conviction As a Criterion. Another criterion is
a general conviction of mankind that a particular act is good or
is bad. Such a conviction must be widespread, embracing many
men in many lands and under different civilizations; it must be
long continued, handed from one generation to another, sifted
by time until the false and unnecessary has been winnowed from
the grain of truth; and it must deal with facts that are evident
to the average man, not with conclusions drawn by a long process
of reasoning.

**148. How Far the Criterion of Universal Conviction Is Appli-
cable.** When these conditions are fulfilled in regard to any moral
conviction we may use it cautiously as a criterion. For man is a
rational animal, and therefore any conviction that is universal
in time and extension and deals with easily ascertainable facts
must have some good reason back of it. We may apply to morals
Lincoln's homely saying about politics: "You can fool all the
people some of the time, and some of the people all the time,
but you can't fool all the people all the time." Mohammedans
may be mistaken about the morality of polygamy; Chinese may
be mistaken about the permissibleness of infanticide; South Sea
Islanders may be mistaken about the desirability of missionary
steak: but pagans and Mohammedans and Christians throughout

absolutely or relatively) because he who unnecessarily exposes himself to a serious danger
of sinning has ordinarily willed the sin. Circumstances excusing from this obligation
would be: (1) Impossibility of avoiding the occasion; (2) when the occasion cannot be
avoided without serious scandal; (3) if the occasion cannot be avoided without grave loss
or other difficulty; (4) when one occasion cannot be avoided without falling into another
equally grave.

the ages are not going to unite in the same error on any simple concrete question.

149. Moral Feelings As a Criterion. The last criterion of morality that we shall consider is that of moral feelings. Everyone who has not destroyed his natural feelings by sophistication, at times feels an impulse wholly unaccountable on rational grounds against a particular line of action. Before having time for reflection there is an instinctive withdrawal from the suggested act. Or, having reflected without being able to discover a solid reason against the act, the feeling of repugnance may persist. Something of the same kind is exhibited in our judgments of people. Despite all they can do to please and win us we sometimes continue to mistrust those for whom at the first meeting we formed an unreasoning dislike.

150. Cautions in Applying. Of course, this criterion can be pushed too far or applied too rigorously. For these feelings can be to some extent cultivated or suppressed, and are often but the expression of certain local or racial fancies and prejudices. A man's sensibility may be so dulled as to look with indifference upon the most horrible crimes, or it may be rendered so abnormally acute as to produce the pathologic condition known as scruples. Also, such feelings frequently refer to the indelicacy rather than to the immorality of acts. In complicated cases, the feeling of repugnance may be aroused by some extrinsic circumstance having no real connection with the morality of the act.

151. Criteria Are Manifestive Not Constitutive of Morality. It must be remembered in regard to all criteria of morality, and especially the criterion of general consequences, that they manifest but do not constitute morality. An act is known to be bad if when raised to a general rule of conduct, it results in evil for the race. But it results in evil because it is bad, it is not bad because it results in evil. Hence any individual act of this kind is a bad act whether the evil consequences follow or not. Nature, for instance, forbids marriages between persons too closely related; and we can know this from the evil consequences which would come to the race if such marriages should become general.

But an individual marriage between a brother and sister is wrong, whether or not the marriage results in deformed children or other evil consequences.

III. DETERMINANTS OF MORALITY

152. The Object. In any human act there are three elements uniting to give it moral color. These determinants of morality are the *object,* the *end,* and the *circumstances.* "By the object is here meant that to which the will primarily and directly tends; that which it determines to do looked at in itself, apart from the circumstances with which the action when done will be clothed; or it is the action considered in the abstract." [7]

153. Circumstances. Accidental determinants, or accidents of an act, without which the act can exist, but which add to it in some way a certain morality other than that which the act derives from its object and end, are called *circumstances.* It is required by the definition that circumstances add a moral quality to the act. Hence not all accidental accompaniments of an act are circumstances. It does not matter morally whether a man steals with his right or left hand; it does matter whether he steals the last cent from a poor widow or a few cents from a millionaire. Circumstances are ordinarily the answers to the questions: *who, what, where, by what means, why, how,* and *when.* It is clear that circumstances may change the morality of an act, because they can change the relationship between an act and the norm of morality. Thus in itself it is good or indifferent to sleep. But to sleep under such circumstances as those of a man employed to watch signals on a railroad is a neglect of serious duty, and hence evil. The morality of an act, as for example, stealing, may be simply aggravated by the circumstances, such as the amount stolen; or it may be changed specifically, as in the theft of sacred vessels, when the sin of sacrilege is added to that of theft. We have treated *ends* sufficiently in the preceding chapter.

[7] Slater, *Moral Theology,* I, 45.

154. Principles Regarding Object, End, and Circumstances. Any one of these elements—object, end, or circumstances—may make an action evil, but only all three together can make it good. The fact that one of these is bad vitiates the whole act and makes it unlawful. To give alms is good; to give them as a bribe is evil, the evil arising from the intention. To aid the poor is praiseworthy, but to steal in order to do so robs the action of its goodness; to save the life of another is an act of charity, but to do it by a lie, an action intrinsically immoral, makes the whole act evil.

155. Distinction Between Material and Formal Morality. But an act rendered evil *materially* by an evil object or circumstance may, however, be perfectly good *formally*. Material morality concerns the action in itself and in its circumstances; formal morality concerns the action as it appears in the mind of the agent. A man who in his sleep shoots another has committed material homicide, but he is not formally guilty because he did not intend his act; and the person who gives a beneficial drink thinking it to be a deadly poison is formally guilty of murder.

156. Material Evil May Be Formally Obligatory. It may so happen, indeed, that what is formally good may be materially evil and vice versa. Hence in order to please God one may sometimes be obliged to commit material wrong or to avoid material good. Whenever through invincible ignorance a man believes some action in itself evil to be a duty for him, he is morally obliged to do it; or if he should think an action good in itself to be evil, he is morally obliged to avoid it. Thus it is said that certain savage tribes consider that filial duty commands the killing of parents when they get so old that they are a burden to themselves; a child who neglected this unless he were more enlightened than his tribe, would be guilty of formal wrongdoing. Or an East Indian widow believing that her wifely duty required that she give herself to the suttee would be bound to this form of suicide.

157. To Make Material Morality Correspond with Formal Is the Chief Object of Ethics. Therefore when we say that an act to be good must be good in its object, end, and circumstances, to be evil need be evil in only one of these elements, we mean it with the qualifications we have just mentioned. The real ethical value for the agent comes from the end, and from the object and circumstances only in so far as their character is known to him. But it is the business of ethical science to establish the objective moral standard and to educate mind and conscience until material and formal morality correspond. The ethician wishes to remove the conscientious obligation under which some persons now labor of committing material wrong in order to avoid formal evil.

158. Can Moral Acts Be Indifferent? Can moral acts considered concretely and in particular, be neither good nor bad, but indifferent? Human acts done without any advertence to the moral order are neither good nor bad; but are all human acts done with advertence to the norm of morality either good or bad? Is the act of a particular individual person done with an end and the other adjuncts accompanying action in the concrete ever indifferent? Bonaventure[8] and the Scotists affirm that there can be indifferent acts, whereas St. Thomas[9] and the greater number of other theologians deny that a particular act can be indifferent. The Scotists argue that when an action (as eating candy) is performed only to satisfy some natural want, it is not good because it is not related to the final end of the agent; nor is it bad because it is not opposed to his rational nature, and hence it must be indifferent. Thomists argue: either the agent intends a good end or he does not intend a good end. Hence he either apprehends the action to be according to the exact norm of reason, and the act is good; or opposed to such norm, and the act is bad. There is no middle conception which adverts to the morality of the action.

159. Is an Act Done Solely for Pleasure Always Evil? This question of indifferent acts has a practical bearing, because some persons interpreting the Thomist doctrine in a very strict way maintain that to be morally good an act must be *positively* re-

[8] In 2 dist. 4a, 1q. 3.
[9] I, II, Q. XVIII, A. 9.

ferred to a good end. If this be true, and there are no indifferent human acts, then acts done for pleasure without this positive reference are morally bad. This view would unsparingly condemn all mere pleasure-seeking. But a milder opinion holds that *negative* reference to the last end—in the sense that the end is not excluded—is sufficient to make an act good, and that acts done merely for pleasure may have this negative reference.[10]

SUGGESTED READINGS

1. Rickaby, *Moral Philosophy,* Ch. VI.
2. Cronin, *Science of Ethics,* I, Chs. IV, V.
3. Ming, *Data of Modern Ethics,* Chs. VI, VII.
4. Hill, *Moral Philosophy,* Pt. I, Ch. III.
5. McDonald, *Principles of Moral Science,* Bk. I, Chs. I, II, VI, VII.
6. Humphrey, *Conscience and Law,* Ch. I.

QUESTIONS

1. What is good? How can moral good be distinguished from non-moral?
2. Is difference between good and evil objective?
3. What are the ultimate and proximate norms of morality?
4. What are the criteria of morality? Distinguish between norm and criteria.
5. What are the determinants of morality? Define each.

[10] Cf. Noldin, *Theologia Moralis,* 6th ed., I, p. 110 ff.

FIVE: *Duty*[1]

I. WHAT IS DUTY?[2]

160. Teaching Regarding Right and Good. We have discussed the essence of right and good. It was said to be conformity ultimately with God's nature and proximately with man's. Further, we considered certain means whereby we can discern if all the elements of an act—object, end, and circumstances—conform with this norm. It was said the failure of any one element to conform rendered the act evil either formally or materially. The distinction between material and formal morality is the distinction between the act objectively and its conception in the mind of the agent. So that an evil object or circumstance makes the act materially wrong; an evil intention or a conception of the act as wrong makes it formally wrong.

161. Distinction Between Righteousness and Duty. But it is not sufficient merely to establish what is right and good. We stand in an essentially different relation to some good from that in which we stand toward other good. The omission of some right acts is wrong; the omission of other right acts is not wrong. It may be a good thing for a particular man to become a priest, but it may not be wrong for him to refuse the opportunity. Only when a distinctly new element enters does the omission become an evil, and that element is obligation. The feeling of oughtness is distinct from the feeling of righteousness. This sense of bounden duty needs further explanation and analysis.

[1] Cf. Cronin, Ch. VIII; Brosnahan, p. 34 ff.; McDonald, Bk. I, Chs. VI, VIII; Rickaby, Ch. VI.

[2] Bouquillon defines duty as "something reasonably due from one person to another because of a necessary connection between the end to be attained and the means used." *Theol. Mor. Fund.*, ed. 2a, p. 188. Here we are simply accepting the universal sense of duty and drawing conclusions from its existence. For a further discussion of duty consult chapter on "Rights, Justice, Duties" in second part.

72

162. Is There a Categorical Imperative? First of all is a sense of obligation ever categorical, or is it always hypothetical? That is, do I feel obliged only on condition that I want to gain a certain end? If I wish to go to Europe, I must take a boat. The obligation of taking a boat depends upon the wish to go. But must I wish to go to Europe? Not at all; the obligation of taking a boat remains hypothetical to my going to Europe. If I wish to enter the army, I must pass an examination. Another hypothetical obligation, because I am not bound to wish to enter the army. If I wish to act rationally, I must not violate my nature. Is this also merely hypothetical, or is there some moral compulsion binding me to wish to act rationally? That is the crux of the question; and unless that ultimate necessity of willing to act rationally can be proven, no obligation can be demonstrated. For a man can logically reply: Yes, but I don't wish to act rationally.

163. Can Unconditional Duty Be Proven? All Scholastic ethicians, of course, agree that man ought to act rationally. But divisions arise when we ask for proof of a moral obligation to use the means to the end of acting rationally. Some, indeed, attempt to offer proof, though hardly with absolute convincingness.

164. Attempted Proofs. Thus Cronin [3] presents three arguments which will not be materially weakened by a little compression. (1) Man's last end is the perfect good. This the will must wish from its very nature. The perfect good it can not help desiring, for in the perfect good there is nothing from which the will can turn away. (2) No will can refuse its adhesion to what we might call the first principle of the will—namely, its last end. (3) The act of the will is essentially an act of movement, of direction towards an end. But movement is impossible unless it begins in something which is firmly fixed. Consequently, our will movement must begin with the desire of some fixed end—some end, that is, on which the will is itself naturally and permanently fixed. If there were no such object or end, the

[3] *Science of Ethics*, p. 208.

will could not begin to move. There is, then, an end which the will desires, not through choice, but because it is fixed on such an end.

165. Criticism of These Arguments. But all these arguments would seem to be either the reiteration of the very thing that needs proof—that we must seek to act rationally—or else prove too much. They prove nothing or they prove the impossibility of formal wrong doing, inasmuch as formal wrong doing is a wilful and known turning away from the last end. But if we mean by the will seeking the last end simply a natural tendency[4] that can be voluntarily frustrated, a position apparently denied in the foregoing arguments, why not grant at the beginning that such a thing as duty exists? It is just as evident and as easily acceptable.

166. Admission That Unconditional Duty Cannot Be Proven. Therefore, it seems better to admit (as do McDonald[5] and Rickaby[6]) that we cannot prove the existence of duty. All that we can do is to place the postulates derived from other sciences before the student and trust to his response. If a man understanding the situation—the relation between a benevolent, good, and wise Being to whose nature certain actions conform while others do not, and a creature owing to Him existence and the power of choice—if a man, grasping this fundamental position, does not realize the duty of acting in "conformity with that nature," then it is useless to say anything more.

167. Moral Resonance. Response to a moral situation has been called "moral resonance," by analogy with the Helmholtz resonators in physics. They are hollow metal spheres with a small hole in one side. Each sphere of given dimensions will vibrate to one tone; and in a lesser degree if the overtone be sounded. When any other tones are sounded, the sphere remains absolutely silent. Corresponding somewhat to this sympathetic resonance or vibration in the acoustic field is the response of different

[4] If the tendency be *natural,* then the obligation is necessarily categorical—the precise point at issue, as already pointed out.
[5] *Principles of Moral Science,* p. 110.
[6] *Moral Philosophy,* Ch. VI, Sec. II.

individuals to moral stimuli. It is often found that a particular human being will respond to one moral argument while another remains absolutely unresponsive. Repetition of the argument affects these others no more than the repetition of a note affects a sphere not attuned to that rapidity of vibration.

II. Sense of Duty Universal

168. Sense of Duty Universal Though Content Varies. So far as we know, however, there is no one who has not this sense of oughtness. We do not mean that all men give the same content to this feeling, that they agree as to what they ought or ought not to do. The specific moral code varies indefinitely from age to age and race to race. "Thou shalt love thy neighbor as thyself" implies obligation; but just what obligation, varies with the definition of neighbor. In earlier ages neighbor meant merely blood relatives. Even in later pagan developments it embraced only members of the same tribe or city. It is Christianity's glory that she has extended its meaning to take in the whole world. Therefore, when we say that a sense of duty is universal, we mean simply that all men, without exception, think they are morally and categorically bound to do some things and to avoid others.

169. How Did Sense of Duty Originate? But admitting the present universality of this conviction of duty (as most thinkers and investigators do admit it), how can it be accounted for? Why do all men feel this sense of obligation, this weight of duty pressing upon their consciences?

170. Scholastic Explanation of Origin of Duty. The Scholastics answer that the sense of obligation is an intuitive perception of a necessity flowing from the nature of things, that we cannot prove it apodictically, but it is written indelibly upon the heart of every individual by the Author of his being. We feel it ourselves; everyone feels it; everyone we can learn about in the past by authentic and sufficient records felt it; hence it is an inseparable part of man's psychology.

171. Utilitarian Explanation of the Origin of Duty. Many modern ethicians, however, are at considerable pains to explain the presence of this feeling on other grounds than the intuitive perception of an essentially distinct and unique *moral* force or obligation. A sense of moral duty, they say, is not in its nature different from a sense of any other obligation. It is the simple result of a mere association of ideas. Its origin can be traced to a sense of constraint connected with certain acts. Either the natural consequences of these acts were painful or an artificial sanction was attached to them by some external authority. There was imposed upon the individual conscience a disjunctive necessity: "Refrain from this action or be punished." Gradually this "or be punished" dropped from the mind and left only the injunction "Do this." [7]

172. Evolutionary Explanation of the Origin of Duty. The utilitarian theory is not changed essentially by increasing the length of time necessary for the process of producing this sense of duty. To throw the question back into remote times does not alter the situation fundamentally. So far as objections are concerned, it makes little difference whether the transition from extrinsic sanction to internal moral necessity takes place in the life of the individual from infancy to maturity, or only gradually throughout many generations. For the contention is that an impassable gulf yawns between a sense of moral duty and any other feeling of necessity. Our consciousness tells us that moral obligation is different from every other kind of compulsion, and that no length of time or process of evolution can change one into the other.

173. Association Is Not a Sufficient Explanation of the Origin of Duty. There are two reasons for maintaining that the sense of duty is absolutely unique. One reason is that mere association can never force our intellects into assenting to any proposition. Thus a color and a perfume may be constantly associated together in our minds, but we do not confuse one with the other. Because

[7] Cf. Spencer, *Data of Ethics*, Ch. VII; Baldwin, *Dict. Phil.*, art. "Duty."

a red rose has a certain fragrance, we do not say that red is sweet. The character of redness and the character of fragrance are kept distinct. Similarly, an action that inevitably brings punishment may be wrong; but wrongness and punishableness are not thought to be identical; and can never come to be interchangeable. We do not conclude that because another act is likewise punishable, it is therefore wrong. If legislation and penalty were the foundation of this sense of obligation, it would attach to many things that are not looked upon as moral or immoral. The cutting of the hair was forbidden for centuries in China, but intelligent Chinese did not look upon the wearing of pigtails as having any intrinsic moral sanction.

174. Even Should Association Explain the Content of Duty It Would Not Touch Its Essence. And even though in individual cases there were a passage from legislation to morality so that what one at first did on the extrinsic ground of command by legitimate authority, he afterwards came to do as intrinsically obligatory, this would account to some extent for the content of duty, but not for its essence. If fear of punishment and sense of duty are not really different in themselves, why do they both exist? Why do men pass from one to the other? Again, one may by a process of reasoning enlarge or decrease the content of his sense of obligation. A particular object before thought moral may later come to be looked upon as immoral. But duty is not therefore a creation of the intellect. Duty *in itself* is independent of the intellect; it is only its content that admits of fluctuations. The intellect does not create the sense of duty, but simply makes it apply to an object heretofore outside of its influence.

175. Problem Is How There Is a Category of "Duty." Similarly, the intellect, habit, environment, authority may make one come to see as true what previously he looked upon as false. The intellect, habit, and the rest have not created truth. In the same way, assuming for the sake of argument, that many Irish persons by long abstinence on Fridays in obedience to the Church have come to look upon eating meat on this day as intrinsically wrong, this ecclesiastical legislation has not produced duty; it has merely taken an act from the category of the morally-unlawful-because-legally-forbidden and placed it in the category in-itself-morally-unlawful. It is evident that this does not touch the question as to how the categories originated. A chemist who breaks up a supposed element, and shows that it really consists of two previously unknown constituents, has not produced or created them. He has simply changed our way of looking at them and has not touched the problem of their original production. In this case, therefore, we wish to know not how anything came to be looked upon as duty, but how "duty" itself originated.

176. These Association Theories Would Lead to Moral Chaos. Another argument against this association idea is that of expediency. While it has been said that such an argument has no force, because the pleasant or unpleasant consequences of a theory do not affect its truth, this is only objected to by those who take too contracted a view of the question. For we assume from natural theology that this universe and everything in it came from the hand of an all-good and all-wise God. Hence any theory that would bring disturbance, revolution, and disorder into society cannot correspond with the objective facts, cannot be true. But if men once became thoroughly convinced that there is no moral obligation back of the code of right and wrong, that it is all a matter of custom, with no better foundation than the varying styles in a woman's dress, all society would be turned topsy-turvy. Legal procedure and police force cannot reach thousands upon thousands of acts that are socially influential; and if the restraining effect of obligation were ever entirely removed from the average man, there would be no power equal to the task of making him a useful citizen. Therefore, an all-good and all-wise God cannot so have designed the world.

III. WHAT VIOLATION OF DUTY DEPRIVES ONE OF HIS LAST END?

177. Does All Sin Mean Eternal Loss? Simply to omit something that is right, is not itself wrong. There must be attached to the right thing the note of obligation, of duty, before its omission becomes wrong. But we may now ask if all violation of duty means the loss of one's last end? Or may there be a violation of duty that is consistent with the ultimate attainment of one's last end, but in a less perfect and complete way? This problem is broader than the lessening of guilt through influences making actions less voluntary. It is perfectly evident that if one is ignorant of the character of his act, there can be no formal sin, and hence no loss of one's last end. The agent is really not turning away from his last end formally. And it is the formal quality of the act that determines its character. The same thing holds true if it is the will rather than the intellect that is affected in such a way as to reduce the formal sin.

178. Mortal and Venial Matter. Our question is rather whether there can be some acts that are perfectly human—that is fully deliberate and done with a thorough knowledge of their character—which, though wrong, are not wrong in such a way as to necessitate the loss of the last end if they are unrepented of. Is the division of wrong acts into serious and slight justified? All Scholastic moralists agree that it is. This is merely the familiar distinction between mortal and venial sins, or rather between mortal and venial matter.

179. More or Less Perfect Possession Last End. And I think that if once we grasp the meaning of the last end and what we must do to attain it, or to lose it, we can see that this distinction between serious and slight matter is perfectly reasonable. The possession of God by our highest faculties, intellect and free will, is the ultimate *end* of our existence. But these faculties are not only limited, they vary with the individual. Hence it seems evident that there may be degrees of this possession, a more and less, a perfect and imperfect. That is true objectively. But is there also a subjective variation? May not only individuals vary, but may the same individual vary? That is, may there be a difference for him between perfect and imperfect? We are certainly on sound ground in answering with all Scholastic moralists that there may be this distinction.

180. Serious Matter. There are three things, then, necessary to make an act of such a nature that its agent forfeits his last end. The first of these is that the act objectively should be serious. Not any slight violation of morality means such complete deordination as to necessitate this loss. If a boy steals a penny, for instance, he is not going to be damned for all eternity for this. The matter is in itself too trivial. And while we may say, indeed, that nothing can be trivial when related to God, and that the slightest offense against Him merits eternal punishment; yet we must also remember that in a certain sense it is not God Who damns a soul, but the soul that damns itself. That is to say, damnation simply follows as a necessary consequence of the act of the individual. Nor is it too lax to maintain that damnation, eternal loss of one's last end, is not a necessary consequence of such a slight turning away from it as is included in stealing a penny.

181. The Race of Life. By putting the situation graphically we can perhaps grasp the idea more clearly. It is not, of course, an accurate description of the actual facts, but we have the example of St. Paul to justify the figure. He compared our life to a race in which we all run for a prize. Geometrically, there is one shortest line between the point where we start and the point where we end. That path may be said to be not only strait, but also straight. The man who keeps to it absolutely will win a greater prize than the man who varies somewhat from this accurately straight line. But one can take a step to the right or left at times while still going in the general direction of the goal. He will end up there, though with a less perfect record than the other man. As long as he does not turn his back on the goal and go in the other direction, he may be said to be making toward it. Full faced turning around may be compared to mortal sin, to complete deordination, to the loss of one's last end; a few steps off the absolutely straight line, while still going forward, may be compared to venial sin, to something short of complete deordination, to a less perfect attainment of one's last end of possessing God with his intellect and will.

182. Knowledge. The second element required in a mortal sin is a knowledge of the seriousness of the matter. We have already emphasized this point sufficiently. And it ought, therefore, to be perfectly clear that if one at the time of acting does not know the nature of one's act, one is not formally responsible. Unless, indeed, one was formally responsible for one's ignorance.

183. Deliberateness. And the third element in complete deordination is full deliberation. This, too, has been sufficiently treated under voluntariness. If for any reason the will does not fully consent, there cannot be the complete turning away from one's last end that is needed to lose it forever.[8]

184. How Many Will Be Damned? How many do turn away from the Infinite in this deliberate and knowing and complete manner? Revelation tells us nothing and reason but little. The only practical conclusion we can draw is that without all these elements entering into one's act one will not lose one's last end; and that when they are all present, and one dies without changing one's will, one damns oneself to a loss of one's last end.

185. Repentance Possible Till Death. There is only one other point to be discussed in this connection. If one has sinned in this

[8] McDonald claiming to have all Scholastic moralists with him, states the matter somewhat differently. He says: "The full concept of sin would represent it not only as an act which is (1) inordinate, and (2) disobedient, but moreover, (3) tends to separate the sinner forever from the enjoyment of the Infinite Good. . . . Mortal sin [as explained by St. Thomas and his school] implies an act of will by which one turns away from the Infinite Good and turns to something finite, weighing one against the other, and freely preferring the finite; thereby giving God a right to confirm the will forever in his choice. . . . Or if you view the sin as an act of aversion rather than as one of conversion, of hate rather than of love—every act of love being, at least implicitly, an act of hate of the evil which is formally opposed to the good which is the object of the love-tendency,—the formal object of the aversion in which mortal sin consists, is the Infinite Good regarded as an evil—as the negation of some finite good towards which one cannot efficaciously tend while tending to the Infinite. This is the very essence of the form of mortal sin—deliberate aversion from the Infinite Good, or free choice of something finite in preference to the Infinite. Unless the will tends by an act of love to the finite in preference to the Infinite—or what is the same thing, unless it tends away from the Infinite towards the finite—there cannot be formal mortal sin, no matter how serious may be the intemperance, or the injustice, or the disobedience, even towards the divine authority, which the faculty embraces." (*The Principles of Moral Science,* pp. 138, 139.) McDonald quotes as agreeing with him in this doctrine of mortal sin, St. Thomas, Suarez, Lacroix, Mazella, and Lehmkuhl.

deliberate, knowing, and complete way, can one repair the injury one has done to oneself? That is, will one inevitably lose one's last end, or can one have another chance of reaching it? As far as reason can analyze our possibilities, it tells us that up to the last breath man can change. One good act does not make it impossible for a man never to sin thereafter; and one bad act, no matter what its nature, does not make it impossible for him afterwards to be good. All around us are examples of sinners being converted. It is the attitude of will, the direction in which it is pointed at the time of death, that counts. And in this, reason is supported by Revelation.

SUGGESTED READINGS

1. Cronin, *Science of Ethics,* I, Ch. VIII.
2. McDonald, *Principles of Moral Science,* Bk. I, Chs. VI, VIII.
3. Rickaby, *Moral Philosophy,* Ch. VI.
4. Spencer, *Data of Ethics,* Ch. VII.
5. Baldwin, *Dict. of Phil.,* art. "Duty."
6. Cath Encyc., art. "Duty."

QUESTIONS

1. What is duty? Can unconditional duty be proven?
2. How did sense of duty originate?
3. Distinguish between category of duty and content of a moral code.
4. Do all formal transgressions of the moral code imply a loss of one's last end?

SIX: *Law*[1]

I. LAW IS KNOWN BY CONSCIENCE

186. How Does Duty Become Concrete? The concept of duty involves three elements: one who obliges; the subject bound; and that to which the subject is bound. So far we have discussed the fact of obligation that flows from the necessary relation between man and his Creator. It remains now to consider the way in which duty becomes concretized through natural law as known by conscience, and through positive law deriving authority from the natural law.

187. The "Eternal Law." A law, in a strict sense, is an ordinance of reason directed to the common good and promulgated by one who has authority over the community.[2] The act of will whereby God wishes that all rational beings should direct their actions according to reason is called the "eternal law." It is eternal and unchangeable, because it flows necessarily from the nature of God, for God cannot do otherwise than will men to act rationally. He was not free to make a different law, given human beings as they are.

188. The "Natural Law": What It Is Not. In addition to the eternal law, moralists speak of another unchangeable law which they call natural. "The natural law is often represented by Catholic writers as some kind of participation of the eternal law, possessed by rational creatures; as some kind of impression on man of the divine light whereby he may be able to discern good from evil; and as a natural innate conception whereby a man may direct his acts in accordance with right reason."[3]

189. What It Is. Such a conception of the "natural law" is apt to lead to difficulties. It is similar to the confusion that arises

[1] Cf. Slater, *Moral Theology,* I, pp. 81 ff.; Brosnahan, VI, VII; McDonald, Bk. I, ch. IX; Cathrein, I. pp. 368 ff.; Rickaby, pp. 126 ff.

[2] St. Thomas, I, II, Q. 90, A. 4.

[3] McDonald, p. 114. In support of his statement, cf. Zigliara, *Ethica,* 24, I; Slater, I, p. 116; Cathrein, I, p. 380; Rickaby, p. 134.

from speaking of conscience as a separate faculty—the voice of God, an inward monitor—somehow independent of the agent himself. McDonald seems to have reason on his side when he goes on to say: "Strictly speaking, the natural law is neither an impression of the divine light on the soul of man, nor a conception of any kind, nor anything like a participation of the act of the intellect or will in which the eternal law formally consists." "As I understand the term 'natural law,' it denotes, not so much an enactment of a ruling will—a law in the strict sense —as an order or relation objectively existing and capable of being expressed in a general formula akin to the laws of motion and other such principles of which we read in physics. It is, for instance, in accordance with the natural law that murder is inordinate; the meaning being that the moral order existing objectively between any two men whatsoever, is such as is expressed in the formula, murder is wrong." [4]

190. Summary of Preceding Paragraphs. The *eternal law,* then, is the act of will whereby God wishes that all rational beings should direct their actions according to reason; the *natural law* is the objective order existing between creatures or between creatures and the Creator.

191. How Is the Natural Law Known? How is this objective order of relationship known? Is a knowledge of it innate in all men? Or is it known directly and immediately by some ethical faculty? Are all ethical truths, that is the whole natural law so known? or only some? or none at all?

192. The Natural Law Is Known Partly Through Intuition. The Scholastic position is that some moral principles are known intuitively; that their number is rather limited; and that a knowledge of the whole natural law can be deduced from these few primary principles. An intuitively known truth is one evident to anyone who apprehends the meaning of the terms.

193. Proof That Natural Law Is Known Through Intuition. It is clear that some moral truths must be so known because

[4] McDonald, pp. 114, 115.

some of our moral beliefs are deduced from other moral beliefs, and all deductions must begin with truths that are self-evident. There cannot be an endless chain of deductions. These primary assumptions of Ethics, or self-evident ethical truths, are not drawn from non-moral principles, because they concern moral goodness and evil, and, therefore, do not form the subject matter of other sciences. There could be no logical passage from the non-moral to the moral.[5]

194. The Natural Law Is Not Entirely Known Through Intuition. This is very different, however, from asserting that all moral truths are known thus directly. It is carrying the principle too far to declare [6] that all men can by means of direct perception and without reasoning of any kind, pronounce correct judgment ordinarily on the morality of particular acts at the moment of action. Such a theory makes moral perception analogous to vision whereby we see immediately whether an object be white or not. It contradicts the universal experience that we reason about some of our moral judgments.

195. The Faculty by Which the Natural Law Is Known Is Reason.[7] The faculty by which we know moral truths, or perceive the natural law is not distinct from the faculty by which we know other truths. A great deal of confusion has been caused in the discussion of morals by speaking of conscience as a distinct faculty independent of the agent. While we know some moral truths intuitively, we know them by the practical reason, and they are so general that we can not immediately conclude that anyone is violating his conscience by acting in a particular way. Conscience is merely the reason giving a decision here and now that a certain act is right or wrong. That judgment may be correct or erroneous, but whichever it be argues no more

---

[5] For a partial enumeration of self-evident moral truths, cf. Cronin, I, pp. 483 ff. Differences of opinion arise when we come to specify these truths. But all authors would undoubtedly agree that "do good and avoid evil," "render to each according to his due," are examples of self-evident principles.

[6] For excesses in this direction, cf. Cronin, I, Chs. XIV, XV; Moore, *Historical Introduction to Ethics,* Pt. II, I to IV.

[7] For general treatment of conscience, see art. "Conscience" in Cath. Encyc.

moral turpitude than a correct or erroneous addition of figures.

196. Conscience Is Influenced by Tradition and Environment.
It is true that in any given society, certain moral truths come so readily to individuals born into that society—synderesis is the scholastic term given to the group of such truths—that they seem to come naturally. But it is difficult to determine how far they are known intuitively, or are easy deductions from such truths, or are imbibed from tradition and the teaching of others. The most reasonable position would seem to be the restriction of intuitively known truths to a few (such as "avoid evil"), and to say that the rest are derived almost entirely from tradition and environment. Otherwise, it is difficult to see how children born in one age have different sets of moral truths from those born in another.

197. Conscience Can Develop. Since conscience is nothing else than reason, it can develop or decay. Every new truth that we attain in the moral field increases the power of conscience just as every new mathematical truth increases the power of the intellect in that branch of knowledge. The more we know the more we can know, applies in Ethics as in other sciences. And conscience can develop by increasing in keenness. Practice makes perfect here as elsewhere. As argumentation sharpens the attorney's wits, so does earnest following of conscience increase its power of discernment until a wonderful sensitiveness is developed.

198. Conscience Can Decay. But as a conscience can develop, so it can decay. Any sickness that weakens the intellect will weaken conscience, and it can be lost entirely by losing one's reason. The power of the intellect, however, can be weakened in any one field, while remaining vigorous in other matters. So we often find men of keen minds but of a dull moral sense. Constant misuse of conscience, or the influence of desire upon thought, can so cripple the mind that it comes naturally to see things aslant.

> "The instinctive theorizing whence a fact
> Looks to the eye as the eye likes the look"

is more widespread and more evident in the sphere of morals than in any other. Conscience can be silenced on almost any given point. Familiarity with vice breeds a tolerance that fast becomes approval.

199. But Conscience Cannot Be Entirely Lost. Nevertheless, there is a limit to the decay of conscience. No one can ever entirely lose his moral sense, except by insanity. What he once considered wrong, he may come to look upon as right; but there will always be something in the category of wrong. The old Scotch brigand mentioned by Sir Walter Scott thought no oath sacred unless sworn on the handle of a certain dagger. But while his conscience was distorted and blunted, he still acknowledged some things as wrong. Many anthropologists have endeavored to show that some savage races have no moral sense, in the effort to prove that the distinction between moral good and moral evil is not natural to man, but an artificial product having no real moral sanction. The attempt has not succeeded. The moral ideals of the savages differ from ours, just as their scientific ideals differ; but all races have some idea of what is bad.[8] The difference no more disproves our moral code than the fact of their different "science" disproves our science. For even if savage man has no moral ideas, the objective truth of certain moral propositions remains; just as the objective truth of Euclid's propositions exists despite the savage's ignorance of them.

200. Conscience Is Supreme. The real lesson to be drawn from this difference of moral ideas and the possibility of the decay of conscience, is an earnest, prayerful guarding of our gift. It is more incumbent upon us that we should preserve and develop our intellectual powers in this field than in any other, because it is the most important. The gaining of our ultimate end depends upon the following of our conscience, and while on the one hand we are justified and even bound to follow a false conscience, on

---

[8] Cf. Cronin, pp. 521 ff. It may be argued that though savages do surround certain moral actions, such as marriage, with ceremonies and sanctions, they may still have no moral sense. From the nature of the case neither side can prove its contention, but the burden of proof would seem to be upon those who wish to contradict appearances.

the other hand we can not excuse our ignorance if we have wilfully neglected to enlighten our conscience. "It is never lawful to go against our conscience," as the Fourth Council of the Lateran says: *"Quidquid fit contra conscientiam aedificat ad gehennam."* [9] But we should do all that we reasonably can to make our conscience correct and to sharpen its powers of perception.

201. Conscience Promulgates Law. The eternal law of God, then is made known to us by the supreme voice of conscience—that is, by the practical reason here and now giving a judgment as to the morality of an action.

202. Other Laws. In addition to the eternal and immutable law that flows from the essence of God, there are various laws depending more or less immediately upon His will. Thus we have the divine positive law, as in the precept to keep holy the Sabbath; we have ecclesiastical law, and we have civil law. They all derive their binding power from the eternal law—that the creature owes obedience to the Creator, that the Creator vests a Church with authority, that a State must have authority to command if men are to live peaceably.

II. Principles for Interpreting Laws

203. The Interpretation of Laws. Where there is a legitimate tribunal to interpret laws, that tribunal must be obeyed. But

---

[9] Quoted by Newman, *Difficulties of Anglicans,* II, p. 247, from Card. Gousset, *Theologie Morale.* Newman continues: "The celebrated school, known as the Salamanticenses, or Carmelites of Salamanca, lays down the broad proposition that conscience is ever to be obeyed, whether the error is the fault of the person or not. They say that this opinion is certain, and refer, as agreeing with them, to St. Thomas, St. Bonaventure, Caietan, Vasquez, Durandus, Navarrus, Corduba, Layman, Escobar, and fourteen others. Of course, if a man is culpable in being in error, which he might have escaped, had he been more in earnest, for that error he is answerable to God, but still he must act according to that error while he is in it, because he in full sincerity thinks the error to be truth. . . . Suppose there was a Papal order to hold lotteries in each mission for some religious object, and a priest could say in God's sight that he believed lotteries to be morally wrong, that priest . . . would commit a sin *hic et nunc* if he obeyed the Pope, whether he was right or wrong in his opinion, and if wrong, although he had not taken the proper pains to get at the truth of the matter." (Pp. 259-260.)

where there is no such tribunal, or recourse cannot be had to it for some good reason, there are certain principles governing interpretation.

204. Custom as Interpreting Law. In the first place, custom is the best interpreter of human law, and can even entirely abrogate a particular enactment. For this, however, certain conditions are required. The legislator must consent at least tacitly; the custom must be reasonable, entered into freely by the majority of the community, and must have existed a sufficiently long time.

205. When Laws Are to Be Interpreted Narrowly. Again, laws establishing an obligation are to be interpreted in the narrowest terms possible, so as to place the smallest inconvenience upon the fewest number of subjects consistent with the wording of the law; laws conferring a privilege are to be interpreted as broadly as possible. To take an illustration from ecclesiastical law: travelers are not bound by laws peculiar to the place in which they are visiting, though they may take advantage of the privileges enjoyed there. Thus one who in his own domicile would be bound to fast upon a certain day because of a special law, and going to a locality where a similar special law enjoins fasting would not be obliged to fast, because the law of his own domicile does not apply beyond it, and the law of the place he is visiting is restricted to subjects of that locality.

206. Dispensations and Epikia. We may sometimes presume a dispensation, or interpret a law not to extend to a particular case on account of special circumstances. This latter is called epikia. It is justified by the fact that no human legislator can foresee all the diverse circumstances in which his subjects will be placed regarding a law. Epikia may be used whenever from the special circumstances one may prudently conclude that the law-giver did not wish to include this particular case. This will be so whenever the observance of the law would be bad or hurtful or too burdensome.[10]

207. When Laws Cease to Bind. Since the eternal law does not depend on God's free will, it binds always and forever. There

[10] Noldin, I, 160.

are no exceptions whatever. It can never be abrogated. But any other law, "even the divine positive law,"[11] does not bind men when great inconveniences would follow from its observance. It is an axiom that necessity knows no law. This is all the more true of positive human law, which must be accommodated to the moral strength of the majority of the people; otherwise it will be impossible to observe it, and nobody can be bound to do what is impossible. Hence, not only physical impossibility excuses from the observance of the law, but also any relatively great difficulty or serious inconvenience which constitutes moral impossibility."[12]

208. Caution in Applying This Principle. Moralists add, however, that such an excuse cannot be applied when the violation of the law would result in public injury, in great spiritual hurt to some individual, or in hatred of God.[13]

209. Laws Cease When Object Cannot Be Obtained. It is also held by some moralists that a law ceases to bind in a particular case when its observance would not attain any of the objects for which it was intended.[14] Hence, laws forbidding interest-taking have become inoperative, because economic conditions have changed to such an extent as to preclude the attainment of their object by keeping them.

III. MORAL SYSTEMS [15]

210. Difference of Opinion in Applying Principles. It does not require much imagination to see that there will be frequently a difference of opinion as to the application of these principles. And if one moralist maintains that there is no obligation under certain circumstances and another maintains that there is, what must the poor lay person do? This difficulty has given rise to

[11] Law made known through revelation and depending upon God's will. It is "positive" even though it forbids certain actions. Cf. Slater, I, p. 83.
[12] Slater, I, p. 104.
[13] Noldin, I, p. 159.
[14] Bucceroni, *Theol. Mor.*, I, n. 172.
[15] Cath. Encyc., art. "Probabilism"; *Catholic Moral Teaching*, by Mausbach, pp. 176 ff.

various moral systems attempting to offer a reasonable principle for action.

211. Systems for Obtaining Certainty of Conscience. All agree that it is never lawful to act with a doubtful conscience. But they suggest different means for arriving at certainty. *Absolute tutiorism* insists that the opinion in favor of the law must be followed, even though a contrary opinion is most probable; *modified tutiorism* maintains that we should follow the opinion in favor of the obligation unless a contrary opinion be most probable; *probabiliorism* allows one to follow an opinion in favor of liberty if it be more probable than that for the obligation; *equi-probabilism* permits one to follow an opinion in favor of liberty when it is equally probable with one for the law; *probabilism* contends that it is lawful to follow any truly probable opinion, even though the contrary opinion be more probable; *laxism* allows the following of an opinion only doubtfully or weakly probable.

212. Condemned Systems. Laxism and absolute tutiorism have been condemned by the Catholic Church.[16] Any other system may be followed, provided the individual using the opinion really agrees with it. One may never act with a doubtful conscience, and unless he has made it certain, either by his own investigations or by the reflex principle that what experts hold to be right must be so, he is bound not to take advantage of the liberty.

213. Probabilism. Practically, however, probabilism is the system most in vogue. It has back of it the weight of St. Alphonsus and the whole Jesuit school. Pascal immortalized it in his famous *Provincial Letters* when he attacked the way in which Escobar had published certain opinions. The principle, however, seems clear; and despite the possibility of abuse, the system justifies itself by its good results.

214. A Doubtful Law Does Not Bind. The basis of probabilism is the contention that a doubtful law has no binding force. It does not bind because one is free unless there is a contrary law,

[16] Denzinger, 1153, 1293.

and the burden of proof is on those who assert the existence of a law. For only a known law can induce an obligation, since the will follows only what the intellect declares to be right. But when the intellect doubts as to the existence of a law, it does not know the law; for true knowledge must be certain. Hence, one who doubts about the existence of a law has no obligation to observe it.

215. What Constitutes a Doubt? Really to doubt, however, the opinion in favor of liberty must have sound probability; and certain conditions are necessary for this. The motive for doubt must be really serious or proposed by weighty authority, and must be able to retain its probability when compared with the reasons for the opposite course.

216. Limitations of Probabilism. Probabilism has application only where there is a question of the lawfulness or unlawfulness of an action, and only when there is a doubt of law. When the case concerns validity or invalidity or a doubt of fact that cannot be reduced to a doubt of law, the safer course must be followed.

IV. Sanction of Law

217. The Sanction of the Natural Law. Every law must have a sanction, and we proceed to enquire as to the sanction of the natural law. Since a breaking of the natural law is simply a turning away from one's last end, the obvious sanction for such conduct is missing of that end. Continued, persistent, final turning away from that end means a failure to attain it unless there be another probation in the next life.

218. What Reason Tells Us of This Sanction. Thus much philosophy can tell us. And some sort of punishment in the next life would seem to be required by our ideas of justice. For all around us we see the wicked prospering and the good suffering. The sins of the parents are visited upon innocent babes. Virtue is not its own reward in this life, and our nature demands adjustment of accounts hereafter.

219. Is This Sanction Final and Eternal? This punishment is *medicinal,* as being a curative process for the individual; *deterrent,* as being an example and warning to others; and *retributive,* as satisfying violated order. Whether or not it is eternal, philosophy cannot say. It might continue for a while and then end in annihilation. Or the punishment might be immediate sinking into nothingness. Nor can philosophy tell us if this punishment be *final,* that is, if it will continue as long as the being exists. For all we know clearly and definitely from natural reason, this punishment might last only for a while, it might be a purifying process resulting in ultimate attainment of God; it might be followed by some other period of probation.

220. Summary of Chapter. The content of duty, then, is the eternal and the natural law with their derivatives as known by conscience. These laws are interpreted according to certain principles, giving rise to various systems, such as *probabiliorism* and *probabilism.*

221. Summary of This Part. This concludes the treatment of *Fundamental Ethics.* We commenced with the definition that Ethics is that branch of philosophy which deals with morality. A consideration of this definition involved a discussion of the ultimate end of human acts, or the knowledge and love of God; the goodness of acts, or conformity with one's last end; duty, or the obligation to do or omit some act; and finally the content of duty contained in the natural law and its derivatives as revealed to us by conscience.

SUGGESTED READINGS

1. Slater, *Moral Theology,* Bk. III.
2. Brosnahan, *Digest of Lectures,* VI, VII.
3. McDonald, *Principles of Moral Science,* Bk. I, Ch. IX; Bk. III, Chs. III, IV, VI.
4. Cronin, *Science of Ethics,* I, Ch. XIV.
5. Cronin, *Science of Ethics,* I, Ch. XVI.
6. Cronin, *Science of Ethics,* I, Ch. XIX.
7. Mausbach, *Catholic Moral Teaching,* pp. 176 ff.
8. Hill, *Moral Philosophy,* Pt. I, Chs. VI, VII, VIII.
9. Ming, *Data of Modern Ethics Examined,* Ch. XI.

QUESTIONS

1. Is the natural law a sort of participation in the eternal law?
2. Is conscience a distinct faculty independent of the agent?
3. Must conscience always be followed?
4. What is the force of custom in regard to law?
5. What is the argument for probabilism?
6. What happens to one who deliberately in a serious matter violates his conscience?

PART II
INDIVIDUAL ETHICS

ONE: *Our Duty Towards God*

I. External, Interior, and Social Religion and Their Abuse

222. State of Question. Having laid the foundation for a philosophy of Ethics by discussing human acts as being free, voluntary, and intelligent; and by showing further, first that these acts will be morally good or bad according as they are or are not in keeping with God's nature; secondly, that certain right acts are obligatory upon man in such a special way as to be known as duties; thirdly, that these duties become concrete through law: we go on now to consider the specific implications of law. First we take up what may be called individual Ethics, as embracing duties to one's self and to God. Some of these duties cannot be rigidly restricted to single individuals. They have their place, too, in any discussion of relations between two or more individuals. But they can be treated more conveniently in individual than in social Ethics as it is necessary to establish them apart from any social relations.

223. Postulates From Natural Theology. God created us, is a postulate that Ethics accepts from Natural Theology. From that postulate flow several important duties that we owe to our Creator. It is not necessary to consider revelation in order to establish certain fundamental obligations incumbent upon us in our relation to God. We cannot by mere reason work out in detail all the ethical truths we know by revelation, but we can arrive at some of them, and those the most important. Apart from revelation, then, we know of some duties of religion which we shall proceed to consider.

224. What We Owe to God. A duty is "something reasonably due from one person to another because of the necessary connection between the end to be attained and the means used."[1] In this case the persons are God and the individual man; the end

[1] Bouquillon, *Theologia Moralis Fundamentalis*, ed. 2a (Bruges, 1890), p. 188.

97

to be attained is the possession of God by man's highest faculties
—intellect and will; and the means to be used is the exercise of
these faculties in such a way that this ultimate and eternal possession of God will be secured. Because the end is to possess God
with our intellect, and the means to be used is such an exercise
of our intellect as will insure this possession, we have the duty
of knowing God here on earth in so far as He has revealed Himself and our natural faculties can attain. Again, because our end
is to embrace God perfectly with our wills, and the means to be
used is such an exercise of will on earth as will make this embracing possible hereafter, we owe God love—since love is embracing God with one's will. Finally, since our end is to possess
God and the means to be used is the exercise of our faculties in
such a way as to accomplish this possession, we owe God service;
for to be rightly used the faculties of a creature must be put entirely at the disposal of the Creator.

225. What Is Religion? The sum of these duties of knowing,
loving, and serving God forms religious worship, or objective religion. Subjectively, religion is a spiritual union between God and
a soul. This spiritual union between God and a soul is developed
and nourished by religious worship, which may be either exterior
or interior.

226. Importance of Subjective Religion. That religion must be
subjective, in the sense of personal and interior, can hardly be
too strongly stressed. For a great many persons ordinarily look
upon religion as something external to themselves with which
they have little or no real concern. They seem to regard the institutions intended to foster religion, and the representatives of
its organized forms, as a sort of poor relation, a country cousin
who is making inconvenient and disagreeable claims upon them.
The greater part of their waking hours is spent in absolute forgetfulness of God and their religious duties. A few prayers said
by rote night and morning and attendance at services on Sunday
constitute the sum of their religious activities.

227. Religion Never Fails. But when sorrow comes, however
they may previously have neglected it, most persons turn to re-

ligion. And then because they do not get the consolation they wish, they blame religion. They think that the church or the ministers of religion have failed them. Perhaps they rebel against God and turn away in disgust from all organized worship. But it was not religion that failed them, because religion (subjectively) is a union between God and the soul. It was themselves who failed because they had not in the days of prosperity patiently built up that union by earnest prayer and by thought on the fundamental truths of existence. They are like a man who has let his revolver rust in disuse for years, and then finds that the mechanism will not work when he attempts to protect himself against a burglar. He is to blame, not the revolver. And so in the case of religion, the individuals, not religion, are at fault.

228. Religion Is the Most Vital Thing in Life. Religion is not something external to one's self which another can administer as a physician does medicine. It is personal and interior, actually in one's soul. Hence, religion is the most vital thing in life. When confronted by the grim realities of death, sickness, loss of friends, of reputation, of wealth, religion is the only thing which remains. Religion is the only thing over which one has full control, and which has power to console. All the material things in which men put their trust may be swept away in an instant by earthquake, flood, lightning, or the microscopic germ of death. And even when these material things remain, how powerless are they to assuage the grief of bereavement.

229. Religion Is the Only Protection Against Sorrow. Since sorrow comes into the life of everyone, and religion alone can protect one against it, the wisest course is to strengthen to the utmost of one's ability this mighty bulwark. Each day one should prepare one's self for sorrow by tightening one's grip on the fundamental truths of religion; whoever believes with his heart and mind, not merely with his lips, that God is all-powerful, all-good, all-loving, that after this vale of tears there is a life of eternal happiness, is indeed armed in proof of steel against the "slings and arrows of outrageous fortune." "Therefore, take unto you the armor of God, that you may be able to resist in the evil day, and to stand in all things perfect. Stand, therefore, having your loins girt about with truth, and having on the breastplate of justice, and your feet shod with the preparation of the gospel of peace: in all things taking the shield of faith, wherewith you may be able to extinguish all the fiery darts of the most wicked one. And take unto you the helmet of salvation, and the sword of the Spirit (which is the word of God). By all prayer and supplication praying at all times in the spirit" (Ephes. VI, 13 ff).

230. Religion Must Be Partly External. In the acquirement of this subjective religion, external worship is useful in many ways. Man owes God exterior worship not because an infinitely pure and perfect spirit needs any man's worship, but because man himself needs to give it. Religion is a process of decentralization of self. The natural man sets up in the center of his consciousness himself to be approved and served before all things. But reason tells him that the Author of that self must be greater; and so, painfully and laboriously, he begins to turn from self-worship to the service of that greater Being. The whole process of religion is comprised in this turning with (conversion) the new light. To assist in this turning, to make tangible this subjective process of enthroning in perpetuity the Supreme in the center of consciousness where heretofore self reigned, exterior worship, praise, prayer, sacrifice, and pious practices are all necessary helps. It is true that God reads the heart perfectly, apart from any exterior sign; and therefore could be content with an interior spiritual worship. But man's soul and body are so closely united that that which he feels in his spirit he naturally expresses in his body. Man's interior affection for God is strengthened by exterior expression, and except in souls far advanced on the definite path of mystical perfection, is apt to decay by default of externalism.[2]

231. Spiritual Worship Needs External Expression. How far one's interior feelings depend upon exterior expression can be

[2] F. W. Foerster, *Lebensfuehring*, pp. 58 ff.

perceived by anyone on a little reflection.[3] Everyone has experienced the result of keeping the chin up and the chest expanded, and it is even seriously recommended by psychologists resolutely to turn up the corners of one's mouth in order to drive away the blues. The influence of music is universally acknowledged. By a strictly enforced ordinance, the bands on all battleships play during coaling operations, because careful investigation has shown that a much larger per cent of coal is thus handled than when the men were left to choose their own pace; and it has been suggested that large factories would find it economical to employ music to intensify the application of work-people.[4] Bands are almost as important in war as rifles and commissariat. In that wild dash across an African plain in the Boer war, the Scotch bagpiper who with both legs shot from under him continued to play "The Cock o' the North" bore no small part in the victorious result of the charge.

232. Liturgy Is a Natural Need of Man. Incense, candles, genuflections, and strange vestments or other externals will always have a part to play in every widespread religion. It may be possible to satisfy the religious cravings of some small groups of unusual souls by the simplicity of a Quaker meeting, but the mass of people will always demand more externalization of their feelings as instinctive dramatic expression and as a stimulus reacting to intensify the feeling. That this is so is shown by the elaborate ritual of Masonry, and other purely human societies. The founders of such organizations knew human nature well enough to understand that an external symbolism is important and they did their best to create a liturgy.

233. Testimony of St. Augustine. "When men pray," says St. Augustine, "they make their bodies share in their supplication, by kneeling, by stretching forth their hands, even by prostrating themselves, and by performing other visible actions, although their interior will, and the disposition of their hearts are known

---

[3] Cf. James, *Psychology.*

[4] Cf. "Working to Music," *Lit. Digest,* Apr. 17, 1915; also L. P. Ayres, "Influence of Music on Speed in the Six-Day Bicycle Race," *Am. Phys. Educ. Rev.,* May, 1911.

to God; and He needs no such manifestations to read their souls.
But man by these acts stirs himself to pray and groan with greater
fervor. And, although I do not know how, since their bodily
movements can only come from some preceding act of the soul,
yet when they are thus visibly performed the interior movement
that gave them birth is intensified, and the heart's affections,
which must have existed already in order to produce these external acts, are thereby increased." [5]

234. The Whole Man, Body and Soul, Should Do Homage.
Besides, since man's body as well as his soul is dependent upon
God for its existence and preservation, his body should share
in the homage. And as man is a social being, his worship of the
Creator should be a social function. Men should unite with their
fellows in doing reverence to the common Father of all.

235. Dangers of Social Worship. It cannot be denied, however,
that there are serious dangers of abusing external and social
worship. Churches are apt on the one hand to degenerate into
mere clubs, and on the other to foster superstition and obscure
the real object of religion. Protestants are beginning to see the
danger of over-socializing the machinery of religion; among
others Dean Mathews of the University of Chicago has raised
his voice in warning on this particular point. And individuals are
likely to conform through business or social reasons, or to make
a hypocritical show that does not really express their interior
attitude.

236. Superstitious Usages.[6] Under the head of superstition come
idolatry, divination, magic, and many forms of occultism. Idolatry need not detain us, as it is no longer a practical issue. But
the desire to know by divination and to do by magic shows itself in every age and nation. The mere enumeration of various
forms—astrology, aeromancy, palmistry, capnomancy, alomancy,

[5] St. Augustine, *De Cura Gerenda pro Mortuis*, No. 7.
[6] For the dangers of superstition, cf. Mgr. D'Hulst, *La France Chretienne dans l'His-
toire*, pp. 644, 645. Quoted in Mgr. A. Baudrillart's introduction to Mgr. D'Hulst's
The Way of the Heart, pp. xviii, xix, xx (N. Y., 1913); W. R. Carson, "The Motherhood
of God," in his *Reunion Essays;* Bp. Bonomelli, *Religious Worship, passim;* Newman,
Difficulties of Anglicans, Vol. I, "The Religious State of Catholic Countries."

cartomancy, anthropomancy, belomancy, geomancy, necromancy, oneiromancy, philters, charms, amulets, lucky and unlucky numbers and days, evil eye, incantations, ordeals, etc.—makes quite an imposing array. Man's curiosity is unlimited, and designing persons have always been able to play upon it in various ways. P. T. Barnum said the American people wanted to be fooled, and what he said of Americans is true quite generally of the human race. Men have been willing to believe in all sorts of false and foolish ways of forecasting the future, from reading signs in the flight of birds, to inspecting the viscera of persons especially sacrificed for this purpose, from the oracles of pagan Greece down to our own gypsies and spiritists.

237. Subjective Guilt Not Easy to Determine. With regard to the subjective guilt attaching to superstitious practices, "it must be borne in mind that no sin is mortal unless committed with full knowledge of its grievous wickedness and with full deliberation and consent. Of these essential factors, the first is often wanting entirely and the second is only imperfectly present. The numerous cases in which the event seemed to justify the superstitious practices, and the universality of such incongruous beliefs and performances, though they may not always induce inculpable ignorance, may possibly obscure the knowledge and weaken the will to a point incompatible with mortal sin. As a matter of fact many superstitions of our own day have been acts of genuine piety at other times, and may be so still in the heart of simple folk." [7]

238. A Natural Explanation for Many Supposed Preternatural Events. And, contrariwise, what is now looked upon by many as superstitious may come to be considered perfectly natural. When Mesmer first practiced the hypnotic sleep, grave and prudent doctors considered that such power could only come from communication with evil spirits. But as time went on, though no satisfactory explanation could be given, Mesmerism came to be admitted as natural. As a general thing, the burden of proof

---

[7] Wilhelm in Cath. Encyc., art. "Superstition," p. 340.

lies with those maintaining a preternatural interference, as no unnecessary forces are to be assumed. Therefore, scientific investigation by competent persons of phenomena generally supposed to be preternatural is not in itself wrong. The deordination of the act consists essentially in attributing to an indifferent action a power that it cannot have, or can have only by some preternatural interference. When the experiment is performed with the object of showing that only natural forces are at work, there is no such deordination.

239. Spiritism Possibly Natural. This possibility of a natural explanation applies even to spiritism. For though many of its advocates call it a religion and boldly insist upon its manifestation of preternatural powers, there are several reasonable hypotheses suggested to explain the phenomena by natural means. Innumerable instances of natural telepathy seem to have been well established, and it is contended that the medium at a spiritistic seance gains information by thought transference from those present or at a distance. Somewhat similar is the theory of an intermediate principle between the soul and the material body. This, according to the theory, accompanies the soul after death and it is through it that the peri-spirit of the medium establishes communication with the dead.[8]

240. Dangers of Spiritism. Whatever the explanation, however, spiritistic seances are accompanied by serious dangers. Mental balance is frequently destroyed and self-control impaired. Raupert, at one time a spiritist, recounts many unhappy issues.[9] Apart, therefore, from the question of superstition, only those who have had the necessary psychological and medical training should attempt investigation [10] of these matters, and all who feel tempted to waste time and money in seeking foreknowledge of a future

[8] For a discussion of the hypotheses, cf. Lodge, *The Survival of Man,* and other works mentioned in the Cath. Encyc., art. "Spiritism."

[9] *Modern Spiritism* (St. Louis, 1904).

[10] Dr. Pace in the Cath. Encyc. thus sums up the attitude of the Catholic Church: "The distinction is clearly drawn between legitimate scientific investigation and superstitious abuses. What the Church condemns in spiritism is superstition with its consequent evil consequences for religion and morality."

mercifully and wisely veiled, should reflect upon the strong words of Father Thurston, S.J.: "In the whole of ecclesiastical history not one satisfactory example can be quoted of a prophet, whether canonized or not, who has clearly predicted any unguessable future event which was of public interest." [11] If Saints have added nothing to our knowledge of future events, it is likely that some obscure palmist or medium should do so? "G. M. Robertson, the Medical Superintendent of the Royal Hospital at Morningside in Edinburgh, the premier institution for the insane in Scotland, feels it is his duty 'to utter a note of warning to those seeking consolation in their sorrow by practical experiments in the domain of spiritualism.' The warning is that the manifestations of mediums, supposing them to be honest, are, if not morbid, yet closely related to manifestations of mental disease that have no element of the occult about them; that indulgence in practices of a spiritualistic nature is apt to awaken a dormant proclivity to hallucination in those who inherit a tendency to nervous disorders; that the belief in spiritualism merges into unmistakable delusion, so that in some cases it is impossible to say where one begins and the other ends. . . . All that Dr. Robertson says I can corroborate from my own experience, and I could add enough to justify stronger opinions, expressed in more positive terms, as to the extent of the evil. . . . To some people—I will go further, and say to many people—spiritualistic practices carry a decided, it may be a grave danger to sanity." [12]

241. Summary. We are, then, obliged to give God interior worship and to avoid certain excesses and errors. By the natural law, however, the kind of worship and the times are not accurately determined. A man must acknowledge God's sovereignty, but whether daily or monthly or yearly cannot be said.[13]

[11] Herbert Thurston, S.J., "The Plague of False Prophets." (*Dublin Review*, Apr., 1915.)

[12] Chas. Mercier, M.D., in *Hibbert Journal*, July, 1917, p. 599, "Sir Oliver Lodge and the Scientific World."

[13] Noldin, *Theol. Mor.*, II, 147.

II. Prayer

242. Daily Prayer Morally Necessary. Though daily prayer or worship may not be absolutely necessary for the attainment of one's ultimate end, it is morally necessary. And if one is to attain his end easily and perfectly, he must pray *always*. To pray always may sound formidable, yet it does not mean that the duties of life must be neglected in order to spend one's time in prayer; nor does it mean that one must go about his affairs in a dazed manner rapt in meditation. In the words of Thomas à Kempis, "to persevere in an upright intention toward God" is equivalent to praying always. In the morning to offer one's self, one's acts, one's intentions to God; in the evening to review the day, to ask pardon for all departures from the resolves of the morning and to consecrate the night to God—this constitutes a day of prayer.

243. Prayer of Petition and of Submission. And one must pray not only by worship or thanksgiving, but also by petition. He must ask of God the help necessary to meet daily temptation.[14] Such prayer should be made with perseverance, confidence, and resignation. The highest form of prayer, in fact, is simple submission to the will of God, and the great object of the spiritual life is to produce this submission.

244. Divisions of Prayer.[15] Private prayer may be either vocal or mental, and the latter may be either meditative or contemplative.

245. Vocal Prayer Has Its Dangers. Vocal prayer is familiar to everyone. In its familiarity, however, lies the danger of its becoming purely mechanical. Some persons begin to say the beads, and because they know the prayers so well, their minds wander off to some profane subject, and they find themselves at the end of their prayer before they realize what they have done. There is less danger of such distraction in conversing familiarly

---

[14] From Natural Theology we know the possibility of prayer of petition and that the answering of such prayers in no way contradicts God's knowledge or wisdom.

[15] Cf. Réné de Maumiguy, S.J., *The Practice of Mental Prayer* (N. Y., 1915).

with God in our own words. Indeed, Mother M. Loyola recommends talking to God about our daily needs, and trials, and pleasures as we would talk to a human friend.

246. Mental Prayer Is Within the Reach of All. Mental prayer, unfortunately, is not so familiar as vocal prayer. There is a very widespread impression that this is something only for priests or religious and that it would be presumptuous for lay-folk to attempt to practice mental prayer. No error, probably, will more effectively hold back souls on the road to perfection. It is a false humility that keeps good souls from using meditation or aspiring to contemplation. Father E. Lamballe, the Eudist, has written a book for the express purpose of combating this humility, and he quotes from the most authoritative saints to support his view.[16]

247. Distinction Between Mental and Vocal Prayer. It is not easy to define and distinguish mental and vocal prayer. If we could call vocal prayer all audible discoursing with God, mental prayer all silent converse with Him, and contemplation a certain immediate intercourse with God without the interposition of words, the matter would be simple. But one who recites the beads silently is not meditating, nor is one who in his own words addresses an interior petition to God. Both cases are merely forms of vocal prayer. Perhaps, the best way to distinguish between meditation and vocal prayer, is to say that vocal prayer is talking to God, and meditation is thinking of God. It is true that one should not talk to God without thinking, but he can, so far as the mere vocal formation of words is concerned; and even when he thinks of what he is saying to God, his thinking is directed to the point immediately at hand—asking a favor or praising God —and hence thinking is not the distinctive characteristic of such praying. One cannot, however, meditate without thinking, and though according to most psychologists the thinking cannot be carried on without words, mental prayer is not so much a petition or a praise as a connected reflection upon some religious truth in

[16] *Mystical Contemplation, or the Principles of Mystical Theology* (N. Y., 1913). Cf. especially Ch. II.

order to apply it to one's self and to vitalize motives for action. On the other hand meditation is distinguished from contemplation by the fact that it must use words; whereas, contemplation is a direct and immediate apprehension of God by the intellect or will.[17]

248. Extraordinary Meditations, or Mystic Contemplation. It is not easy to describe the higher forms of mental prayer. "The theological notion of contemplation is far from clear,"[18] and those who have experienced it are rather helpless in trying to make it known to others. All are united, however, upon the teaching that the practice of meditation gradually leads, in certain gifted souls to a higher form of prayer, which, for want of a better name, is called contemplation. "It is, above all, an *experimental* knowledge, which teaches us more than books or any amount of reasoning. No one knows God like those who have experienced the union of love. Before they had heard of Him; now they know Him by experience, because they have felt, tasted, and as it were, touched with their fingers His goodness, His kindness, His infinite condescension, His character."[19]

249. The Essence of Religion and Prayer Is Humility. It must be constantly remembered, however, that the essence of religion and of prayer is submission to the will of God. We have said this before, but we come back to it at the close of this chapter in order that it may be strongly impressed upon the mind. No matter what seeming devotion one may have, no matter what visions and ecstacies, they are all vain without the fundamental of the spiritual life—absolute resignation. And resignation is based upon humility, upon a recognition of our complete dependence on God, and of our weakness. Humility and resignation are practically the same. One cannot be humble without being resigned, one cannot be resigned without being humble.

[17] Lehodey, *Ways of Mental Prayer,* thus divides prayer: "Vocal prayer is that which is made by using words or signs, or perhaps more exactly by using some approved form of words which we read or recite. . . . Mental prayer is that which is made without employing words or formulas of any kind." P. 5.

[18] Lamballe, *op. cit.,* p. 1.

[19] Lehodey, p. 297.

250. God's Majesty Should Make Us Humble. Numerous motives lead us to resignation and humility. First and foremost, of course, will be a consideration of God's power and majesty; how He brought us out of nothing; how He keeps us in existence; how without Him nothing can be done in this world—all these considerations teach us to humble ourselves in the presence of the Almighty.

251. Our Weakness Should Humble Us. Again, our own weakness should sink us in the dust before the power and the purity of God. What are we but a little slime of the earth for a moment gifted with the frail breath of life? Even the length of time this body of ours shall live does not depend upon us. It is subject to infirmity and sickness. A microscopic germ of death may rob us of it in an instant. At last analysis we are mere worms of the earth. And if a consideration of our bodies humbles us, much more so should reflection upon our weakness. An honest facing of how often we have offended the Creator in the past, of how we are apt to offend Him in the future, of how weak are our strongest resolutions, should be sufficient to make us resigned to anything God may send us in the way of pain and suffering.

252. Joyousness a Mark of Humility. In proportion as we gain humility and resignation, we shall also gain peace of mind that will exhibit itself in a certain serenity and even cheerfulness. Inevitably a joy will show forth in our lives in somewhat the same way that it did in the life of St. Francis of Assisi, the great Troubadour of God. In our own small way we should all be troubadours of God, constantly singing His praises, constantly bright, cheerful, and happy. As some savage tribes tattoo their bodies with the totem of their tribe to indicate their consecration to their deity, so we should always wear the badge of our religion—cheerfulness. Our religion must be one of sacrifice and suffering, but not one of sadness. Suffering and sadness do not necessarily go together. They are entirely distinct. St. Laurence, roasting upon a gridiron, was doubtless suffering considerably, but he was not sad. He was cheerful and happy, and joked with his torturers, telling them that as he was done enough on one side to please turn him over.

253. Sadness Hurts Us Spiritually and Physically. Sadness is wrong in itself, as indicating a lack of resignation and humility. But besides being wrong in itself, it leads to serious consequences. Even from a selfish standpoint, sadness robs us of joy. We cannot be sad and happy at the same time. "Cast sadness far from thee," wrote Ecclesiasticus, "because it has killed many and is good for nothing." (XXX, 24.) If indulged in, it will become such an ingrained habit as almost to defy eradication; and it will even lead to physical complications that are the foundation for numerous diseases.

254. Sadness Hurts Our Neighbor. Again, sadness will lead to anger and quarrelsomeness with our neighbors. We cannot live at peace with them if we are sad. Inevitably, we shall be irritated at what otherwise would be passed over without notice. The sweet charity of association will be destroyed. Naturally we shall become marked as kill-joys, as persons always with a grouch, and to be avoided as much as possible. With those who cannot avoid us, our life will be a continual quarrel.

255. Prayer the Best Means of Gaining Humility. For all these reasons we should do our best to cultivate a spirit of joyousness. What we have said regarding habits will show that it is possible to do so. Largely, it is a question of forming the right habits and of inhibiting the wrong ones at the start. A cheerful disposition can be acquired by constant effort. Among the tools to be used in its acquirement is meditation. Reflection upon God's will, upon our absolute creaturehood, upon our weakness, will bring humility and resignation, and with them happiness and joy.

256. Summary. According to the natural law, then, we owe God love, service, and knowledge, which are fulfilled and fostered by worship both interior and exterior, individual and social. The danger of social worship is that it may become too largely mere human association; of exterior worship that it may become mechanical. True worship may sin by excess, in superstitiously attributing power where it is not; false worship by attributing to creatures what belongs to God, or by commerce with God's enemies of the spirit-world. Individual worship may be exterior (vocal prayer) or interior (mental prayer), which latter is divided into meditation and contemplation. The highest forms of prayer lead to a personal union with God that is almost absorption of the finite into the Infinite.

SUGGESTED READINGS

1. De Sales, *Introduction to a Devout Life,* Pts. I, II.
2. Lehodey, *Ways of Mental Prayer,* Pt. I.
3. Underhill, *Mysticism,* Ch. I.
4. Bonomelli, *Religious Worship,* the whole.
5. McSorley, *The Sacrament of Duty,* ch. on "Openmindedness."
6. Newman, *Difficulties of Anglicans,* ch. on religious condition of Catholic countries.
7. Carson, *Reunion Essays,* on "The Motherhood of God."
8. A Kempis, *Following of Christ,* Bk. I.
9. Thurston, *Spiritualism and Its Dangers,* Studies, Sept., 1919.
10. Johan Liljencrants, *Spiritism and Religion,* Ch. IX (N. Y., 1918).

QUESTIONS

1. Distinguish between objective and subjective religion.
2. When apparently religious folk collapse under trial, what has really failed?
3. Can religion be completely internal?
4. What are the excesses of the religious temperament?
5. What is the best kind of prayer?

TWO: *Truthfulness*

I. Negative Duties

257. The Duty of Truthfulness Has a Positive and a Negative Side. One aspect of duty regarding truth concerns the obligation of volunteering the truth, of dissipating error, of enlightening ignorance; and the other aspect concerns the obligation of speaking the truth according to one's light, when one cannot avoid speaking, or when one voluntarily speaks. We shall first consider the negative aspect.

258. Material and Formal Falsehood. Falsehood may be either *material* or *formal*, or both material and formal. *Material* falsehood is a disagreement between the object and the terms used to express or describe the object. If one swears in a court of justice that he saw a certain man commit a crime when in reality the man did not commit it, there is a disagreement between the objective facts and the sworn statement; that is, there is material falsehood. Should the witness be perfectly sincere in his conviction that he saw this man commit the crime and be merely mistaken as to his identity, the falsehood is only material. But if he knows that this man did not commit the crime, then the falsehood is formal as well as material.

259. A Formal Falsehood May Be Materially True. However, falsehood to be formal need not necessarily be materially false also. Thus a man adopted in infancy and brought up in the belief that he is the real son of his supposititious parents, would be telling a formal falsehood if he denied their parentage, even though his words actually agreed with the objective facts.

260. Definition of a Lie. It is of the essence of a formal falsehood, then, that one should speak against his own mind,[1] that there should be a discrepancy between his words and his con-

---

[1] Speak is used here as any method of communicating with our fellow man, whether by speech strictly so-called, writing, gestures, or silence.

ception of what is true; it is not essential that there should exist a discrepancy between the words and the actual facts. A formal falsehood is a lie, when one utters it with the intention of deceiving. Some authors[2] maintain that it is not necessary for a lie that one should have the intention of deceiving. But it would seem to create unnecessary difficulties to include in the definition (and, therefore, in the unconditional condemnation of lying) a speaking against one's mind that is not intended to deceive and does not deceive. It is better to make the intention part of the lie.

261. Ethicians Are Concerned Only With Formal Falsehood. There is no moral quality in a mere material falsehood. The ethical interest comes from its formality.

262. Kinds of Falsehood. There are many kinds of formal falsehoods and of lying, from almost innocent flattery to false witness against one's neighbor. It has been said of sin in general that

> "The course of evil
> Begins so slowly and from such slight source
> An infant's hand might stop the breach with clay.
> But let the stream grow larger and Philosophy—
> Ay, and Religion, too—shall strive in vain
> To stop the headlong torrent."

And this is particularly true regarding falsehood. One commences with the desire to please that makes him flatter others with whom he wishes to stand well. Then he tries to see how much persons will believe, even though he does not care what they think of him. From flattering others, he flatters himself. His virtues are magnified, his faults diminished. Exaggeration grows upon him until he is continually indulging in "fish tales." From exaggeration it is an imperceptible step to a lie of excuse. Habits of falsehood generate facility, and it becomes easy to lie out of a difficult situation. Promises are made unthinkingly, and broken without a scruple. Appointments are not kept, because "some-

[2] Cf. Rickaby, p. 225.

one" came in just as one was starting; favors are not conferred, duties are not done, for this pretended reason, or that. A certain carelessness in handling the truth soon leads from innocent gossip to scandalmongering, and from the repeating of real scandals to the retailing of what is supposed to have happened, or may have been done, or probably occurred; and before one knows it one has calumniated someone and robbed him of his reputation. Gossiping does not begin through malice, but it ends in *malice,* and if a strong temptation comes, it will be backed by perjury.

263. Importance of Truth-Telling. It has been said that the surest way to develop strength of will is by forcing one's self to a scrupulous adherence to the truth. Contrariwise, the quickest way to become spiritually flabby is to neglect such accuracy. We can see this working out every day in individuals and in nations. The strongest are the most truthful.

264. Lying Is Morally Wrong. No difficulty presents itself in condemning lying in general. All ethicians, though differing somewhat in estimating the reasons for such a condemnation, are agreed that lying is morally wrong. Some base their condemnation entirely upon social grounds, some entirely upon our relationship to God, but all agree upon the main point.

265. Lying Wrong Because of Our Relation to God. To us it seems advisable to consider lying intrinsically wrong, because it violates our own nature and our duties to a God Who is Truth itself. For this reason, we are treating the subject here, rather than in social Ethics where it would otherwise belong. Lying is wrong whether or not it violates the right of another human being. It will be remembered that the proximate norm of morality is our own nature and the ultimate norm is the nature of God.[3] Hence, the problem is to show that God's nature requires that He be true to Himself; and that, therefore, conformity to that norm requires us to be true to ourselves.

266. God's Nature Demands Truthfulness. We know from

[3] Pt. I, Ch. IV.

Natural Theology that God is infinitely perfect. And since truth-fulness is a perfection, God must be eminently truthful. But aside from that, it would seem metaphysically impossible for God to speak against His own mind. For there is nothing acci-dental in God; everything is essential. We speak of God's will and God's mind as if these were separate, but only for con-venience. In reality God is absolutely simple. Hence, the acts of God's intellect and will must represent or correctly express His nature.

267. Good of Society Demands Truthfulness. The social argu-ment, while not strong enough by itself to prove the intrinsic evil of lying, is nevertheless a helpful subsidiary proof. For all social intercourse is based upon trust in our fellow men. If we could not depend upon the truthfulness of the average man under ordinary circumstances, all trade, all government, all helpful as-sociation whatsoever, would be at an end; for in proportion as suspicion increases, association becomes hurtful or impossible. Those countries are most comfortable and pleasant in which the inhabitants are frank, honest, and sincere. Likewise, they are the strongest, because reliability is the foundation of commercial and national strength. The countries whose inhabitants cannot be trusted, where prices mean nothing, and contracts are mere verbiage, are not pleasant to live or travel in. And such countries are among the weakest in the world.

268. But All the Truth All the Time Is Socially Hurtful. The fact that if the plain unvarnished truth were always told, society would just as surely be disrupted,[4] does not destroy the force of this argument. There is a great deal of room between telling a lie and not telling the whole truth. A man must smile, and smile again, when he feels like striking another; the avoidance of social friction requires conventionalities, such as, "I am glad to meet you," when in reality one is extremely bored. All this, however, merely militates against an absolutely rigid rule of truth-telling, not against the proposition that in general one must not tell a

---

[4] *Atl. Monthly,* Vol. 95, Mch., 1905, "An Unlovely Virtue."

formal falsehood. Whatever force the objection has, indicates only that a reasonable mean should be followed. What that mean is we shall consider shortly.

269. Lying Is Cowardly. Another argument in favor of truthfulness is that lying is cowardly. Whether cowardice be morally wrong or not, no one wants to be considered a coward. Cowardice is universally condemned; hence, lying that is based upon cowardice should be condemned. The lie of excuse springs from a desire to avoid the unpleasant consequences of one's actions. It is an attempt to escape them because one is not strong enough to take one's punishment. The lie of exaggeration rises from the desire to get credit which is undeserved, and which the liar generally is not man enough to win for himself. Lying and cowardice almost invariably go together. A man who is a liar will usually be a coward. Lying and cowardice are twin brothers whom you seldom find separated. All lies are based upon cowardice, acquisitive cunning, or protection of self or others. Cowardice is weakness, physical or moral. The liar who has not strength to make or take the thing he wants, or to acknowledge his own weakness, or to face the consequences of his own actions, worms his way underground to that which he seeks. The liar of acquisitive cunning may be strong and even brave; but something—circumstance, right, or the will of another—proves stronger, and he uses misrepresentation to accomplish his ends. The man who falsifies in order to protect himself or others is the only one whom the ethicians would to some extent uphold. Various opinions are held by the different schools as to the degree in which this privilege is justifiable.

270. Some Lying Offends Against Justice. Other kinds of lies, such as calumny, back-biting, perjury, are sins against justice and are wrong upon that ground also. The malice of such lies and the duty of making good any injury done by them will be considered when we come to treat of social Ethics.

271. Is All Deception Wrong? All ethicians, then, agree that lying is wrong, as they agree that murder is wrong. They also agree almost unanimously that there are certain circumstances when the deception of others is justifiable. And the consensus of all nations supports such exceptions. Must a physician, for instance, tell a patient the effect of a certain medicine on his condition, or may he use language that he foresees will deceive the patient for his good? May a soldier deny his identity to escape death at the hands of an enemy? Is it lawful to tell a child that Santa Claus will come soon in a sleigh with reindeers to bring a sled?

272. Different Answers of Various Authors. These are simply concrete examples of the general problem. If it be sometimes right to take the property of another, and in some cases right to kill another, may it not also be right and reasonable to deceive another? Practically all ethicians answer affirmatively. They vary, however, as to the principles by which they justify such untruthfulness and in their judgment as to the limits to which it may go. Scholastic authors, in general, stand by the proposition that a formal falsehood, intended to deceive, is never justifiable; and call their exceptions mental reservations or equivocation. Some non-Scholastic authors, on the other hand, and a very few Scholastic ones, frankly admit that formal falsehoods intended to deceive are sometimes lawful.

273. Grotius' Principles Regarding Lying. Thus, Grotius, adding to our definition of a lie the element of "discrepancy with some existing and permanent right of the person to whom the words or signs are addressed," allows any formal untruthfulness that does not violate such a right. This right "may be taken away either by the express permission of him with whom we deal; as if anyone has announced that he would tell falsehoods, and the other has permitted it; or by tacit permission, or by permission presumed on fair reason; or by the opposition of another right which, by the common opinion of all, is much more important." [5]

274. Grotius' Application of His Principles. From these principles he concludes that "though anything be said to an infant,

[5] *De Jure Belli et Pacis,* Lib. III, Cap. I, n. XI.

or a person out of his mind, which has a false signification, it does not involve the guilt of a lie. The common sense of mankind allows the thoughtless age of childhood to be deluded."[6] This would justify the Santa Claus legends. And it is, perhaps, worthy of note that the northern races which have this custom are more truthful than the southern which have it not. He also allows formal untruthfulness "when it is certain that he who is addressed will not be dissatisfied with the disturbance of his liberty in judging, but rather will be gratified at the course taken, on account of some advantage which follows therefrom."[7] This may be presumed by a physician encouraging a patient who is dangerously ill. The right to hear the truth is superseded also when "he who has a supereminent right over the rights of another, uses that right either for his private, or for the public good."[8] "A fifth case may be when the life of an innocent person, or something of like value cannot otherwise be preserved, and when another person cannot otherwise be withheld from the perpetration of a wicked act."[9]

275. Paulsen and Lying. Paulsen states the problem: "Is deception under all circumstances morally indefensible? Or are there some circumstances under which it is permissible and even necessary?"[10] In practical life, he answers, there is no doubt as to the answer. Everyone agrees that lies are sometimes necessary. It is only a problem for the theoretical moralist, and if he cannot square his theory with the facts, his theory must be discredited.[11]

276. Some Examples of Deception Allowed by Paulsen. Paulsen's own answer is perfectly consistent with his principles. Basing the malice of lying upon the social ground of destroying trust and working harm to society,[12] he justifies deception when these results do not follow. As an example, he instances a housebreaker or murderer. So long as a man follows such a calling he is anti-

---

[6] *Loc. cit.,* n. XII.   [8] *Loc. cit.,* n. XV.
[7] *Loc. cit.,* n. XIV.   [9] *Loc. cit.,* n. XVI.
[10] *System der Ethik,* Band II, Buch III, kap. XI, p. 187 (Berlin, 1894).
[11] *Op. cit.,* p. 189.   [12] *Op. cit.,* p. 182.

social and has no claim to that trust and sincerity which are necessary for right association.[13] A similar principle applies to warfare. The art of deception is part of the art of war. A general need have no scruples in deceiving an opponent regarding his numbers, position, or intention. To make war with cards on the table would be an absurdity. But he does not go so far as to justify the violation of treaties or armistices.[14] About the same applies to diplomacy. Some deception is necessary and expected. Let those who play the game keep their eyes open. A physician should sometimes deceive his patients for their good.[15] And it is frequently the part of virtue for a man to appear cheerful when his heart is heavy. Such a deception is not the less deception that it is done with the eyes or a forced smile, yet what moralist will be rigorist enough to condemn it?

277. Scholastic Authors and the Lawfulness of Deception. Such are the ways in which two prominent non-Scholastic ethicians have met the problem of necessary formal untruthfulness. The Scholastic method at present is usually somewhat different. "The historical course of thought upon the matter has been this: The Greek Fathers thought that, when there was a *justa causa,* an untruth need not be a lie. St. Augustine took another view, though with great misgiving; and, whether he is rightly interpreted or not, is the doctor of the great common view that all untruths are lies, and that there can be *no* just cause of untruth. In these later times, this doctrine has been found difficult to work, and it has been largely taught that, though all formal untruths are lies, yet that certain equivocations, when given in a just cause are not untruths." [16]

278. A Lie Is Never Justified. In the first place, then, Scholastic moralists now usually take their stand firmly upon the proposition that a lie is never allowable—that is, a formal falsehood, or speaking against one's mind, with the intention of deceiving the person addressed is never justified. "We are never justified in

13 *Op. cit.,* p. 190.   15 *Op. cit.,* p. 193.
14 *Op. cit.,* p. 190.   16 Newman, *Apologia,* note G, p. 349.

telling a lie, not even if the life of another, or the safety of the world depended upon it." [17]

279. But Deception Is Sometimes Allowable. However, many of them go on to say that *when there is sufficient reason,* then the difficulties involved in telling the plain, unvarnished truth may, under certain restrictions, be avoided by *mental reservation* or *equivocation.* These terms must be carefully defined,[18] and their application strictly conditioned, since any looseness or laxity gives an opening for a powerful attack upon Scholastic Ethics.

280. Definition of Mental Reservation. Mental reservation consists in attaching to one's words certain restrictions or reservations which give them a meaning different from the sense that they have on the surface—a meaning, too, which the victim of the reservation is not likely to surmise. Such reservation is *artificial* when it is entirely mental and cannot reasonably be guessed from any external circumstances; it is *real* when one may reasonably infer from the circumstances that reservation is being practiced, and what it is.

281. When Mental Reservation Is Allowable. Artificial or *purely mental reservation is never allowable,* and real mental reservation is allowable only when it is the sole means of avoiding serious inconvenience, and the questioner has not a right to know the whole truth. Moreover, when used it must not be with the intention of directly deceiving the other person, but for the purpose of allowing him to deceive himself. The speaker's words must be true and their true meaning must be discoverable by pru-

---

[17] Slater, *Moral Theology,* Vol. I, 465.

[18] Cf. Newman, *Apologia;* Mausbach, *Catholic Moral Teaching and Its Antagonists,* Chs. I, IV. The latter says: "It cannot be denied that many mistaken, subtle, and ridiculous things have been written upon this subject [by Catholic authors]; many things, in fact, that we should consider morally doubtful if they had been intended for the general public, who would have understood these things only on their lax and gross side. I need only draw attention to a few points that ought to put us on our guard against rash and unfair judgments." (P. 113.) "Even later moralists are not so consistent in their adherence to these principles as to exclude from their concrete instances all purely mental reservations. . . . Herrmann rightly condemns an attempt discussed by Gury and others to justify a denial of adultery by the argument: Se non fregisse matrimonium si quidem adhuc persistit." (P. 115, note.)

dent persons either from the words themselves, or from the circumstances of person and matter in which they are spoken.

282. When Equivocation Is Justified. Equivocation is the use of an expression that has two meanings to dodge the telling of the plain truth. The conditions that make it justifiable are the same as for real mental reservation.

283. Applications of the Foregoing Doctrine. Ordinary examples of the application of these principles are: To anyone enquiring about what may not be revealed, one may answer that he does not know—that is, know for communication. This applies especially to persons in an official position, such as confessors, physicians, and lawyers. Or a person being requested to make a loan, might reply that he had no money, meaning that he did not have it to lend on such security. Servants may tell visitors that one is "not at home," because custom gives the necessary gloss, "at home to you," or "ready to receive you." Since what is said with these reservations and equivocations is actually truthful in a real sense, it may be affirmed upon oath for any just reason.[19] This is particularly true in the case of those who are obliged to protect the interests of others.

284. Some Scholastic Moralists Find Difficulty in Doctrine of Mental Reservation. But not all modern Scholastic moralists are satisfied with the solution of the problem by mental reservation or equivocation. The Casuist, after quoting Berardi's statement of the difficulty, goes on: "If a theologian as competent as Berardi finds difficulty in applying the theory of mental reservation, it will be readily understood how the simple and ignorant are quite unable to use it as a means of concealing a truth or keeping a secret from those who have no right to know it. In the face of this insurmountable difficulty many moralists think that the definition of a lie, as commonly given in the textbooks ought to be revised; that is to say, it ought to be made to read something like this: A lie consists in speaking contrary to one's mind, with the intention of deceiving one *who has a right to the truth.*

---

[19] Noldin, *Theol. Mor.,* Vol. II, art. 640, p. 651.

If the person has no right to the truth it ought not to be called a lie if the truth is concealed from him by saying the thing that is not in one's mind.

285. Another Scholastic Solution of the Problem. "Such speaking against one's mind might be called an untruth, but not a lie. Not every taking of human life is murder, and not every taking of another's goods is stealing, and, therefore, not every speaking contrary to one's mind ought to be called lying. And as there is taking of human life that is justifiable, and, therefore, not sinful, and as there is taking of another's property that is not stealing, and, therefore, not a sin, so there must be untruths that are not lies, and therefore, not sinful. There are many occasions when a person has no right to know the truth and to deny the truth to such a person is justifiable, and, therefore, not sinful." [20]

II. Positive Side of Truthfulness

286. Responsibilities of Possessing Truth. Difficult as is the negative side of truthfulness, the positive side is even more ticklish. But it must be faced. It is a serious and inexcusable mistake to imagine that one's duty towards truthfulness is fulfilled merely by never lying. Over and above the obligation not to speak against our mind, there is sometimes the additional duty to speak our mind. The possession of truth often places upon us an obligation to make it known; and ignorance of truth may produce the duty of seeking enlightenment.

287. Obligation of Seeking Truth. In general, each one has the obligation of using to the full measure of his ability the truth-attaining faculty God has given him. By will and intellect man is made higher than a beast; to drift aimlessly without exerting his will-power, to fritter away his time in mere animal gratification is to fail in one of the most fundamental duties of life. He will be judged for culpable failure to seek and to attain truth, for high gifts and capabilities are not given merely for his own

[20] *The Casuist*, Vol. III, p. 48.

temporal enjoyment, but that they may be employed for the honor and glory of the Giver.

288. Special Duty of Seeking Religious Truth. This duty of seeking truth is particularly weighty and important in the religious sphere. We know from Natural Theology, that there is a God, and that this God may have spoken to man in a special way, may have made a revelation; hence each one is bound according to his ability to ascertain whether or not such a revelation has been made, and what it is. Nor is one's duty of seeking truth completely fulfilled by some attenuated connection with an organization entrusted with that revelation, assuming for the sake of argument that there be such. There are varying degrees of knowledge of this God, as we saw in a previous chapter, and each one is bound at least to some extent, to live up to his opportunities of knowing God.

289. Duty of Communicating Truth. Having attained truth one's self, there is an obligation to communicate it, to share it with others, to help them to reach the same height. Ordinarily, the duty will be one of charity. The general principle of neighborly love requires us to show this interest. There is a story told of two Pennsylvania Dutch farmers that illustrates how one may fail in this regard. One met the other on the road one morning and said his horse was sick. "So was mine" was the reply. "What did you do for it?" "Gave it turpentine." A few days later they met again. "My horse died," said the first farmer. "So did mine," said the second, whose horse had been dead before he had told the other in their previous meeting that he had administered turpentine. What he said was true, he had given turpentine, but a little more charity in communicating the truth would have added the fact that the remedy killed the horse.

290. How This Duty Can Be Conditioned. The duty of communicating truth, however, is based upon two conditions: that one is sure he is right, and that the neighbor will probably accept the truth. There is no obligation to cast pearls before swine. If people are not in the frame of mind to receive truth, it is better not to give it to them. Great tact is required in enlighten-

ing other persons. Knowledge is frequently power to do evil as
well as good, and to give information indiscriminately may harm
rather than benefit.[21]

291. When an Invincibly Ignorant Sinner Should Be Enlightened. When a person is in invincible ignorance regarding the nature of a sinful act he is committing, and no reform can be reasonably expected from the enlightenment, even those who stand in an official relation to him should, ordinarily, say nothing. For of two evils the less is to be chosen, and material sin is less than formal sin. The same holds true when the revelation would result in serious injury to a third party, as in disclosing the invalidity of marriage. But when the fact that a man sins in ignorance would cause injury to someone else, his ignorance should be dissipated, at least by those who stand in an official relation to him—even if no reform is expected.[22]

292. This Duty May Be One of Justice. The duty to communicate truth will usually be merely one of charity, but it may happen that this obligation will be one of justice. One's official position, as that of a physician or attorney, may compel the giving of advice to those who stand in the relation of patient or client. Or it may happen that by some mistake a serious punishment will be meted out to an innocent person unless the guilty person confess. In such a case there would be an obligation to reveal the truth, if it could be done without proportionately serious inconvenience; and even an absolute obligation if the guilty party were responsible for suspicion attaching to the other. How far he would otherwise be bound will be clear from the discussion of co-operation.[23]

293. Nobility of Preaching Truth. While there may be no strict obligation to reveal truth publicly or privately when serious inconvenience may follow, as in the case of Galileo, it is the nobler

---

[21] For a discussion of the advisability of enlightening children upon sexual matters, cf. M. Gillet, O.P., *Ignorance et Innocence* (N. Y., 1917); Gatterer & Krus, S.J., *Educating to Purity* (N. Y., 1912). Both books advocate a progressive initiation by the parents or other superiors of the children.

[22] Noldin, *Theol. Mor.*, Vol. III, No. 400, p. 463.

[23] Cf. Ch. III in Social Ethics.

thing to do. But while honoring heroes of investigation and discovery, we should not too severely condemn those who may have persecuted them. For it seems a psychological necessity that new truth—whether in religion, science, or politics—should be resisted. The old conceptions are at the basis of all institutions of society, and to change these conceptions too rapidly would be anarchy instead of progress. Structures must be modified gradually, and a certain conservatism is necessary as a brake even upon truth.

294. Why New Truth Is Not Easily Received. Again, personal interest frequently inclines to the maintenance of old policies and ideas. That inclination is apt to blind the keenest intellects. Those who have privileges, whether monetary or of honor, wish to keep them. Truth may interfere and therefore they are prejudiced against truth. The masses resist truth, because it means the acquirement of new habits of thought, new ways of looking at things. Few men can accept new ideas after they are forty, not from intellectual dishonesty, but from a natural inability. All these reasons combine to make the acceptance of a new truth a slow process, and its preaching a painful road to glory. Society has always rewarded its greatest heroes with martyrdom. Those canonized today were persecuted during their lives. A prophet is without honor in his own country.

295. Is Truth Always Good? A further consideration is the very pertinent question: Is truth under all circumstances good and error evil? Bishop Spaulding of Peoria has said: "Knowledge cannot be evil. If earth were a hell, and life a curse, and the universe but a cinder, it would still be good to know the fact." [24] And again, "the saddest truth is better than the merriest lie." But while such epigrams sound well, it may be doubted if they are wise in practice. Even the most ardent advocate of preaching truth would probably admit that Enoch Arden followed the nobler and wiser course in keeping his knowledge to himself, and

[24] *Means and Ends of Education,* Chicago, p. 23.

that Philip and his wife were the happier and better for his concealment.

296. Practically Error Is Sometimes Better Than Truth. Paulsen points out that the natural science of Aristotle, while mostly false, was useful and stimulating to the Middle Ages; whereas, the science of today, while nearer to absolute truth, would have been an enigma to the minds of that time. Truth while absolute in itself is in its utility relative. What is truth and useful for one man, may not be useful for another. In itself, the truth remains the same, but the old Scholastic saying: "Whatever is received is received according to the nature of the recipient," must not be forgotten. Truths are not material possessions that can be handed over to another at will. That other person must work to acquire them, must get such a mental hold on them that they really will be true for him.

297. Absolute Truth Can Be Relative Error. Those, therefore, who have the obligation of teaching—professors, preachers, and the like—must remember that truth can become error if administered unwisely. There is an analogy here between the mind and the body. As what is one man's meat is another man's poison; so what is one man's truth may be another man's error. It is recognition of this paradox that makes the Catholic Church so careful of her little ones. Books, that may proclaim only things that are true, are sometimes forbidden the uneducated, because they are strong meat unfit for intellectual babes; certain historical facts are not preached from the pulpit, because they would scandalize some weaker brethren; innovations of science are almost discouraged for fear of the results of pushing their acceptance too rapidly.

298. Summary. A lie is speaking against one's mind with the intention of deceiving. All ethicians agree in condemning this as a general thing. But non-Scholastic authors allow deception under certain conditions and Scholastic authors when it can be reduced to real mental reservation or equivocation, and there is a just cause. In addition to the duty of not telling a falsehood, there is a positive duty sometimes to tell the truth.

SUGGESTED READINGS

1. Rickaby, *Moral Philosophy,* ch. on "Veracity."
2. Slater, *Moral Theology,* Vol. I, Pt. VIII, Ch. IV.
3. Mausbach, *Catholic Moral Teaching and Its Antagonists,* p. 113 ff.
4. Newman, *Apologia,* Note G.
5. *Atlantic Monthly,* March, 1905, "An Unlovely Virtue."
6. Grotius, *De Jure Belli et Pacis,* Lib. III, Cap. I.
7. Paulsen, *System of Ethics,* Bk. III, Ch. XI.
8. Walsh, *Popes and Science,* Appendix I (N. Y., 1911).

QUESTIONS

1. Give original example how formal falsehood may be materially true.
2. Give original example of situation justifying deception.
3. Suppose a friend is ignorant of the moral wrongfulness of a particular act he contemplates, are you obliged to enlighten him?
4. What do you think of the statement: Knowledge cannot be evil?

THREE: *Temperance*

I. Food

299. Definition of Temperance. Temperance is the reasonable use of food, drink, and medicine. It is the reasonable rather than the moderate use, because the immoderate use is sometimes justifiable and does not offend against the virtue of temperance. And a very moderate use of certain drugs, judged by the amount taken, may be very intemperate.

300. Gluttony, or the Immoderate Use of Food. Gluttony may be a serious sin. This is so when eating becomes the end for which persons live. The Romans who deliberately practiced vomiting in order to relieve themselves of one meal that they might enjoy the sensation of eating another, were seriously violating the virtue of temperance. One who eats what he likes, knowing it will render him unfit to perform his ordinary duties, will be grossly intemperate no matter how small the amount taken. To spend more than a reasonable sum upon food, whether or not one eats a great quantity, is likewise gluttony. An abstemious meal of peacock tongues would be inordinate on account of the value of the food. No one person has a right to pay for one meal what would support a dozen families, as the King in Shelley's satire:

> "I fear your sacred majesty has lost
> The appetite which you were used to have.
> Allow me to recommend this dish—
> A simple kickshaw by your Persian cook,
> Such as is served at the great King's second table.
> The price and pains which its ingredients cost
> Might have maintained some dozen families
> A winter or two—not more. So plain a dish
> Could scarcely disagree."
>
> (Swellfoot the Tyrant.)

301. Importance of Being Temperate. The question of intemperance in food is second only to that of intemperance in drink;

128

in a way, it is more important, because it is more insidious. Intemperance in drink brings its consequences immediately, and they are self-evident. The effects of gluttony are slower and more hidden. Over-eating may go on for years without the results being attributed to the real cause. Physicians tell us that as a nation we over-eat, that we should be better off bodily, mentally, spiritually, financially if we would cut down the amount of our food.

II. Drink

302. Drunkenness. Intemperance in the use of alcoholic liquors is so wide-spread, and has such disastrous consequences both for the individual and for society that it has come to appropriate the term intemperance. Most persons think only of drink when they think of intemperance, because it is the most prevalent form of this vice.

303. Drunkenness Is Morally Wrong. The malice of drinking to excess is partly intrinsic and individual, partly extrinsic and social. To take so much of any liquor as to lose one's reason is, in itself, seriously wrong, unless there be a sufficient justification. It is true that one loses control over himself temporarily every night in sleep. It is a fact that about one-third of his existence is spent in this condition. But this is a natural need of one's body. Not to take this rest would mean a complete and permanent loss of one's reason. There is a justifying cause that makes this perfectly lawful.

304. When Intoxication Is Lawful. When there is sufficient motive, as in offsetting a poison, one may lawfully drink until he temporarily loses his reason. Without some such motive, however, it is a violation of right order for man to deprive himself of the faculty that distinguishes him from the brutes. Reason was given to man that he might consciously direct his actions; to give up that direction, to place one's self in a condition where one not only cannot control one's self, but is most likely to commit some grave sin of impurity, blasphemy, or anger, is a very serious deordination. One who is guilty of it, is guilty not only of the sin of drunkenness, but also of all the other sins that he commits while in that condition provided only that he has at least a dim foresight of their commission.

305. Drinking As an Occasion of Sin. How serious this latter consideration may be is evident to everyone who has had any experience with those given to drink. It applies, also, to a large extent even when liquor is used in moderation. The effect of liquor varies with the individual, but it is safe to say that a large number of the sins against purity, innumerable quarrels leading to physical violence and bloodshed, untold sins of cursing, swearing, and blaspheming would never be committed without the demoralizing stimulus of liquor. Even a little of a strong intoxicant, such as whiskey or brandy, lessens one's self-control and opens the gate to all sorts of wrong-doing. What has been called the "great sin of great cities" would be greatly reduced if liquor were abolished.

306. Drinking and the Social Evil. For it is not simply the loss of self-control that leads to debauchery. It is the companionship into which drinking leads. And it is a well-known fact that a new psychology comes into play when men form into groups. Those who individually may be rather decent and self-respecting become dominated by a certain group personality and will do what they would not have thought of doing had they been drinking by themselves.

307. Alcohol and Gasoline Do Not Mix. Moreover, in this machine age even a small amount of liquor, much less than required to cause intoxication, may have serious consequences. When there are ten deaths a day and several times that many serious injuries from automobile accidents, no one should increase the danger of accident by drinking just before or while driving a high-powered car. Some persons are exhilarated by even one drink, so that they drive faster than they otherwise would and take unnecessary chances. Tests have shown that a small amount of alcohol reduces one's motor responses a fifth of a second, and at sixty miles an hour a car will travel nearly twenty feet in a fifth of a second. Hence failure for one-fifth of a second to respond to the sign of danger may mean the difference between safety and an accident. It would seem that one who drinks at all while driving is offending against the reasonable care he owes to his own health and the health of others.

308. Intemperance Injures Health. Another consideration making it wrong for the individual to drink to excess, apart from any scandal or violation of duties due to others, is the impairment of health and shortening of life. Physicians may not be agreed as to whether alcohol is a food, or even a useful medicine, but they are unanimous in affirming that it is physically injurious when taken in excessive quantities. And, as we shall learn in the next chapter, each one has the duty of taking care of God's most important gift to him in the natural order, his life and health. Wantonly to squandor it for the sake of one's palate, or for the sensations accompanying the use of intoxicating liquors is a grave wrong against the Author of that gift.

309. Drinking Forms Unbreakable Habits. Again, a person who drinks to excess does not simply lose the use of his reason at the time of intoxication. He has permanently weakened his will. He has begun the formation of a habit that unless broken at the start will knit for him cables that Samson could not break. As Poor Richard says, it is easier to resist the first desire than all which will follow if that is gratified. Let him continue his dissipation for a year or two, and he will be bound hand and foot. It takes almost a miracle to free a drunkard from his slavery to drink. Various cures are advertised, but those who have had any dealing with inebriates know how rarely they are permanently cured. The effect may last for a few months, but men once addicted to drink are almost sure to go back to their cups. Sometimes a man who has stayed away from liquor for years will succumb to a temptation, and the last state of that man is worse than the first. It is the old story of one devil being driven out, and returning with seven more to find the house swept and garnished.

310. Alcohol a Habit-Forming Poisonous Drug. It should never be forgotten that alcohol is a habit-forming drug. Moreover, it is one of the few poisons that may affect the germ plasm. Taken in sufficient quantities it is a lethal poison. The wisest course is to avoid alcohol as one avoids opium or cocaine.

311. Delirium Tremens. The Greeks, it is said, used to make their slaves drunk as an example to their sons. That may have been effective with the Greeks; it is not effective with Americans. Even the sight of those with delirium tremens does not keep men from going and doing likewise. One would think that if anything could show men the folly of drink it would be to see the human beasts locked up in cages in a ward for inebriates. It is hard to imagine anything more disgusting than the antics through which these poor creatures go. They are not simply drunk—they are temporarily crazy, and their insanity takes the most revolting forms. But all this has no effect upon our young men. They always imagine that they are the exceptions, that they can safely play with what has been the downfall of so many others. The start is made with the intention of being a moderate drinker. Total abstinence is only for the weak wills who cannot take one glass without taking too many; whereas they are strong. And they die in a drunken brawl, or in a cell with iron bars, raving maniacs.[1]

312. Every Drunkard Once a Moderate Drinker. Of course, it is perfectly true that many persons remain moderate drinkers as long as they live. But it is also true that each year a certain number of moderate drinkers pass over into the class of drunkards. No moderate drinker can be sure that he may not be of this number. The only absolutely sure way of never becoming a drunkard is never to drink. If one could be sure of never contracting cancer simply by avoiding one article of food or drink, he would be foolish to indulge in that item. But alcoholism is worse than cancer. It may lead to death, and it is certain to spell a moral collapse, a breakdown of character.

[1] For a statement of the case in favor of moderate drinking, cf. *Alcohol—The Sanction of Its Use,* by Dr. Starke (N. Y., Putnam); on the other hand, *The New Internat. Year Book* (N. Y., 1913) thus sums up recent studies and experiments regarding alcohol: "While it may have its uses, especially in illness, to encourage its use, especially in daily life, on the grounds of nutritive necessity would be indefensible." (Art. "Alcohol.")

313. Private Intemperance Wrong. The above reasons make intoxication wrong in itself. They effectively meet the excuse of those who say: "I drink only in my own room. Nobody sees me drunk and I hurt only myself." A man loses the use of his reason in his own room as well as in a saloon, and he has no right to shorten his life and injure his health privately any more than he has publicly.

314. Intemperance Is Not an Individual Matter. But the excuse does not touch upon some very important considerations affecting the drink problem. It is not a matter which concerns an individual alone. Few of those who drink to excess are considerate enough to indulge only in private, nor can they so indulge themselves even privately without neglecting duties to other persons. The horror of the drink problem does not consist so much in its effects upon the drinkers themselves as in the ruin of those connected with them. If only the drunkards suffered, a great deal of the thought given to these questions would be wasted. Men who deliberately court danger might be allowed to take the consequences, if the consequences affected themselves only.

315. Drinking Drags Down Others Than the Drinker. But no man can live to himself alone. We are members one of another, and the man who drinks to excess is bound to drag others down with him. Sometimes it is an innocent wife and children; again it is an aged mother; frequently it is some companion who is led astray by his example. And so the evil grows. Each one is taught to drink by someone else; and having learned, he becomes a source of corruption for others.

316. Inebriates Flock Together. Drinking is usually a social affair, and being social its influence for evil is enormously larger than if it were merely individual. It is probably the most social of all vices. Men do not congregate to steal, or to murder, or even to debauch, in the same open way as they do to drink. Narcotic drugs are usually taken in comparative secrecy. But intoxicating liquors are consumed very largely as a social matter, offered as an attention of friendship, shared in sociability.

317. Ethics of Legal Drinking. And even if one's drinking is within his own home, yet this may easily be more than an individual matter. A wife or child may thus acquire a habit that will lead to destruction. And besides the moral consequences, they may lose sight or life through bootleg liquor. The same consideration applies, too, if this legal product is offered to guests. One cannot enter into the hearts of his guests; one cannot know their characters sufficiently well to judge if it be prudent to expose them to this danger. Perhaps a temptation is being offered to a guest who is too weak to resist, who is struggling with all his strength to keep away from liquor entirely as his only salvation, and who will succumb to this temptation offered in a private home. Because the law recognizes such drinking as lawful, does not really change its character, does not ennoble it.

318. The Motive for Total Abstinence. It is true therefore, that everyone, no matter how strong he may be, can find a weighty motive for total abstinence from intoxicating liquors. However, the weight of this motive will depend upon many things. One may have more or less reason for distrusting his own continued power or resistance, or the weakness of those with whom he drinks. Again, the closeness of co-operation between occasional or moderate drinking and the traffic that ruins body and soul should be considered. The keener one's social conscience, the more clearly will he realize his duty in this regard. As we come to appreciate more fully the solidarity of society, we are coming to understand more clearly how each one is his brother's keeper.

319. Obligation of Total Abstinence Is Not Absolute. Only the most radical temperance advocates, however, will at present go so far as to say that the individual must never, under pain of serious sin, take so much as one drink. We prefer to hold up total abstinence as an ideal that the best should strive for from a sense of responsibility for their weaker brethren, and with an obligation binding under slight inconvenience. The strong, who do not for themselves need total abstinence, should practice it as an example to those who do need it, and to create an atmosphere in which it shall be considered right and proper and best to abstain entirely. If only weak men abstained, it would be a confession of weakness; and the weak would be ashamed to make that confession. Therefore, men who themselves are cool-headed enough to drink in moderation owe it to their weaker brethren to abstain.

III. Drugs

320. Habit-Forming Drugs. What has been said of intoxicating liquors applies *mutatis mutandis* to the use of all drugs which induce a loss of consciousness or self-control. To induce sleep or relieve pain, an opiate may be given when there is sufficient reason, but no possible doubt should exist in the minds of the patient or physician as to the sufficiency of the reason. Of those who contract drug habits, a very great number begin the use of the drug as a medicine. For this reason physicians should be most careful in prescribing habit-forming drugs. Each patient should be studied, and as far as possible the probable effect upon him as an individual foreseen. In cases involving extreme pain the therapeutic exigencies of the moment may demand an opiate, but the conscientious physician will not be content with immediate results. He will take into account the future as well as the present welfare of his patient. In cases of insomnia, for instance, he will exhaust every device of hygiene, such as fresh air, exercise, special baths, hydro-therapy, and relief from indigestion before ordering even the least harmful opiates. For, the wise physician well knows that a temporary relief is dearly bought at the price of a possible life-long bondage.

321. Tea and Coffee. Nor are the effects of more common drugs to be despised. Caffein and tannin are dangerous and injurious, though of course in a lesser degree than alcohol and opium. Their ill-effects are not so noticeable, but they exist nevertheless. A man who cannot do without coffee in the morning is a slave to this beverage; a woman who is always sipping tea is undermining her health and contracting a habit she will find hard to master. But whether or not tea and coffee are as injurious from a moral standpoint as some would claim, no one should give up his liberty to any drink—whether it be whiskey, tea, or Coca-Cola. It is not manly to submit one's will to a habit.

322. Tobacco. This same argument applies against the use of tobacco. Few can use it, without using it to excess. They either spend too much money on it, or they injure their health, or they become addicted to it in some form so that they are miserable if circumstances prevent their getting it. A man who is unhappy because he has not a cigar, pipe, or cigarette between his lips has done something unworthy of a man in making his happiness depend upon a mere weed.

323. All Stimulants. David Starr Jordan insists with truth that, "As a drop of water is of the nature of the sea, so in its degree is the effect of alcohol, opium, tobacco, cocaine, kola, tea or coffee, of the nature of mania. They give a feeling of pleasure or rest, when rest or pleasure do not exist. This feeling arises from injury to the nerves which the brain does not truthfully interpret. . . . One and all these various drugs tend to give the impression of power, or a pleasure, or an activity, which we do not possess. One and all their function is to force the nervous system to lie. One and all the result of their habitual use is to render the nervous system incapable of telling the truth. One and all their supposed pleasures are followed by a reaction of subjective pains as spurious and as unreal as the pleasures which they follow. Each of them, if used to excess brings in time, insanity, incapacity, and death. With each of them, the first use makes the second easier. To yield to temptation makes it easier to yield again. The weakening effect on the will is greater than the injury to the body." [2]

IV. Hypnotism

324. What Is Hypnotism? Hypnotism is an artificial sleep induced by external means and exhibiting certain abnormal characteristics. It is well known now how this sleep may be induced, and extensive experiments have been made to determine just

[2] *The Strength of Being Clean*, pp. 28, 32.

what can be accomplished by it. But no completely satisfactory explanation has yet been given of the nature of this influence. Whether it be due to some magnetic fluid, or to imagination, or to suggestion may never be determined; but some progress has been made, if only this, that we are now able to consider these phenomena as within the realm of the natural law instead of thinking them, as formerly, a result of witchcraft, or demoniac activity.

325. Consent Is Necessary for Hypnotism. The general consensus of modern opinion is that persons cannot be hypnotized for the first time without their consent. Having once undergone hypnotization, however, they can be more easily subjected to it a second time. It is even said [3] that the operator can then put a person to sleep at pleasure. Probably the hypnotic sleep cannot be induced at a distance.

326. Possible to Suggest Crimes. How important the question of hypnotism is for Ethics is evident when we consider what is possible through its means. The subject becomes dominated by the suggestions of another. He will go through the most foolish antics, or perform the most immoral actions. "It is a generally recognized fact that criminal or unlawful acts have been, or can be committed on sleeping subjects. . . . Women have been made the victims of attempts on their honor, and even of rape. Sometimes, too, by means of suggestions, the subject is made to consent to the crime, as criminal records show. We have no properly ascertained cases of fraud or theft successfully practiced by means of hypnosis, but such things are nevertheless possible. The evidence given in all such cases should be regarded with mistrust; the subject may be deliberately trying to deceive, or he may be mistaken in good faith, and so accuse an innocent person." [4]

327. Suggestions May Be Followed upon Awakening. It seems possible to suggest during hypnotic sleep that a certain action should be performed after awakening, when designated circumstances arise. If that be possible, then clever criminals could make

[3] Cath. Encyc., VII, p. 606.
[4] Cath. Encyc., VII, p. 609.

perfectly innocent persons their accomplices and go scot-free; or they might be able to suggest to hypnotized persons that they have committed a certain crime and have them confess to it. Some years ago there was a famous murder case in which several notable authorities claimed that hypnotism figured. A young married woman, Mrs. Bessie M. Hollister, was brutally murdered in Chicago, in January, 1906. Richard Glines Ivens was arrested for the crime and almost immediately confessed. But Professors James, Muensterberg, Christianson, and Max Meyer claimed that he was hypnotized when he made this confession.[5] Whether their contention was true or not, it shows what those best qualified to judge believed may happen through hypnotism.

SUGGESTED READINGS

1. *New International Year Book,* 1913, art. "Alcohol."
2. Dr. J. Starke, *Alcohol: The Sanction for Its Use.*
3. Cath. Encyc., art. "Temperance."
4. Cath. Encyc., art. "Temperance Movements."
5. Cath. Encyc., art. "Hypnotism."
6. Maher, *Psychology,* Appendix B, "Hypnotism."

QUESTIONS

1. Is it ethically wrong for one to dig his grave with his teeth?
2. Does opium have a worse effect on Chinese than alcohol has on Americans?
3. Does the use of opium lead to debauchery and crimes of violence as does the use of alcohol?
4. Are there any dangers connected with total abstinence?
5. Does the fact that we live in an automotive age affect the quantity of alcohol that may reasonably be called intemperate?
6. Look up latest statistics on auto accidents due to drunken driving.

[5] Cf. *Current Lit.,* Vol. 42, p. 221.

FOUR: *Duties Towards One's Self*[1]

328. State of Question. There is no question of duties of justice towards one's self. For an injustice cannot be done to one who willingly accepts the damage; and in the case of self-inflicted injury the agent and recipient being one and the same, the recipient must acquiesce in the act. All moralists are agreed, therefore, that one cannot, strictly speaking, commit an injustice against one's self.

329. Duty to Love One's Self. But can one have a duty of charity towards himself? Schopenhauer[2] says: "No," because one cannot help loving himself and duty can be only where there is freedom. Others have claimed that one cannot love himself, because love implies *union,* and union is impossible where there is identity. While this is true, the Scholastic position is that, "in another way we may speak of charity in its proper character and essence, as it is the friendship of man with God primarily, and secondarily with the creatures that are of God; among which the man himself counts who has charity. In this way, among other things that he loves in charity as belonging to God, he also loves himself in charity."[3]

330. Division of Duties Towards Self. Nor is this self-love, so long as it is well-ordered, inconsistent with the self-renunciation preached by Christ, for Christ did not teach an absolute self-denial. We shall now, therefore, proceed to consider what are the duties of well-ordered self-love. These fall into three classes as distinguished by the object of the love: (1) in relation to the

---

[1] Cathrein, *Moralphilosophie,* Pt. II, Sec. 1, Bk. II; Rickaby, *Aquinas Ethicus,* II, II. Q. XXV; Willems, *Philosophia Moralis, Pt. II, Bk. II, Ch. II; Pascal, Philosophie Morale et Sociale,* Vol. II, Bk. II; Schiffini, *Philosophia Moralis,* Pt. II, Disp. I, Secs. III, IV; Noldin, *Theologia Moralis: De Praeceptis;* Gousset, *Traité du Decalogue,* Pt. V, Art. V; Lehmkuhl, *Theologia Moralis Specialis,* Bk. II, Div. I, Ch. I; Slater, *Moral Theology,* Bk. VI, Pt. V.

[2] *Die beiden Grundprobleme der Ethik,* II, No. 5, p. 126, quoted by Cathrein, *Moralphilosophie,* II, p. 53.

[3] Rickaby, *Aquinas Ethicus,* II, II. Q. XXV, A. IV.

soul; (2) in relation to the body; (3) in relation to external goods, such as honor or material objects.

I. Duties of One's Self to His Own Soul

331. Duty Is Summarized by Natural Law. The highest good of a man, it has been proven,[4] is union with God hereafter. Hence, a man's first and highest duty towards himself is to order his acts in such a way as to attain this union. And as this union is dependent upon a keeping of the natural law in so far as this is formally known, there follow, at least as indirect duties, all duties prescribed by that law.

332. Duty of Cultivating Intellect. But as man knows the natural law through his intellect and obeys it with his will, it is incumbent upon each one as a duty to himself to develop these faculties. In relation to the intellect each one is, therefore, bound to acquire the knowledge which is necessary to enable him to fulfill the duties of his state in life. To this class belong, above all, a knowledge of God and of the duties of religion as previously explained.[5] In addition he should know the special obligations placed upon him by his particular office, such as physician, lawyer, parent, servant. Beyond this necessary vocational knowledge, one is not strictly bound to go in his spiritual education.

333. Duty of Seeking Knowledge. Yet it is praiseworthy to develop one's powers and to extend one's knowledge as far as possible. This is certainly in accordance with God's plan in giving us faculties capable of such indefinite increase, and placing us in a universe that at every turn besieges us with questions and riddles. And it is certainly useful in smoothing out the rough places of life, in furthering civilization, in making life on earth more comfortable and worthy of human beings.

334. Seeking of Knowledge Should Be Well-Ordered. But this seeking after knowledge should be reasonable and well-ordered.

[4] Cf. Pt. I, Ch. III.
[5] Cf. Pt. II, Ch. I.

It should correspond to our capacities and our station. Over-education may be a curse to the individual and to society when it unfits a person for the only thing he has a chance to do in life. Again, there is an idle curiosity that acquires a certain encyclopedic, but useless information that seemingly enables one to gossip about any topic under the sun, but which forever remains mere information and is never digested into faculty or wisdom.

335. Will Must Also Be Trained. Hand in hand with the acquisition of knowledge must go a training of the will to seek good, lest one become merely a clever knave. For it is not sufficient, as was said previously, merely to know the good in order to do it. The will must be set in the direction of virtue, certain good habits must be acquired by long practice. This is true character-building, without which all the knowledge in the world is worse than useless, since it is positively harmful. By actual efforts the will must bridle anger, root out pride, conquer avarice, give everyone his due, in short, keep the whole moral law.[6]

336. The Duty to Work. Here it will suffice to mention more at length only two specific duties. The first of these is to work. Man is born to labor as the bird is to fly. There are in every man certain needs that can be satisfied only by somebody's work, and in most cases by one's own. But even where it is possible to satisfy these needs without working one's self, work is nevertheless necessary for the avoidance of moral pitfalls. For there are few truer sayings than that idleness is the devil's workshop. An inevitable moral deterioration takes place in anyone who spends his life or a major portion of it without work of some sort, and frequently one of the greatest curses imaginable is to be left an income one does not earn.

337. The Evil of "Society." Hence, the duty to work is universal. No one is morally permitted to spend his life in idleness. To fritter away day after day and year after year in toilet making, elaborately long meals, theater-going, card-playing, attending

---

[6] For a very practical treatise on the virtues and vices to be acquired and avoided, cf. St. Francis de Sales, *Introduction to a Devout Life*. Scaramelli, *Directorium Asceticum*, a much larger work, is probably the classic on this subject.

concerts, newspaper and magazine reading, autoing, and sleeping, is unworthy of intelligent human beings, no matter what "the world" may say of such matters.

338. The Order of Work. In order that work should be well-ordered there should come first what is *necessary,* then what is merely *useful,* and finally what is *agreeable.*

339. Duty of Courage. The second virtue to be mentioned more at length is courage. God placed man in a world where there is a great deal of pain and suffering, and each man has his portion. Why He so designed the world we do not know. No one has ever intelligently solved the problem of the existence of evil. But practically, the solution is to accept it bravely and cheerfully. To keep one's eyes to the front, one's chest out, one's chin up, one's lips firm is the only truly worthy way of meeting the difficulties of life. Bravery is a virtue demanded by Scholastic Ethics as well as by Stoicism. No man should be a whiner or a coward.

II. Duties in Regard to Life and Health

340. Duties in Regard to the Body. Duties in regard to life and health naturally divide themselves into positive, which command certain things favorable to health and life; and negative, which forbid what would be hurtful. Among the negative duties, the prohibition of suicide takes first place.

341. Suicide. *By suicide we here mean the deliberate and directly intended taking of one's life by one's own authority.*

342. Sometimes Lawful Indirectly to Intend One's Own Death. We say directly intended, because it may sometimes be lawful to perform an act from which one's own death will follow. Thus a soldier may light a mine knowing that he will almost certainly be destroyed.[7] But he does not directly intend his own death and the desired end is not produced by his death. In the same way it is lawful for a woman to defend her honor by leaping from a window when there is no other way to escape.[8]

---

[7] Cathrein, II, p. 62.
[8] Cf. Noldin, *De Praeceptis,* p. 349.

The principle on which this is allowed is that the action is indifferent, two effects proceeding from it with equal immediacy, that the bad consequence does not cause the good, and that there is a sufficiently serious reason affecting public or private good.

343. May Be Lawful to Execute One's Own Self. It is necessary to specify that suicide is the taking of one's life by one's own authority, to distinguish it from cases where a condemned criminal may act as the State's executioner. Some moralists maintain that it is lawful in this case for a man to take his own life, as it would be lawful for him to take the life of another criminal if he were acting by the State's authority.[9]

344. Suicide Is Never Lawful. With the above distinctions in mind, Scholastic moralists maintain that suicide is never justifiable.

345. But Reasons for Unlawfulness Not Conclusive. But while moralists agree that suicide as defined is unjustifiable, the reasons they adduce for such a position are not conclusive. "For," as Cardinal De Lugo says: "though its [suicide's] turpitude is immediately apparent, it is not easy to find the foundation for this judgment. Hence (a thing that happens in many other questions), the conclusion is more certain than the reasons adduced by various authors for its proof."[10]

346. Traditional Arguments Against Suicide. The usual reason adduced to prove the unlawfulness of suicide is that God has not given to man an unlimited dominion over his own life. In support of this proposition one may point to the normal feeling of mankind. The deep-seated instinct of self-preservation, seen frequently in the unhappiest wretches, indicates a lack of that sense of power completely to dispose of one's self which men have in regard to brute animals.[11] The argument loses some of its force, however—referred to by Cathrein—from the fact that some 50,000 men in Europe alone annually suicide [12] and that in

[9] Noldin, *De Praeceptis*, p. 348.
[10] *De Just. et Jure*, Disp. X, Sec. I, 2.
[11] *Op. cit.*, II, p. 65.
[12] Quoted from Masaryk by Cathrein, II, p. 63.

Prussia, between 1883-1903, 1,125 school children suicided.[13] Nor
does the social argument that man injures society by taking his
own life [14] appeal particularly. For it may be just as advantageous
to society to have a criminal suicide as to hang him. In fact, it
would save the cost of a trial and the ill effects of the morbid
publicity given such things. And if the act be done secretly, there
is no bad example set, no encouragement given better people to
do likewise.

347. Metaphysical Argument Against Suicide. It seems better
to confine one's self to the metaphysical reason that one can
have dominion only over that whose end he is. As man is not
his own end,[15] he cannot have full dominion over himself.

348. When Self-Mutilation Is Unlawful. From the unlawfulness of suicide, it follows that self-mutilation is also forbidden.
As a man is not master of his person, so he is not master of his
members. For since man is made up of various parts, if he were
master of the individual parts, he would be master of the whole.
In case, however, the amputation of some part is necessary for
the health of the whole, the amputation is entirely lawful. And
St. Alphonsus does not condemn at least one form of serious
mutilation for the good of the community.[16] By the same reasoning, one might, it would seem, allow certain experiments to be
performed upon himself for the sake of scientific investigation.
A man who allows mosquitoes to bite him in order to prove a
theory of yellow fever transmission, and who dies as a result,
should not be adjudged guilty of suicide.[17]

349. Misuse of Organs. In the same way that the mutilation
of one's members is prohibited by self-love, so is the abuse of
an organ. It is not lawful to use any organ against its purpose.
Hence, certain solitary sins against the Sixth Commandment are

---

13 *The Nation*, Oct. 31, 1907, p. 403; quoting report of Prussian Cultus Ministry.
14 Rickaby, *Aquinas Ethicus*, II, II, Q. LXIV, art. 5.
15 Cf. Pt. I, Ch. III.
16 *Theologia Moralis*, n. 374.
17 For advocacy of the lawfulness of suicide, at least under some circumstances,
cf. Hume, *Essays on Suicide;* Paulsen, *System of Ethics;* Ziegler, *Sittl. Sein und
sittl. Werden;* Steudel, *Der religioese Unterricht.*

forbidden and should be treated here if it were within our scope to go into such matters. Something, however, should be said, for ordinarily we speak in such roundabout terms of such sins that many growing boys and girls go through agonies of conscience thinking they have committed horrible crimes when they are perfectly innocent; while others in invincible ignorance contract habits that may lead to very serious consequences in after life. Hence, we deem it necessary and prudent to state frankly the principles for regulating conduct in this most important sphere of practical life.

350. The Angelic Virtue.[18] In unmarried persons, all directly intended and deliberately willed sexual pleasure is sinful, and since the days of Aquaviva practically all Scholastic moralists have maintained that it is seriously sinful. Whether the pleasure is caused by word, look, or touch, it is wrong. On the other hand, what does not cause this excitement is not sinful. It will thus be seen that there is a strong personal equation to be reckoned with. What would be wrong for one person may not be for another; what is wrong in one country may not be in another; because in the one case it would cause this excitement, in the other it would not. Some persons, for instance, can look upon paintings of the nude with perfect innocence, others cannot. Each one must be governed largely by his own nature.

351. The Need of Prudence. But while this is true, one should not experiment with himself. It is best to accept as dangerous what others come to look upon as such, and avoid it. Do not run risks. To play with this passion is to play with fire. And in this case the burnt child does not dread the fire—he wants more burning. The best rule is not to think about sexual things except when necessary. All knowledge and anything else which comes within the conditions specified in the preceding paragraphs would be lawful. But here more than anywhere, he who does all that is lawful will do more than is lawful. As St. Paul says: "All things are lawful to me, but not all things are expedient."

---

[18] Cf. Martindale, *The Difficult Commandment.*

352. Freud. On the other hand, the Freudian emphasis on sex is undoubtedly an exaggeration. Sex is not responsible for all of our ills and the psychoanalytic searching for this element would seem itself often to be a morbid manifestation of sex. If it is ever practiced on any large scale, it is likely to lead to serious consequences. Certainly, patients should be very loath to submit to any such searching into their past or private lives. The ordinary answer to such questioning should be that it is none of the physician's business. Moreover, the Freudian scorn of restraint, if followed to its logical conclusions, would lead to all sorts of sexual excesses.

353. One Should Not Be Scrupulous. On the other hand, however, one should not become scrupulous. One ought not always to be wondering if one has fallen. That is to break the rule not to think about such matters. A person should keep occupied with other things, and if doubts arise, decide them promptly according to the principles laid down—that only directly intended and deliberately willed sexual pleasure is sinful. The excitement must be deliberately willed. What may come from one's natural disposition of body apart from any volition is not formally wrong. What comes as a consequence of another action lawfully willed, as of a physician performing an operation or one bathing, is permissible on the principle of indirect volition.

354. Temptations to Impurity Sometimes Physical Rather Than Moral. Abnormally strong temptations to impurity sometimes come from physical defects which can be remedied. One afflicted in this way should consult a physician to see what is possible for relief.

355. Sometimes Lawful to Desire One's Death. But though suicide is forbidden under all circumstances, it is lawful to desire one's death in order to avoid a greater evil than death, or to gain a greater good than life. Instances would be: desire to be rid of very serious pain, or to enjoy the Beatific Vision.

356. How Far Must One Preserve Life? Positive obligations to preserve life and health do not go beyond the use of ordinary means to that end. If the means necessary in any particular case are extraordinary on account of danger or pain, immoderate expense, or for any other good reason, there is no strict obligation to use them. Thus, one may refuse to undergo an operation if it would be extremely painful, or if it would impoverish him too much. Nor is one bound to undergo an operation for which one has great horror, as a woman for certain surgical operations at the hands of a man.[19]

357. Life May Sometimes Be Shortened. For a just cause, it is lawful indirectly to shorten one's life, even by a considerable period. A just cause would be *moral necessity,* or the *exercise of virtue.*[20] Hence, laborers may engage in certain kinds of labor that are known to shorten life. Nor is one bound to abstain from particular kinds of food or drink upon the opinion of a physician that their use will subtract slightly from the probable length of life.[21]

III. Duties to Non-Rational Beings

358. Duties Regarding Inanimate Objects. Besides these duties directly to himself, a man has certain duties as regards the use of external objects, whether inanimate or animate. He has a duty, for instance, to acquire the material goods necessary for the proper nourishment of his life. Also, he has a duty to preserve his good name.

359. Duties Regarding Animals. More important probably, because more open to abuse, are a man's duties regarding the use of brute animals. These are in the world for man's good, it is true, and have no rights, strictly speaking, of their own. But though man's use of them, therefore, is limited only by his duty to God and himself, he is just as really limited as if the brute animals had strict rights.

360. Vivisection. The most hotly disputed question regarding the use of animals is concerned with what is known as vivisection. Literally, vivisection is the dissection of a living animal.

[19] Noldin, *op. cit.,* p. 346.   [21] *Id.*
[20] Noldin, *op. cit.,* p. 350.

More generally, it is an experiment performed upon an animal under abnormal conditions. Are such experiments lawful when performed on brutes?

361. Vivisection Does Not Violate Animal's Rights. Scholastic moralists agree that these experiments are not a violation of any of the brute animal's rights, for brute animals not being persons cannot be the subjects of rights.

362. Is Vivisection Lawful? The question still remains, however, as to whether or not the experiments are immoral on account of man's duty to use the brute and inanimate kingdoms wisely and in accordance with his own ends? The question of vivisection, therefore, is one of fact. Does vivisection minister to the welfare of the human race? If it does, then it is lawful, for irrational animals are intended for use.

363. Gains From Vivisection. Despite some vigorous denials, it seems well established that medical science has benefited considerably by vivisection. The circulation of the blood, practically everything we know about the brain, the action of certain poisons and serums, and the usefulness of innumerable surgical operations could never have been demonstrated except by such experiments. It seems impossible, therefore, absolutely to condemn vivisection on moral grounds.

364. Vivisection Lawful, But Should Be Limited. But vivisection should be limited and regulated so as to have the experiments performed in the way least painful to the animals. This has been done by various legislatures and is a very laudable exercise of governmental authority.

365. Hunting and Duties to Animals. On a par with torturing birds to get feathers for a hat, is the sport of hunting. It is a strange thing that men pride themselves upon their skill in killing defenseless animals, and in doing it not for food, but merely for "sport." In fact, they despise the men who are engaged in hunting for food. A true sportsman will have nothing to do with a "pot-hunter."

366. Cock Fighting. But the worst form of cruelty to animals is probably in cock, dog, and bull fighting. These minister only to the lowest instincts in a man's breast and cause very considerable pain to the animals. It is not a swift shot that puts the victim out of pain quickly; it is prolonged torture to gratify the whims of barbarous spectators. Such fighting can probably be condemned as morally unlawful upon the ground that it fosters cruelty, hardens the heart, and brings the beast in man uppermost. The other practices that we have enumerated, though far from praiseworthy, cannot be condemned as morally wrong. Nevertheless, they should be discouraged, and it is laudable for persons to set their faces against such things. At least Christians, who themselves do not wish to live up to this higher standard, should not brand those who do as cranks. Rather they should do everything they can to strengthen their hands.

367. Summary. Everyone has a duty to love himself. As regards the soul this implies the avoiding of sin and an appropriate training of his intellect and will. As regards the body, love of self means proper care of health and life. Suicide is never lawful. The duty of loving one's self implies, further, the reasonable use of brute animals. They should not be tortured for fashion or sport. Vivisection, however, when performed by competent persons with as little pain as possible to animals is justified.

SUGGESTED READINGS

1. Rickaby, *Aquinas Ethicus,* II, II, Q, XXV.
2. Dewey and Tufts, *Ethics,* Pt. II, Ch. XVIII.
3. Carver, *Essays in Social Justice,* Ch. III.
4. Cath. Encyc., art. "Suicide."
5. Cath. Encyc., art. "Vivisection."
6. John S. Vaughan, *Thoughts for All Times,* Ch. IX.

QUESTIONS

1. May individuals have too much education?
2. May one who cannot read or write nevertheless be educated?
3. May one hold a college degree and yet be uneducated?
4. Should everyone work?
5. Is it ever ethically lawful to take one's own life?
6. May a woman suffering torture from cancer wish for death?
7. What do you think of euthanasia?

PART III
SOCIAL ETHICS

ONE: *Introductory*[1]

368. Summary of Preceding Chapters. So far we have discussed a man's duties to God and to himself. We have outlined the duties of external, interior, and social worship, with their attendant dangers; we have pointed out the duty of seeking and of disclosing the truth, as well as of never lying, though real mental reservation or equivocation may sometimes be lawful: the duty of moderation in eating and drinking, and especially of never becoming intoxicated; the duty of developing one's intellect and will, and of taking proper care of one's life, and we have determined the standard of conduct in our relations with brute animals. All these duties are individual in the sense that they are based upon our relation to God and not upon any right residing in our fellow men. With the exception of lying and social worship, they can be fulfilled independently of our neighbor, and they would exist even if there were only one human being in the world, or for a man who lived entirely to himself, as Robinson Crusoe before discovering Man Friday.

369. The Need of Social Ethics. But as there are many human beings, and they do not live absolutely separated lives, there follow many rights and duties that would have no concrete existence and would not need to be discussed by ethicians if there were only one man, or if men never came in contact with each other.

370. The Fact of Society. That men do associate together would seem so obvious as to merit no extended discussion. Indeed, the first fact that strikes our notice in a study of human population is aggregation or grouping. "Neither in savagery nor

[1] Cf. Urwick, *Philosophy of Social Progress;* Stuckenberg, *Introduction to the Study of Sociology;* Small, *General Sociology;* Montesquieu, *The Spirit of the Laws;* Bagehot, *Physics and Politics;* Pascal, *Philosophie Morale et Sociale;* Page, *Trade Morals;* MacDougall, *Social Psychology;* Deploige, *Le Conflit de la Morale et de la Sociologie;* Antoine, *Cours d'Economie Sociale;* Ross, E. A., *Sin and Society, Social Control;* Devas, *Key to the World's Progress.*

in civilization do men live normally in isolation." [2] Of the total population of this country, about one-third live in cities, and in the North Atlantic section about fifty per cent.

371. Attempts to Explain Society. For a great many centuries this fact of aggregation and association was accepted for what it was worth, and it did not occur to scholars to attempt an explanation of the obvious. It seemed so necessary and natural that this appeared the final word to be said about it, and to be as useful as any other possible theory as to its origin. But with the advent of evolutionary ideas, sociologists turned to primitive men and to brute animals to find some clue as to why men really do associate. So much time and effort have been expended in this direction with so little result that it is well at the outset to recall Professor Small's warning:

372. Best Course Is to Study Contemporary Men. "For revelation of man as man there is not a clump of neighbors in any rural community or city block that does not offer vastly more evidence toward explaining primitive men than the same number of primitive men can ever afford to explain our neighbors. It is a grotesque hallucination that men in stages of arrested development—men, moreover, about whom all the available evidence is woefully meager—furnish the only clues to human nature. In fact, a handful of knowledge of today's men, just as they are, is worth, if properly sifted, more than a ton of the sort of information we can get about men of any other period. Rate as high as we will the value of the past in explaining the present, we may set it down as certain that the present will prove a hundred-fold as useful in explaining the past." [3]

373. Animal Society. And what Professor Small says of our knowledge of past men is even more applicable to our knowledge of animals. "It is a grotesque hallucination" to imagine that tracing evidences of aggregation in brute beasts is any more of an explanation of human association than the frank admission

---

[2] Giddings, *Principles of Sociology*, p. 81. For an account of exceptions he refers to Numholtz, *Cave Dwellers of the Sierra Madre*.

[3] Small, *General Sociology*, p. 100.

that such association is natural. The study of any group of contemporary men living under the conditions with which we must deal is a million-fold more useful than the most learned investigation of animal instinct. Even though human society be the result of a gradual evolution of the packs and herds of beasts (a point that has not been proven), the little we can learn regarding animals will throw only a very faint light upon human association under present conditions.[4]

374. Spencer's Theories.[5] One of the first to go back to the analogy of animal life for an explanation of human society was Herbert Spencer, and his work in that respect is still largely typical. The animals of some species live together, says Spencer, while those of others live apart, because these customs further race or individual maintenance in the respective species. Thus animals of a predatory kind, subsisting on food that can easily be caught and killed, profit by living alone. As help is not needed to get the food, there is no need to share it when caught. Other animals that kill larger prey go in packs. In each species the size, strength, means of defense, kind of food, manner of rearing offspring, etc., must variously co-operate and conflict to determine how far a gregarious life is beneficial and how far a solitary life.

375. Spencer Does Not Really Explain Society. But does this really *explain* the fact of human society? It reduces itself to the statement that man belongs to a species of animals which have certain elementary needs making life in groups easier than life in solitude. At bottom it is the expression of the age-old dictum that man is a social animal. The language is modern but the idea is ancient.

376. Supposed Origin of the Moral Sentiments. All this, too, fails to distinguish the fundamental difference between human and animal association—that one is moral and the other is not. It is true that some sociologists essay to trace the moral senti-

---

[4] Cf. Kropotkin, *Morality and Nature*, Nineteenth Cent., Vol. 57, p. 407; Espinas, *Des Sociétés Animales.*

[5] *Principles of Psychology*, Pt. VIII, Ch. V.

ments back to these brute instincts, but the attempt ends in failure. Starting from the facts we have just quoted from Spencer, they go on to say that habit and survival of the fittest will tend to strengthen this rudimentary sociability or gregariousness wherever beneficial. After a time there will develop a pleasure from the company of those of the same species—what Giddings calls a consciousness of kind; and simultaneously with mental states produced by the *presence* of others, there come into being mental states produced by the *actions* of others. Thus expressions of fear on the part of one will produce like feelings in others; joyous actions will produce joyous feelings. This is nothing less than sympathy, they claim, and to sympathy Adam Smith traces all *moral* feelings.[6]

377. Sympathy Is Not Identical with Sense of Duty. But Smith fails, as does Spencer, really to bridge the gulf between the instinctive sentiments of fear, sympathy, and so on, and strictly *moral* ideas. Among moral ideas is the sense of duty, which is essentially distinct from sympathy or a recognition of utility. A man may realize the advantage of uniting with others in building a house, but he does not look upon it as a duty; he may sympathize very keenly with a man on a sinking ship and give him his place in a life-boat, thereby insuring his own death, but he does it out of sympathy, not from any sense of moral obligation. If a man failed to do either of these things he would not reproach himself with having failed in his duty. On the other hand a woman who has absolutely no sympathy with a faithless man she has married and a great deal of sympathy with another man, may yet refuse to take advantage of the laws of her country to marry a second time, because she feels bound to this first man. Here we have a sense of duty clearly independent of and even opposed to sympathy. And hence sympathy cannot be a satisfactory explanation of all moral ideas.

378. Professor Giddings' "Consciousness of Kind." Nor is Professor Giddings any more successful when he attempts to trace everything back to what he calls "consciousness of kind." Assum-

---

[6] *Theory of the Moral Sentiments.*

ing the same explanation of gregariousness in man as Spencer, Giddings [7] goes on to say that this is always supplemented by association if the individuals are not too unlike. At the first encounter there is a recognition of unlikeness, since "likeness can be distinguished from identity only through perception of difference, and, therefore, cannot be known until after some degree of unlikeness is apprehended." In this encounter between two individuals, any act or expression of the one is a stimulus to the nerve centers of the other. "Therefore, unless the action of those nerve centers is inhibited by the will, or by a counter stimulation, they must discharge themselves in movements that must more or less closely copy the originals." [8] Hence, "it is the factor of imitation in the conflict that gradually assimilates and harmonizes." [9] Yet imitation creates new conflicts, since imitations inevitably become differentiated. Antagonism, however, is self-limiting, and "necessarily terminates in the equilibrium of toleration." [10]

379. All Such Theories Unsatisfactory. Just how all these high-sounding phrases account for the fact that men like to be together, that they form governments, and recognize certain actions as *morally obligatory,* others as *morally right,* though not obligatory, is probably not entirely clear to the reader. Nor will it be any clearer, we venture to say, if he reads diligently the learned authors of these various theories. In fact, most sociological thought about the origin of society seems to be an elaborate and unnecessary explanation of a very simple thing. It can best be described as bosh. And the sooner "consciousness of kind," and "sympathy," and "imitation" (as all-sufficing keys to social phenomena) are confided to the limbo of Spencer's organism [11] and Hobbes' *Leviathan* and Rousseau's *Social Contract,* the better

[7] *Principles of Sociology,* p. 100 ff.

[8] *Op. cit.,* p. 110.

[9] *Op. cit.,* p. 109; Tarde, *Les lois de l'imitation,* makes imitation the explanation of all social forms.

[10] Giddings, *op. cit.,* p. 113.

[11] Spencer's wordy development of the analogy between an organism and human society is fortunately so completely discarded by modern sociologists that it is not necessary to do more than mention it here.

for the science of sociology. Until arrives that "consummation devoutly to be wished," there will be some justification in describing sociology as "a tale told by some idiot, full of sound and fury, signifying nothing." [12]

380. Traditional View of Society's Origin Is Best. The simplest, and at the same time the truest and most useful, explanation of the origin of society, is the old traditional biblical view. God created man (whether immediately or by a process of evolution does not matter) with certain social desires and tendencies. These work out naturally in aggregation and association, begetting certain social contacts. Such contacts, in accordance with the density of aggregation and the complexity of association, result in certain institutions to govern social action. Of the actions consequent upon association, some are required for conformity with the norm of morality, and are, therefore, morally obligatory; others are not required for conformity with this norm, and, therefore, are not morally obligatory.

381. Various Elements of Man's Existence. As Professor Urwick expresses it, we "are all members, as it were, of five different universes, each with its own conditions of existence. In all five universes we live our lives, subject at every moment to the laws of each, to the limitations and powers, the helps and hindrances, which the conditions of each universe impose or grant. First, and least important, there is the material universe of which we are a part, with its conditions of force and energy by which our powers are circumscribed, and also, by right use, enlarged. Secondly, there is the universe of living things, with its laws of life and growth, of health and disease, of birth, development, decay and death, from none of which we can escape, and all of which must be learned and obeyed. Thirdly, there is the universe of

---

[12] Sociology is commonly described as the science of social life. I do not believe that sociology is or can be a science. . . . What passes for sociology is a collection of generalizations of very varying value; and it is inevitable that most social generalizations shall be more or less dignified guesses, and more or less disguised expressions of the hopes and fears, the prejudices and beliefs, of their originators." Urwick, *A Philosophy of Social Progress,* p. vii. Professor Urwick is director of the School of Sociology, London. This book is one of the sanest and most brilliant pieces of writing in the field of sociology.

human minds, with its special laws of feeling and thought, sympathy and repulsion, planning and achieving. Fourthly—and very closely connected with the third—there is the universe of social units, in which are brought to bear all the laws governing the life of a homogeneous, co-operative, organic society, of whose tissue and structure we all form a part, in a mutual dependence, from which there is no escape, each affecting all others by every action, each drawing from the whole much of the stuff that makes our conscious life, much of the significance that makes our life worth while. And lastly, though far first in importance, we are all part of a spiritual universe, to whose laws of social growth our souls are subject, from which we draw all that is best in our resolves, our aspirations, our living faiths and our determinations to find the good." [13]

382. Scope of Social Ethics. Any comprehensive sociology must consider all these universes. In social Ethics we are chiefly concerned with the last three. The material and organic universes interest us only in so far as they indirectly affect man's relations with his fellows by becoming the object of rights and duties.

383. Division of Social Ethics. From an ethical standpoint association may be either of charity or justice, as the action accords with or violates one or the other virtue. Charity requires that we should have a well-regulated love for our neighbor; justice that we should give to each his due. It may frequently happen that we ought to do from charity what our neighbor has not the right to exact. Association may be between one individual and another, or between an individual and a group, or between groups. Hence, the division of social Ethics will be first into the broad cleavage between charity and justice, and each as affecting the relations of individuals; secondly, the relations of the chief social institutions—the family, State, and Church—to the individual; and finally, the relations between group and group, as the Church and State, or State and State—international Ethics.

[13] Urwick, *op. cit.,* pp. 13, 14.

384. The Age-Old Problem of the Individual and Society. This brief outline of the field indicates innumerable points of possible conflict between the individual and society. All the rights are not on one side and all the duties on the other. The reconciliation of the rights of the individual and the rights of society has ever been a delicate and complicated question. Theorists and politicians have frequently overstressed one side or the other. Relations of men in society being in a constant flux, readjustment is continually necessary. Today the situation is not as acute, perhaps, as it has been in some periods in the past, but it is sufficiently serious to arouse attention and alarm.

385. Social Theories of Plato and Aristotle. From the days of Aristotle we find two clearly marked currents of thought—the individualistic and the socialistic. Aristotle coincided rather closely with American public opinion. We find him criticizing the suggestions of Plato that property should be common, that marriage should be arranged by the State, and that children should be reared by professional nurses instead of their own parents. To Plato's mind such measures would have made for the efficiency of the State, and, therefore, they were advisable. His admiration for Spartan manhood seemed to blind him to certain inherent defects of absolute State supremacy.

386. The Individualism of the Eighteenth Century. Throughout history we see these two attributes struggling with each other for supremacy. Now a nation representing one view-point leads the world, now another. With the break-up of feudalism and the socialized guilds of the Middle Ages, political philosophers imagined that they had found the solution to this problem in a radical individualism. According to them every individual was free and equal and perfectly able to take care of himself. The State was to keep hands off and never interfere in industrial relations and as little as possible in any other affairs. *Laissez faire* was the great word summing up their philosophy. The "natural freedom of the individual" exhibiting itself in "enlightened selfishness" was expected to work out automatically to the advantage of all.

387. Excesses of Individualism. Such an exaltation of the individual speedily led to his degradation. The strong oppressed the weak to the full measure of their power, and the period between the Industrial Revolution and the Reform Bill—1785 until 1834—forms one of the blackest of English history. When we read over the history of those times we can hardly believe that such things were tolerated, since even their recitation is harrowing. Lord Byron was probably not exaggerating when he said in his maiden speech in Parliament (1812): "I have traversed the seat of war in the Peninsula, I have been in some of the most oppressed provinces of Turkey, but never under the most despotic infidel governments did I behold such squalid wretchedness as I have seen since my return to the heart of a Christian country."

388. Socialistic Tendencies of the Present. Today we seem about to go to the opposite extreme. The State is assuming more and more authority, becoming more and more paternalistic. We take, as a matter of course, State interference which would have produced a revolution in 1776. It will need clear thinking and courageous acting to prevent a repetition of past failures in the way of over-socialization, to save the mass of individuals from horrible tyranny at the hands of society.

389. The Via Media of Scholasticism. As we review the history of thought upon these questions, one fact stands out above all the rest: that on this question as on many others, truth lies in the middle. It is not a weak spirit of compromise, it is not an attempt to carry water on both shoulders, but a realization of the good in each, that leads to seeking a principle of organization between these two extreme views of Socialism and Individualism. Individualism emphasizes the value and importance of the individual—a great and noble truth—but overstresses it. Socialism emphasizes a necessary subordination of the individual to society —an equally great and noble truth—but also overstresses it.

SUGGESTED READINGS

1. Page, *Trade Morals,* Chs. I to V.
2. Deploige, *Le Conflict de la Morale et de la Sociologie.*

3. Ross, E. A., *Sin and Society*, Ch. I.
4. Pesch, *Lehrbuch der Nationaloekonomie*.
5. Garriguet, *Social Value of the Gospel*.
6. Urwick, *Philosophy of Social Progress*.
7. Antoine, *Cours d'Economie Sociale*, introduction and Ch. I of Pt. I.
8. Devas, *Key to the World's Progress*, Pt. I, Ch. I.
9. Poock, *Socialism and Individualism*.
10. Slater, *Questions of Moral Theology*, art. on "Modern Sociology."

QUESTIONS

1. Consult some standard textbook of sociology and discuss the author's explanation of the origin of society.
2. Is there a middle ground between individualism and socialism?
3. To which extreme—individualism or socialism—is there more danger of the World going today?
4. What is the difference between communism and Communism?

TWO: *Of Charity in Association*[1]

I. DISTINCTION BETWEEN JUSTICE AND CHARITY

390. Summary of the Preceding Chapter. We have seen that men are social beings bound together in a most complex organization known as society, and that there is constant conscious and unconscious association between them. Now we go on to discuss certain moral implications following from this association.

391. Social Ethics Depends on Use of Goods. All association implies the use of one's own and one's neighbor's goods in some way. Good, it will be remembered, was defined as "being considered as desirable." It should be evident, therefore, that one human being cannot associate with another without using innumerable goods. Indeed, the very fact of association is itself a very precious good. And even in its simplest form association is inextricably bound up with goods of memory, speech, assemblage, education, and of a dozen or more other kinds. Hence, social Ethics must necessarily concern the use of one's own and of one's neighbor's goods.

392. Division of Goods. At the outset we must distinguish between various kinds of goods. This division is important, because, as is evident, in a conflict of rights regarding goods, the question must often be settled by the nature of the goods to which the respective rights appertain. Rights to goods of a higher order will naturally take precedence over rights to goods of a lower order. Therefore, taking a broad survey of goods, we find that goods may be divided into goods of soul, goods of body, and goods of fortune.

393. (A) Goods of Soul. Our first division embraces *goods of soul,* such as memory, education, morals, personal development,

---

[1] Reports of the National Conference of Catholic Charities; Fr. Cuthbert, *Catholic Ideals in Social Life; Catholic Charities Review, passim; The Survey, passim;* Cath. Encyc., art. "Charity."

and free expression. A right [2] to each of these goods is inherent in everyone, but it is not unlimited. For an unlimited right in any one individual would mean a corresponding limitation imposed on someone else. A free press, for instance, is a great good, but it must not be used for libel. The nice balance of personal rights so as to secure for each one the maximum development and freedom consistent with the public good is a delicate social problem requiring continual adjustment to changing conditions.

394. **(B) Goods of Body.** By goods of body we understand health, life, and all means necessary to protect and preserve them. A right to these goods is inherent, as expressed in our American Declaration of Independence,—"We hold these truths to be self-evident, that all men . . . are endowed by their Creator with certain inalienable rights; that among these are life, liberty, and the pursuit of happiness." Each one also has over his body a right forbidding its use in immoral ways. But a relationship voluntarily entered into with another person under certain conditions may give an intimate and exclusive mutual right over each other's bodies.

395. **(C) Goods of Fortune.** All external objects are goods of fortune. They are subdivided into real and personal. A right to any specific external object is always an acquired right. Hence it cannot have the same inalienable basis as an inherent right. And the fact that any one man has a right to a specific external object to that extent excludes the right of other persons. All men can be individually healthy. The fact that one man is healthy does not mean that another cannot have this same good. But the fact that one man has a diamond means that nobody else can have it at the same time. This natural limitation of the supply of certain external goods and their appropriation by individuals has given rise to some of the most insistent ethical problems of today. Socialism, single-tax, monopolism, all center around the private ownership of external goods.

396. **Importance of This Division.** This division of goods, as we have said, is important as influencing the obligation to help

2 Cf. Pt. III, Ch. IV.

persons in need and as determining priority in conflict of rights. Other things being equal, goods of soul take precedence over those of body, and goods of body over those of fortune. Thus a man who needs spiritual goods in the same degree as another needs those of fortune should be helped first. In the proper place, these questions will be gone into more fully. Now it is important to fix this division in the mind.

397. Justice and Charity. Obligations regarding the use of goods as affecting others spring from two different sources. In so far as others have a strict right to certain goods, we have a duty of justice to respect that right; in so far as they have not a strict right, whatever obligation we have comes from brotherly charity, from the love we are bound to have for our neighbor. Charity may induce just as real and serious a duty as justice, but it is necessary to distinguish between the two because *only commutative justice binds to restitution*.

398. Justice, Charity, and Restitution. This difference between justice and charity can probably be brought out clearly by an example. If you refuse a beggar alms, you may have violated charity, but no matter how serious your obligation to help him at that time, if you meet him again when he is no longer in need of your assistance, you are not obliged to give him the alms you should have given formerly. That is because he had not a strict right to any particular good in your possession, and his right to have you help him ceases with his need of your help. But if you defraud a man of a hundred dollars, you are bound to repay him no matter how wealthy he may be or become. The reason is that he has a strict right to the specific good which you took, and that right persists even though actual possession may have passed to you. This distinction between the consequences of violating justice and charity is important and has constant application in the field of social Ethics. The difference, however, is in the consequences. A violation of charity, though not inducing an obligation to restore, may be just as wicked morally as a violation of justice.

399. Definition of Charity. Because a violation of justice implies an obligation to repair the injury, more complicated problems develop in discussing justice than in considering charity. Therefore, as it is usually advisable to proceed from the simple to the complex, we shall first consider the question of charity. By charity we mean an attitude of mind whereby one wishes well to another human being. As distinguished from justice, charity means that one wishes well to another over and above what he has a strict right to have. Charity may be *affective,* resting merely in the attitude of mind; or *effective,* proceeding to action.

400. How Far Is One Obliged to Charity. Immediately the question arises, towards whom is one bound to have charity and is it to be effective or only affective? The answer is that one should love his neighbor affectively, or with an internal act of benevolence; and effectively in so far as one's neighbor stands in need of succor one can give without too great inconvenience. By neighbor is meant every rational being capable of eternal beatitude. But one may be obliged to love one neighbor either affectively or effectively more than he loves another. Hence arises the necessity of considering the order of charity; that is to say, when there are several neighbors in need of help, which one should be helped first?

II. The Order of Charity

401. The Order of Charity. The order of charity depends upon three elements:—the kind of need, whether of spiritual, bodily, or external goods; the degree of need, whether extreme, grave, or slight; and the relationship of the one in need to the one who can help. Generally speaking goods of soul are to be preferred to goods of body, and goods of body to goods of fortune. Hence, spiritual need of the same degree as of body is to be helped first. To make the question clearer, we may divide need as to any class of goods into three degrees, *extreme, serious, slight.*

402. Degrees of Spiritual Need. *Extreme spiritual necessity* is found when a person without external help cannot or can only with greatest difficulty escape perpetual loss of his ultimate end. Thus to one who believes in the necessity of infant baptism, the unbaptized infant in danger of death is in extreme spiritual necessity. *Serious* spiritual necessity is when one can avoid this loss of his ultimate end only with great difficulty. An example of serious spiritual need would be a saloon keeper. He can only with great difficulty avoid co-operating in the serious sins of others, and hence he is in grave spiritual need of getting into another business. *Slight* spiritual necessity arises from any situation that endangers the attainment of one's ultimate end, but in such a way that the danger can easily be avoided. For example a mature well-instructed man working in the factory of an unbeliever might be in slight danger of losing his faith.

403. Degrees of Bodily Need. *Extreme bodily necessity* is found when one is in danger of death, as a man without medical attention suffering from small-pox. *Serious* bodily necessity is when one suffers a grave evil but not perpetual, as a severe toothache, or if perpetual not grave in itself, as chronic indigestion. *Slight* bodily necessity when one undergoes an evil but not a very serious one, as loss of teeth.

404. The Order of Obligation to Help One's Neighbor is as follows:

(a) Extreme spiritual necessity.

(b) Grave spiritual necessity.

(c) Extreme corporal necessity (though it may happen that extreme corporal necessity should take precedence over grave spiritual necessity).

(d) Serious corporal necessity.

(e) Slight spiritual or corporal necessity.

405. Order Between One's Self and His Neighbor. In the same class of goods one may (and is even sometimes bound to) love himself in preference to others. He is bound to love himself as regards spiritual goods in preference to his neighbor as regards the same goods. While he is not bound to love himself before his neighbor in relation to corporal goods, yet he may lawfully do so, unless there is some accidental reason to the contrary.

More specifically, a neighbor in *extreme spiritual necessity* is to be succored even at danger of life. If he be only in *grave spiritual necessity* one is not bound to risk life or grave temporal loss unless obligated *ex officio*. A neighbor in *extreme temporal necessity* is to be helped, but need not be assisted at the risk of life or equally valuable goods. A neighbor in *grave temporal necessity* is to be helped at slight inconvenience.

406. Order Between Neighbors. When several persons are in the same degree of necessity, those to whom one is more closely related are to be loved more affectively and effectively; but if someone less closely related be in greater necessity, then he is to be succored first. Those standing in a particular relationship to one, however, are to be preferred to others only as regards the goods that the bond concerns—whether spiritual or temporal. Thus a parent in temporal necessity is to be helped before one standing in no such relationship; but it may be that someone else related in a spiritual way would have a greater claim to spiritual help. For instance, a man standing in the relationship of pastor to a congregation at a distance from his father is bound to minister to his congregation in preference to his parent. It would be a grave violation of duty for him to go to his father to the neglect of the spiritual needs of his congregation, because spiritual needs are to be preferred to temporal, and his relationship to his father is temporal rather than spiritual. Presumably his father is in spiritual relationship with some other man, who is thereby bound to minister to him in this way.

407. Love of Enemies. Even by natural law one is bound to love his enemies. The obligation binds to the common signs of affection, such as persons of the same condition and relationship ordinarily yield each other, but it does not bind to any extraordinary manifestation. If one has offended another, he is bound to put aside all hatred and seek a reconciliation.

408. Mercy. The act of charity towards a neighbor in distress is called *mercy*. Everyone is bound, according to the preceding order, to show mercy. But he is not bound to enquire into the condition of his neighbors, since it is incumbent upon them to make known their need. When he stands in some special relationship, however, as that of direct or indirect employer, he will have the obligation of enquiring. A great development of conscience regarding this obligation has taken place since the early years of the Industrial Revolution. Employers are beginning to recognize that at least they are the keepers of those of their brothers whom they employ.

409. Division of Mercy. As goods are divided into goods of soul and of body, so mercy may be divided as it concerns the soul or body. *The works of mercy* usually enumerated under each head are: *Corporal* works—to feed the hungry, to give drink to the thirsty, to clothe the naked, to receive travelers, to visit the sick, to redeem captives, to bury the dead; *Spiritual works*—to teach the ignorant, to counsel the doubtful, to comfort the sorrowful, to forgive offenders, to bear with injury, to pray for the living and the dead. Changed conditions have made some of these works obsolete by providing socially for their performance; but there is still much to be done by the individual; and many of our social problems would be solved if every person calling himself Christian would only practice these works to the best of his ability.

III. Material Relief

410. Almsgiving. In order to be obliged to give alms, one must be able to do so; and his neighbor must be in need. The degrees of necessity have already been enumerated. Here it should be pointed out that need may arise *involuntarily in se* and *in causa;* or *voluntarily in se* and *in causa* through devotion to a worthy cause; or *involuntarily in se* and *voluntarily in causa,* as by laziness. One is obliged to help in the first two cases.

411. Principles Governing Obligation of Almsgiving. The obligation of helping one's neighbors depends upon their degree of necessity and one's power of helping—that is, having superfluous goods with which to help. It will, therefore, be necessary now to determine various degrees of superfluity whereby obligations arise corresponding with various degrees of need. For evidently no one is bound to make himself poorer by almsgiving than is the neighbor he assists. Hence we distinguish between goods necessary to life, goods necessary to one's station, and goods necessary for the appropriate upkeep of one's station. *Goods necessary to life* are those without which one cannot live, and any other goods are superfluous to life; *goods necessary for one's station* are those without which one cannot maintain his position in the community; goods *necessary for becomingness of station,* are those without which he cannot live as befits his condition.

412. When Almsgiving Is Obligatory. A neighbor in *extreme necessity* is to be helped from goods necessary to the decency of one's station. For according to Noldin,[3] one is not obliged to lose one's station in life in order to prolong the life of another. If one's neighbor be in *serious* or *common* necessity, he is to be helped from goods purely superfluous.

413. The Principle of "Station in Life." At first sight, this seems like a heartless doctrine. Why should not a rich banker whose station in life demands an expenditure of $10,000 a year be obliged to help a poor laborer, even though the assistance does reduce him to the way of living of prosperous but small merchants? An analysis of the situation will show us why. If he would be obliged to, then logically those in a class below would be similarly bound, and the lowest class of self-respecting and self-supporting workmen would be so bound. This would mean, really, that no one had a right (in the face of a neighbor's need) to more than what was necessary for his own life. But if that were so, there could be no progress among the working classes, their standard of living would always remain at the minimum. For only the recognition that, when a class has for a reasonable length of time actually attained a standard, that class has a right to this standard, makes us fix a minimum wage for an American laborer as greater than for a Chinese coolie. As far as bare existence goes, the American could probably get along on rice and fish if obliged to do so, but no minimum wage commission would ever say he had a right only to rice and fish.

[3] Noldin, *Theol. Mor.,* Vol. II, art. 91, p. 104.

414. Limitations of the Principle of Station in Life. Yet we must admit that this principle can be abused. Extremely fashionable women, for instance, will think it necessary to spend $25,000 a year on dress in order to maintain their station. It is hard to fix a limit logically, yet limit there should be. I do not know of any better way of fixing it than by an application of the principle of social utility. As long as it is socially useful that there should be a station in life requiring a certain expenditure, so long is it justified. Thus a physician whose profession necessitates an office, a conveyance, a certain outlay for books, instruments, and so on; or a gentleman of leisure whose culture adds an invaluable element to a community though at the same time it represents a certain outlay in money: these should feel no qualms of conscience because they do not give up this expenditure and with it their position in society in order to feed the hungry. In our nation, at least, the need of such sacrifice on their part indicates a social maladjustment for which they are not responsible, and which would not be remedied by these heroic methods. Mere social butterflies, however, have no justification, and they should be ruthlessly reduced—or elevated.

415. Must Alms Be Given to Those in Common Necessity? Moralists differ as to whether there is ever a grave obligation of giving alms to those who are only in common necessity. It would seem probable that there is no such obligation.[4]

416. Should Alms Be Given Directly or Vicariously? Having determined how far one is bound to give alms and in what order, there is still a further question as to how the alms should be given. Is it better for one to give directly to a beggar or to give through some organization? Circumstances have become so complicated with the growth of cities that it requires great prudence and experience to dispense material relief without doing more harm than good. There is danger of pauperizing the deserving and of subsidizing the unworthy. No matter how we may regret the simpler conditions under which alms were given directly, the poor man's heart beating with gratitude and the rich man's

---

[4] Noldin, *op. cit.*, Vol. II, art. 92, p. 105; St. Thomas, *Summa*, II, II, Q. 32, A. 5.

warming with Christian charity, we cannot wisely go back to those days. We know too well that the blind man often has as good sight as his dog, that some cripples if properly stimulated can do a hundred yards in twelve and two-fifths. "Be wisely generous" is a good motto; to live up to it, we must ordinarily give through expert investigators. Thus the tendency in current social thought is to make giving impersonal. One subscribes to a fund or pays taxes to support charitable institutions and imagines that his duty is done. And it is largely fulfilled.

417. State Philanthropy. But not every organization conducted by paid workers is worthy any more than every beggar is worthy. In some cases, the salary is the main incentive. Undoubtedly there are parasitic organizations whose "workers" live in comparative luxury and turn over to the poor in material relief and service only an insignificant fraction of what they collect. Therefore, the most advanced states and municipalities protect contributors not only from undeserving individuals, but also from undeserving organizations. And it is seriously proposed to make all care for the unfortunate come through State agencies and be paid for by State taxes. For at present the charitable business man must not only pay taxes for such State institutions as we have, but is also the victim of what is often an ill-concealed hold-up by private philanthropies [5] while the miserly man escapes the voluntary contributions and perhaps the taxes.

418. Private Philanthropy Under State Supervision. Under the present conditions of society, however, it is probably inadvisable to give the State a monopoly of charitable work or to allow it to do very much directly. The field offers too great a temptation to grafting politicians. It is better that the institutions needed for relief work should be under private control, but subject to supervision by the State. These private institutions should be supported partly by private subscriptions, partly by State aid. Where the nature of the institution lends itself to the system, as in the case of an orphan asylum, short time contracts whereby the State

[5] Cf. pp. 66 ff. Bulletin Texas State Conference of Charities and Corrections, Jan., 1915.

obligates itself to pay a fixed sum for every person committed by it to the institution is probably the best way of arranging matters.

419. Religion and Charity. By keeping the institutions in private hands, we are enabled to secure an invaluable element in dealing with many situations. It is immeasurably better that young children should be surrounded by religious influences in an asylum than that they should be brought up without religion in a State institution. Especially where there has been a moral breakdown, as in the case of delinquent girls, religion is a powerful force and should not be neglected. Yet in our country the State cannot directly get this religious element. Because of our fundamental principle of separation of Church and State, it is impossible in State orphanages and other institutions to bring the same effective religious influences to bear upon the persons as is possible in private institutions.

420. Charity Obliges to Preventive Measures. But one has not entirely fulfilled his duties towards his neighbor by giving of his superfluous goods to those in need. There is also the obligation of preventing as far as possible the arising of that condition of need. We must not be content with nursing the sick in hospitals —every hospital should also be a center for teaching hygiene and bringing about better living conditions so as to reduce disease. It is a noble thing to build orphanages, but it is nobler still to force employers so to guard their machinery and maintain sanitary conditions that there will be no unnecessary orphans.

421. Imagination Necessary in Charity. It is natural, perhaps, that the visible misery of people should excite more active reaction than the probability of persons suffering unless certain preventive measures are taken. But that is because we lack imagination. And certainly the nobler souls who are striving with all their might to live up to God's law of charity should realize their obligation in this regard. They have but to face conditions as they are to realize that mere remedial charity gets us nowhere. Unless we go down to the roots of the trouble, we shall have ten (if not twelve) poor people to feed next week where we had five to feed today. And though the obligation to prevent poverty is not as strong as the obligation to relieve it, nevertheless it exists. If we are to make any progress, we must recognize this. Preventive philanthropy, therefore, is the great hope of the future; and those who profess to be charitable should be among its leaders. It should be insisted upon that though the obligation to give alms may bind only as stated, there is the additional obligation to do what one can by voting, by writing, by public agitation—to remove by appropriate social action the possibility of anyone being in need of the actual necessaries of life.

422. Summary. We have seen in this chapter that the duties of men to each other revolve around goods—which may be of soul, of body, or of fortune. So far as charity means succoring one's neighbor, it depends upon the neighbor's need—whether extreme, serious, or slight—in regard to these goods; one's relationship to him; and one's own ability to help from goods superfluous either to station or life. Material assistance should be given usually through professional workers conducting private institutions supervised by the State. In addition to relieving need according to its degree and one's relationship and ability, one is also obliged to take what measures he reasonably can to prevent poverty and distress.

SUGGESTED READINGS

1. Walsh, *Thirteenth, Greatest of Centuries,* Ch. XXI, p. 337.
2. Walsh, "The Story of Organized Care of the Insane and Defectives," *Cath. World,* Nov., 1916.
3. Somerville, "The Apostle of Organized Charity," *Cath. World,* June, 1916.
4. Walsh, "Care of Children and the Aged," *Cath. World,* Oct., 1916.
5. Cuthbert, *Catholic Ideals in Social Life,* pp. 99-126, 209-248.
6. Cath. Encyc., art. "Charity."
7. Report Nat. Conf. Cath. Char. 1910, pp. 166-194, 285-352, 383-420; 1914, pp. 35-43, 55-78, 101-128, 269-284; 1916, pp. 114-198, 367-370.
8. Walsh, "Care of the Dependent Poor," *Cath. World,* Sept., 1916.
9. *Catholic Charities Review, passim.*

QUESTIONS

1. Does charity involve restitution?
2. Towards whom must one have *affective* and *effective* charity?
3. Make a diagram showing the order in which one's neighbor must be helped.
4. How does "station in life" affect the obligation of almsgiving?
5. Do you think that the State should assume the whole burden of relieving poverty?
6. Do you think that the Good Samaritan is the highest ideal of charity?

THREE: *Offenses Against Charity*

423. State of Question. So far we have considered the subject, object, and terms of charity—that is to say, who should have charity, about what, and to whom. Certain principles have been enunciated to determine how one's conduct should be governed in various circumstances. By implication, this establishment of positive duties of charity rules out all offenses against this virtue. Nevertheless, it will be well to treat in some detail the vices opposed to charity.

424. Envy. First in order of the offenses against charity comes envy, which has well been called one of the capital sins, as it so easily leads to anger, hatred, detraction, and slander. Envy is sorrow at the good fortune of another, inasmuch as the mere fact of his prosperity is considered an injury to one's self. It implies a dog-in-the-manger spirit. Not one's actual but one's relative loss causes envy. One grieves at his neighbor having what he himself cannot have; or one is sorry because another acquires what he himself already has, even though his neighbor's acquisition does not in the least diminish his own possessions. This element of the loss being purely relative is of the essence of envy in a strict sense.

425. Limitations of Envy. Hence it is not envy, strictly speaking, for one to sorrow at the fact of another possessing goods which he will use unjustly for one's own harm, as a political rival owning a newspaper with which he will blast one's aspirations for office. The same holds true of one's feeling in regard to goods which will be used wrongfully even though one's self does not thereby suffer. Neither is it envy to regret that another possesses goods of which he is really unworthy, as an uneducated boor falling heir to a magnificent art collection. Theoretically, too, it is not envy to be sorry that another has attained an object in so far as his attainment deprives one of what one might otherwise have had, as an opponent in an election winning out over one.

176

We say "theoretically" because it is so easy to deceive one's self where one's own interests are concerned. And while sorrow under the conditions we have described may not be sinful, nevertheless it is best to avoid it. The passage from allowable to unallowable in this regard is so easy and imperceptible that the brakes should be shoved on long before the precipice of wrong-doing is reached. In all this, too, it should be remembered that the order of charity should be preserved. As was specified in the preceding chapter, charity sometimes requires us to love our neighbor even to our own material hurt.

426. Dangers of Envy. From a selfish standpoint, too, envy (whether taken in a strict or a loose sense) is a dangerous emotion to allow into our hearts. Sometimes the very fact of our being in the right adds to its sting. Particularly when envy takes the form of jealousy, it becomes veritable torture. We should avoid it as the plague. Never give it encouragement, or it will soon be a habit. Once it has been welcomed, there is always something to feed the fuel of envy. No one is so well off but that he may find someone who is better situated, and if he once allows this vice entrance it will grow to enormous proportions and lead to all sorts of other lapses.

427. Remedies Against Envy. The best remedy against envy is detachment from the things of this world. One who realizes fully the real end of man—to possess God for all eternity—and the uselessness of material things to gain this end, will never envy another his possessions. Rather, he will pity those who are unfortunate enough to be in danger of having the realization of their ultimate end obscured by the satisfaction they are obtaining in this world.

428. Anger. Second only to envy in importance and extent is the vice of anger. In itself it is a violation of charity and of the order which restricts vengeance to the proper authorities. Anger is an inordinate appetite for vengeance. As consequences of anger come indignation and such tumult of the mind as leads sometimes even to temporary insanity, blasphemy, cursing, abuse, quarrels, personal violence, murder.

429. Dangers of Anger. In the definition, we called anger an *inordinate* appetite for vengeance. This implies, of course, that there may be an ordinate desire for vengeance. And while this is true, as in the case of a parent punishing a child, what was said of envy applies likewise to anger. It is a dangerous lodger to have in one's heart. For anger grows steadily. The more it is indulged, the more uncontrollable it becomes. Starting from mere trifling impatience, it will gradually take such possession of a man that he will no longer be responsible for his actions. He will do the most outrageous things, and the most foolish. It is told of an English admiral that in his rage he would bite pieces out of a tumbler and chew them to bits until his lips were covered with blood. Children will frequently roll on the floor when angry and become little demons with murder in their hearts. And as the manifestation and power of the passion increases, the stimulus necessary to produce the fit decreases. One who has allowed himself free rein in this regard will be thrown into a rage by any little thing: it may be a mislaid letter, a pin on the floor, a cloudy day.

430. Conquer Anger Early. In children anger frequently exhibits itself as a sort of poutiness. If they are crossed in any way they become moody and withdraw into themselves. If such a disposition is allowed to grow, it will completely destroy one's ability to associate pleasantly with one's neighbors. One's sensibilities will constantly be offended, and the tendency will be to mix with people as little as possible. Conquer this weakness as soon as you realize that it is in your heart. And if you have charge of those who show that spirit, do everything you can to force them to overcome it. Nothing will wreck a life quicker than this oversensitiveness, and it shows a lack of real religion—for it is the essence of the religious spirit that one should be willing to suffer.

431. Conquest of Anger a Slow Process. There is no royal road to conquer anger. The more often it has been indulged, the more violent have been its outbursts, the harder will it be to overcome. New channels must be patiently cut in the brain, the old ones choked up, before the stimuli will naturally motivate according to reason. Constant watchfulness, strong exertion of the will, are required for this conquest. But the battle is worth winning. Even from a selfish standpoint, anger destroys peace of mind, mars the judgment, and brings opposition and disgrace.

432. Resignation the Best Remedy Against Anger. The best remedy is to prepare for war in time of peace by accustoming one's self to absolute submission to the will of God. Whoever realizes that the action which causes his anger is permitted by God—and, therefore, to that extent comes from Him—and is completely resigned to God's will, must bear patiently whatever happens, no matter how irritating.

433. Particular Examen Useful. In conquering anger, as was said in speaking of the passions, it is best to divide the enemy. Pick out some hour of the day, for instance, and put all your energy in being patient during that time. Concentration counts here as well as elsewhere. The myriad rain drops falling on a weedy soil simply increase the crop of weeds. But gathered into a single stream of small dimension and directed against a particular point, they will uproot the mightiest oak. So it is with the will. If your power is directed against a whole field of moral weeds, it will be so diffused that your failure will merely multiply your faults. But if you gather up what force you have and drive it with all your might against one special part of a sin, there is no limit to what they may in time accomplish.

434. Hatred. Envy and anger soon lead to *hatred*. Strictly speaking, hatred is enmity for a person so that one rejoices at the evil he recognizes in his neighbor, because it is an evil for him. This is always sinful and from its nature seriously so.

435. Aversion. But hatred is different from having an aversion to a person because evil is recognized in him. That is lawful and laudable. It may also be lawful sometimes to wish evil to another, if it is wished not as evil to him but as good to someone else. An example would be that of a patient, struggling wife wishing the death of a worthless, drunken husband in order that she may bring up her children in greater security.

436. Cursing. One form which hatred frequently takes is that of cursing. When one curses his neighbor seriously and deliberately, really wishing him some grave injury, as injury, and not merely from a careless habit, it is a serious sin. Frequently, however, cursing loses its gravity through lack of matter, defect of consent, or inadvertence to the nature of the evil wished.

437. Scandal: Its Definition. As by the virtue of charity we are forbidden to take certain attitudes towards our neighbor or to commit certain actions against him, so we are obliged not to give scandal to him, using the word scandal in the strict and scriptural sense, as in the phrase, "if any man scandalize one of these little ones." St. Thomas [1] has defined scandal as a wrong—or apparently wrong—word or deed offering occasion to another of spiritual hurt. The action need not be wrong itself, but may have only the appearance of wrong.

438. What Is Included in Scandal. By *word* or *deed* is understood not simply a positive external act, but also the *omission* of some act when this furnishes the occasion of sinning. The act must be bad or at least have the appearance of being bad. For if it is not bad even in apearance, then not the act but the other person's weakness is the occasion of the sin. It is not necessary to the essence of scandal that the occasion furnished by it be embraced. If the persons to whom the occasion is offered are foreseen as being drawn to sin by one's word or act, scandal has been committed.

439. Division of Scandal. Scandal is divided into *direct* and *indirect,* according as the one giving scandal does or does not intend the sin of the other.

440. When Is Scandal Allowable. The desire to avoid scandal which may follow upon acts prescribed by a negative law of nature will never justify their omission. [2] It is difficult to imagine an act which will have the appearance of evil commanded by a negative law. But if there be any such, their omission is never justifiable, because negative laws bind always and at all times.

---

[1] *Summa,* II, II, Q. XLIII, A. 1.
[2] Noldin, *op. cit.,* II, 106.

A case in point might be that of a child telling the truth about a parent in order to free an innocent person from imprisonment. This might seem unfilial to those who do not know all the circumstances and, therefore, be the occasion of a sin of rash judgment, but the child would be obliged to speak if his remaining silent would deceive.

441. When Scandal May Be Obligatory. What is commanded by positive law, whether divine or human, *may* be omitted; and indeed there may sometimes be an obligation to forego such actions. Thus a wife who could fast without injury to her health might forego fasting because a following of the law would anger her husband. While good in itself, the act might have the appearance of evil to him if he thought the attempt would really injure her health.[3] *One should* forego what is good or indifferent but not commanded, provided no serious inconveniences would follow.

442. Special Questions Regarding Scandal: Women's Dress. The principles here laid down regarding scandal will be clearer if we consider a few specific cases, and most important, perhaps, is that of women's dress. In this connection the custom and the intention play prominent parts, for hardly any way of dressing is in itself sinful. Thus moralists say that to paint the face through lasciviousness is seriously sinful, to do so in order to feign beauty is only slightly wrong, and to paint in order to hide a defect is perfectly lawful.[4] All decent dress or ornaments in accord with the customs of one's country are permissible, even though they should be the occasion of sin for others. Custom has a great part in determining what is and what is not allowable, for the usual has less effect than the unusual.

443. Scandal Largely Relative. It may thus happen that what is lawful in one country or at one time may be unlawful elsewhere or at a different season. In tropical countries a certain exposure of the person is customary that would be immodest farther north. There is in Latin lands, a frankness in meeting natural

[3] Noldin, *loc. cit.*
[4] Noldin, *op. cit.*, II, 107.

necessities that in English speaking sections would merit the police station. The difference in dress in our own United States between August on the beach and December in a ball room is very marked. Each is proper in its place because custom has justified it. But to reverse the practice and to appear at a dance in such a skirt might be immodest and scandalous. Such considerations should make us keep our heads in judging new fashions. Custom can justify almost anything from an abbreviated bathing suit to the habit of a Sister of Charity. The first to introduce certain styles may thereby commit sin, but those who simply follow established styles may generally do so conscience free. The ultimate principle of modesty is that any exposure of the person is wrong which will be the occasion of sins against purity, after due allowance has been made for all the circumstances and for the experience of the persons concerned.

444. Special Questions Regarding Scandals: Pictures and Statues. Custom has much the same extenuating force in regard to artistic representations. Those accustomed to paintings and statues of the nude are not likely to be sinfully affected by them. And so Aertnys would allow the collection and exhibition of what would ordinarily be considered immodest statues if they are of great artistic value and age and if kept in galleries reserved for mature artists. But while painting from the nude may not be an occasion of sin for the particular artist doing the work, nor for the purchaser of the work, it may still be an occasion of sin for the model. And at least the buying of such pictures and the painting of them by artists foster a custom that leads inevitably, human nature being what it is, to much sin. Art students congregated in great cities, such as Paris, have an unenviable reputation for immorality, and their conduct justifying this reputation is probably partly due to painting from the nude. Hence, there would seem to be quite a serious obligation upon artists and connoisseurs to discourage the practice of using nude models. The following principles may be laid down: (1) whoever makes notably obscene pictures or statues except for the purpose of anatomical instruction commits grave scandal; (2) as also whoever exposes such works publicly, whether in his office, house, grounds, etc.; (3) and those who place statues, less gravely obscene but still indecent, in public squares, sin gravely.

445. Seduction. Closely related to scandal is seduction, for seduction is an external act by which another is explicitly and directly provoked to sin.[5] The provocation may be given by speech, writing, or gestures. Seduction has this in common with scandal, that they both excite a neighbor to a sin which he had not already decided to commit. But it differs from *indirect* scandal in that it is always joined with the intention of leading another into sin; and from *direct* scandal inasmuch as scandal is an *occasion*, seduction a *cause* of another's sin. Seduction is serious or slight according as the sin induced is grave or slight.

446. General Principle Regarding Seduction. In connection with seduction, we lay down the general principle that it is not lawful to seek from another what he cannot give without sin. The only exceptions to this rule are when the thing itself can be given (though not by this particular person) without sin, and when there is a just cause for asking. Thus it is an additional sin for a priest not in the state of grace to administer a sacrament, and one who knows of his sinful state should not seek it from him except for a serious reason. When there is a just and adequate reason for such a request, it may be made, as is clear from the previously explained principle of two effects following from one cause.

447. Application of Principles Regarding Seduction. One of the most interesting cases of seduction may be stated in this way: When a person is determined to commit a certain sin, if it be impossible to deter him in any other way it is lawful to persuade him to commit a lesser sin of the same species against the same person provided that he be already prepared for the lesser sin. For he is not persuaded to commit a sin, but to choose a lesser instead of the greater, and, therefore, the persuasion is good. Thus if a man is determined to kill Peter in order to rob him,

[5] St. Alphonsus, *Theol. Mor.*, No. 57; cf. DeLugo, *De Just. et Jure*, Disp. 19, n. 44; Ballerini, *Theol. Mor.*, III, 365.

it is lawful to persuade him simply to rob Peter. A more complex and difficult problem arises when the lesser sin is not directed against the same person. When, for example, John is determined to get a hundred dollars by theft, and has fixed upon a poor widow as his victim, it may be asked if one can lawfully persuade him to rob a millionaire instead? Noldin seems to answer affirmatively.[6] And finally, what are we to say when the lesser sin is not of the same species? For instance, would it be lawful to persuade a man bent on homicide, to commit adultery, instead?[7] St. Alphonsus seems to justify even this.

448. Co-operation in a Lesser Sin. And not only do theologians maintain that under the above conditions it is lawful to persuade a man to commit a lesser sin; they justify other forms of co-operation in its commission provided the greater sin cannot otherwise be prevented. Thus it would be licit to help a robber get away with a certain article if by doing so a greater injury than this loss would be averted from the owner. But according to Noldin[8] it would not be lawful to provoke a man bent on homicide to get drunk, since it is never lawful to do evil that good may come of it; though Génicot[9] thinks that this provocation would not in itself be evil, and, hence, would be lawful.

449. When Another's Sin May Be Permitted. For a just cause it is lawful not to remove an occasion of sin that one might remove, or it is lawful even to place the occasion. Thus a watchman may hide himself in order to give an opportunity for attempts at theft so that he may catch the culprit and deter others from stealing; or parents may expose money before their children so as to have the opportunity of correcting them should the money be taken. The reason is that the sin of others is not caused but permitted in order to prevent greater sin in the future.

450. Restitution on Account of Scandal or Seduction. There exists an obligation of repairing as far as possible the injury done by scandal or seduction. If there be an obligation to procure the reform of the sinner much graver is the obligation when one has

---

[6] Noldin, *op. cit.*, II, 113.
[7] *Theol. Mor.*, Lib. III, No. 57.
[8] Noldin, *op. cit.*, II, 113.
[9] Genicot, *Casus Conscientiae.*

been the occasion or cause of the sin. The obligation thus arising comes from charity or justice according as one or other virtue has been offended by the action. Public scandal should be publicly repaired.

451. Co-operation: Definition. In a wide sense, co-operation means any *concurrence* in the action of another; in a strict sense, co-operation means *formal* concurrence with another in a bad or unjustly injurious action.

452. Co-operation: Division. Co-operation may be either *physical* or *moral,* according as it influences the act or will of the agent; *negative* or *positive,* according as it consists in the omission or commission of acts influencing the agent or the action; *formal,* if the co-operation is both with the intention and the act of the other, *material,* if only with the act; *immediate* if with the act, *mediate* if with what prepares the way for the act.

453. Liceity of Co-operation. Formal co-operation in another's sin is always unlawful. Material co-operation is also unlawful except with an act either good or indifferent and for a proportionately serious cause. The proportion must exist between the gravity of the sin, the nearness and necessity of co-operation, and the obligation of preventing the sin. Co-operation in a sin that leads to the harm of Church or State is never licit. *Remote* co-operation is excused by slight inconvenience; *closest* co-operation is excused only by very or most grave inconvenience. An example of *serious* inconvenience is fear of a great pain or loss of a notable sum of money; danger of death, or loss of an important member of the body, such as an eye, would be a very serious inconvenience.

454. Co-operation of Merchants. No one is allowed to sell what is in itself evil and can have only an evil use. Indifferent things may usually be sold with a good conscience. But when it is certain that the buyer will gravely misuse the article (*e.g.,* a revolver) and will be prevented from committing the guilty action by withholding this article, then a serious reason is required to excuse the sale. A most serious reason is necessary to justify selling things indifferent in themselves, but of such a nature as rarely to be used for a good purpose, such as idols.

455. Periodicals. A slight reason will excuse buying a single copy of a bad paper or magazine, but a serious reason is necessary to justify becoming a subscriber. Editors formally co-operate, and, therefore, cannot be excused. Ordinary writers co-operate more or less closely according to the degree of help furnished by their articles. When their co-operation is close, only the need of money for their own or family's support will excuse them from sin.

456. Booksellers and Publishers. It is not lawful to sell books that can have only a bad use. For a serious reason one may sell a bad book that may also have a good use. A publisher may not issue a bad book, since this would be *formal* co-operation. Typesetters and proofreaders co-operate most closely and hence require a most serious reason to justify their co-operation. Those who tend presses, fold sheets, or bind the books co-operate only closely and hence are excused for a serious reason. Mere monetary gain excuses those who sell the paper, type, presses or other articles used in the manufacture of such a book.

457. Dances. In itself dancing is perfectly lawful, and it is probable that comparatively few people who dance sin thereby. But some dances are of such a character as to be an *occasion* of sin for almost all; others, though proper in themselves, are dangerous to some few people. Hence, the question of dancing sometimes involves scandal and sometimes co-operation in the sin of others. Ordinarily, therefore, one may dance and one may invite others to dance with good conscience. But those who invite others and who dance, sin gravely if the dances are of a gravely sinful character. Musicians may play for such dances only because of a very serious reason; those who rent the hall may co-operate in this way for a slight reason.

458. Servants. Remote co-operation of servants, such as the preparation of wine for a master who will drink to excess is excused by the mere fact of service; closer or closest co-operation, such as the carrying of illicit love letters, is justified only by a proportionately serious reason.

459. Modes of Co-operation. Co-operation may take place in nine ways: *command, counsel, consent, coaxing, receiving, sharing, silence, not opposing, not revealing*. The first six are positive, the last three negative.

460. Co-operation by Command. Anyone who orders another to injure a third party in his name is said to co-operate by command. It does not matter whether the action be done for pay or gratis, or whether or not the one commanding be the agent's superior. When such a command really influences the will of the agent, it is a true cause of the injury and induces an obligation to restore—(1) Towards the injured party: All damage done by force of the command must be repaired, even the injury done by the agent through invincible ignorance and beyond the intention of the one who gave orders. Should the one commanding fail to restore, the obligation falls upon the agent. (2) To the agent there are no obligations, provided that he freely accepted the commission. But if he was forced through fraud or grave fear, then the commander is bound to repair any injury received in the execution of the command, provided that it was foreseen at least dimly. The commander is not bound to repair injury occurring accidentally, as when an agent commissioned to rob a man falls from a horse and breaks his arm while on the road to the place determined upon for the robbery.

461. Co-operation by Counsel. Whoever by his persuasion moves another to commit a sin is said to co-operate by counsel. Counsel differs from command, in that the agent in the one case acts in his own name, in the other in the name of the commander. Hence, the agent in a case of counseling is the *primary* cause of the act, in a case of commanding is the *secondary* cause. The distinction between *"naked"* counsel and that *"clothed"* with reasons for the act is important, as the one ceases to influence by mere retraction; whereas the influence of the other continues unless contrary reasons are brought forth. Hence, mere retraction of "naked" counsel before the accomplishment of the act absolves from the duty of restoring; but not so as regards "clothed" counsel.

462. Duty to Retract Counsel. If one has given wrong counsel, whether in good or in bad faith, he is bound to retract. The obligation arises from justice or charity, according as the act counseled is forbidden by the one or the other virtue.

463. Duty of Counselor to Restore. Towards the injured party, a counselor is bound to restore all injury done *in virtue of his counsel*. If the agent was already determined to commit the act, or the influence of the counsel is doubtful, he is bound to nothing.

464. Duty of Counselor Toward the Agent. To the agent no restitution is due for injury incurred in carrying out the counsel, unless the counsel was given by fraud or lies, or the counselor was bound in justice to give good advice. Lawyers, and all who stand in similar relations to others, as confessors to penitents, are bound in justice to advise their clients wisely. Hence an attorney who ignorantly gives advice which results in unnecessary loss to his client is bound to restitution if information that he might reasonably be expected to have would have saved the situation.

465. Co-operation by Consent. Whoever by his external approbation, vote, or opinion influences an action towards another, is said to co-operate by consent. Examples of such co-operation would be—a jury concurring in a decision, a legislator voting for a certain bill.

466. Duty of One Who Has Consented to an Act. If one has given consent to a wrong act, he must withdraw the consent. Should such withdrawal be accomplished before the act, one is bound to no restitution, even though he in the first place acted in bad faith. If one acted in good faith, one is bound to nothing, even though one cannot retract one's consent and injury is accomplished; on the principle that only formal co-operation binds to restitution. For since one is in good faith, one does not co-operate formally with the evil.

467. Co-operation by Voting. Is one who casts an unjust, but unnecessary, vote for a wrong act bound to restitution? (1) When the voting is by agreement (as in a conspiracy), or at the same time (as by rising), or secretly (as by ballot) all are equally bound to restore. This is because in a conspiracy the agreement influences others to vote in a particular way; when the vote is by rising, none are first or last; and when it is by ballot no one can tell beforehand that his vote will be unnecessary. (2) When voting is public and successive certainly those who first cast a sufficient number of votes are bound to restitution; and other voters are probably not bound. (3) If a man's vote in favor of a particular injurious act is the only way of preventing a greater injury, he is not bound to restitution; and if the matter is not intrinsically evil he even acts licitly.

468. Co-operation by Coaxing or Threats. Whoever by praise or blame moves another to the commission of a wrong act thereby co-operates in the evil done. His obligations with regard to reparation for the harm done are the same as those of one counseling evil.

469. Co-operation by Receiving. Whoever knowingly and in such a way as to affect the wrong-doer's action affords security to one who injures another, co-operates in the injury. This co-operation may be given either by receiving a stolen article, or by protecting the wrong-doer. Since under the definition it is necessary to influence the will of the wrong-doer, those are not receivers who admit malefactors into their homes as friends or relatives, or as hotel keepers to avert a serious injury to themselves; nor lawyers who legally defend such persons. But when one has by receiving been the efficacious cause of an injury, he is bound to repair it.

470. Co-operation by Sharing. One may co-operate with another either by sharing in the booty or by participating in the act itself. In the one case he is bound to restore what he has received; in the other case he must restore that part of the loss for which he was efficiently and culpably responsible.

471. Co-operation by Silence; Not Opposing, Not Revealing. Co-operation by *silence* is effected when one does not by his words impede the act, as when one does not scare off thieves by shouting; co-operation by *not opposing* is given when one does not by his deeds prevent the act, as when one does not frustrate robbery by defending property; co-operation by *not revealing* takes place when, after the act, one does not reveal the fact or culprit to the proper party.

472. Duties of Negative Co-operators. Those who are bound in justice to prevent an injury and do not do so, when without serious inconvenience they could, are bound to restitution.

473. Restitution. Restitution *in toto* is when one is obliged to repair the entire injury. This is *absolute* when one is primarily bound to restitution and others are bound only in case he neglect; *conditional,* when many are bound primarily, and the duty of complete restitution devolves on one only when the rest refuse or fail to do their part in making restitution. *Pro rata* restitution is the restoring of the proportionate share for which each was responsible.

474. Principles Governing Restitution. In general, one is bound *in toto* only when he is the cause of the whole injury. This would be when with others he is the *equal* cause of the *whole* injury. In this case he is bound absolutely to repair only his share and the whole upon condition that others do not. Those are equal causes who form a *conspiracy,* or whose co-operation is *necessary,* or who posit a *moral cause in itself sufficient* to produce the whole injury. Whoever with others is the *partial cause of injury* is bound to restitution in proportion to his influence upon the action. A partial cause is one neither sufficient nor necessary to effect the action.

475. Order of Restitution. If all have co-operated in the same degree to produce the complete injury, each is equally immediately bound to restore his part. If they have co-operated in different degrees, then they are bound in this order: (1) the *possessor* of another's goods; (2) the *commander;* (3) the *agent;* (4) other positive co-operators; (5) negative co-operators. Hence, if the principal or one of the secondary causes restores, the others are not bound to restitution, though the principal must compensate the secondary cause who restores; but if one of equal causes restore the whole, the others are bound proportionately to him.

Also, if the principal cause be forgiven, others are bound to nothing; but if a secondary or equal cause be forgiven others are not therefore forgiven and are still bound to restore.

SUGGESTED READINGS

1. Scaramelli, Treatise III, Arts. VIII, X.
2. Scaramelli, Treatise II, Arts. V, VII, VIII.
3. Rodriguez, Treatise III, Vol. I.
4. Rodriguez, Treatise III, Vol. II.
5. Thomas à Kempis, Bk. III, Chs. XIX, XXII, XXXIII.

QUESTIONS

1. From your own experience or your reading of fiction give an example of consequences of anger.
2. What is scandal? Is one ever justified in putting before another an occasion of sin?
3. Give examples of ways in which one may co-operate in the act of another.
4. Distinguish clearly between *formal* and *material* co-operation and give example of each.
5. Is one who has co-operated in injuring another bound to make restitution?

FOUR: *Rights, Justice, Duties*

476. Various Uses of the Word Right. Right, like a great many words in common use, is difficult to define. It is used in several senses and with a looseness that is fatal to clear thinking. Perhaps one of the most remarkable popular uses of the word is found in the South. Here it frequently takes the place of duty, by a curious twist coming to mean something entirely opposed to its primary signification. Thus a motorman who runs into a cart will say to a driver: "It was all your fault. You had a right to get out of the way." Even among ethicians it is sometimes restricted to external conduct, sometimes made to apply both to interior motive and external acts.[1] And when we come to get back of the word to the basis of the idea, there is still greater confusion. Some authors would make all rights dependent upon the State, some upon custom, while others contend that at least some rights are based on nature in such a way as to be independent of custom and human legislation.

477. Right as an Adjective. Perhaps we shall get a clearer conception of right if we commence with the meaning of the word adjectivally. As we saw in fundamental Ethics, those actions are "right" which are in accordance with the ultimate norm of morality—that is to say, with God's nature. Further than this, however, we saw that actions which are in accordance with God's nature are in accord with the natural and with the eternal law. For the eternal law is simply the divine decree by which God must will that every human being should act consistently with his rational nature; and the natural law is merely the objective relationship which should exist between Creator and creature and between creature and creature.

478. Right Implies a Law. A right action, therefore, implies a law. Without law there would be no rightness as there would be no wrongness, because there would be no decree of God that

[1] Cf. Cronin, *Science of Ethics*, I, Ch. XX, p. 637.

we should act in one way rather than another. Hence a right action is based on law. This gives us the true clue to the meaning of "right" as a noun. For if a right action is one that is in accordance with law, then a "right" implies a way of acting which will not violate the eternal or the natural law. The right is not exactly the way of acting. Rather a right is a power of acting in such a way as does not violate a law. As an adjective "right" indicates the fact that a particular act conforms with the norm of morality; as a noun it means the power a person has of acting in a particular way without violating any law.

479. Might Is Not Right. As we are speaking of moral acts, we mean, of course, a moral power. One may have the physical power to do what he has not the right to do. And contrariwise, one may have the right to do what he has not the physical power to accomplish. Might is not necessarily right, in spite of many ethicians to the contrary. It is true that they do not usually put the matter thus baldly. They do not maintain that because a thief has the power to snatch your purse, therefore he has a right to it. But some do maintain that because citizens have not the physical power to vindicate claims against the State, therefore they have no rights in the matter; and that if a State can impose its will upon its own subjects or upon others, it has a right to do so.

480. Rights Are Natural. All rights go back to the natural law ultimately, and some go there so directly that they are inalienable and con-natural. The importance of this fact is evident if we are to protect the individual personality against tyranny on the part of other individuals or of the State. As we pointed out in the first chapter in Social Ethics, there has been a constant warfare between the individual and society, between individualism and socialism. It is to the glory of a sound Ethics that it has maintained the proper medium between these rivals. All social justice is based upon a right conception of this doctrine of rights. Rights must be natural if we are to work out the proper freedom for individual development. If they were due merely to custom or physical power, the individual would have no inviolable rights, and there could be no real injustice.

481. Definition of Right. We define *right,* therefore, as *an inviolable moral power of doing, having, or acquiring something.* A right is a moral power, because it means that the exercise of the power is in accordance with the norm of morality; it is inviolable because no one can violate it without coming into conflict with this norm of morality. Therefore, since a right is a moral power, only those who are by *nature* capable of moral acts can possess rights. Hence, as we saw in treating of vivisection, brute animals can have no rights in a strict sense. Men may be obliged to refrain from treating them cruelly, but it is not on account of the rights of the animals. On the other hand, infants and insane persons, though *de facto* incapable of moral acts, are nevertheless endowed with a *rational nature* and hence have rights in a strict sense.

482. So-Called Conflict of Rights. But though a right is an inviolable moral power, it is not unlimited. It may happen therefore, that one right may be superseded by another. Rights are based on law, and since the natural law is the objective relation existing between Creator and creatures, between creature and creature, the whole field must be taken into consideration before determining how far one right can be pushed against another. There is sometimes a so-called conflict of rights. In reality rights do not conflict, but claims do. What from a narrow view of the situation would seem to be a right is seen on taking a broader view to be no right at all. Thus ordinarily a citizen has a "right" to private property which is recognized by the law of the land, but when the community demands the taking over of this property by the duly constituted authorities, his rights ceases.

483. Elements in the Idea of Rights. Four elements are to be considered in any right: (a) the *subject,* or who has the right; (b) the *object,* or to what he has a right; (c) the *title,* or *foundation* of the right; and (d) the *term,* or who is bound to respect the right.

484. Division of Rights. Rights are either *con-natural* or *acquired, alienable* or *inalienable, perfect* or *imperfect, real* or *personal*.

485. Con-natural and Acquired Rights. *Con-natural rights* belong to a man by his very nature. Of this kind are the right to life, liberty, and the pursuit of happiness. Our immortal Declaration of Independence specifies these rights as inalienable, yet its assertion is hardly in accordance with strict logic. For one may forfeit or alienate his right to life by the commission of a crime to which the death penalty is attached. If the right to life were absolutely inalienable, the State would commit an injustice by inflicting capital punishment. *Acquired rights* are those superadded to what one has by his nature. These may come to him by his own exertion or in some other way, as by gift.

486. Alienable and Inalienable Rights. Inalienable rights are those which cannot be ceded or superseded. Strictly speaking, there is only one such right, and that is the right to whatever is necessary to attain one's last end. No one may justly yield this right to another, not even a mother to her dearest child. Alienable rights are those which can be ceded or superseded.

487. Perfect and Imperfect Rights. Perfect rights are those based on commutative justice. A violation of such a right binds *per se* to restitution. Imperfect rights are such as flow from some source other than commutative justice, and do not give a claim to restitution. Thus a deserving beggar has a right to alms, but no claim to restitution if one does not give them.

488. Real Rights. A *real* right, *jus in re,* is a legitimate power which anyone has in or over his own objects; as, for example, in regard to objects acquired by purchase. Whoever has a real right has the thing itself obligated and bound to him, so that he can prosecute this right in court against anyone and recover it wherever found. Three conditions are required to constitute a real right: a just title, as gift or purchase; that the thing should be determined individually; and (usually) a handing over of the object.

489. Personal Rights. A *personal right, jus ad rem,* is a legitimate power held by a person whereby something may become his own. Of this kind is the right to something promised, or to the payment of a debt. This does not immediately affect the object itself, but the person actually possessing it, so that he should hand over the object. Hence one who has a personal right does not hold the thing itself, but a person bound and obligated to him to deliver the object; wherefore, such a right gives action against the personal debtor, but not against the thing, nor against a third party who may perhaps possess the object. For acquiring a personal right (called also an inchoate right) nothing else is required than a just title.

490. All Rights Derivable from Natural Law. All rights, we said, depend ultimately upon the natural law. Some, however, are derived proximately from human law. This is because the natural law, or rather our understanding of the natural law, is not sufficiently clear and detailed to decide all the questions concerning the relations of one man with another. Where reason does not speak decisively as to rights in human association the civil law may step in to define. These rights, nevertheless, are based ultimately on the natural law, because the natural law demands authority in human association. Without authority there would be anarchy. Those regulations, then, which are necessary in order to insure an orderly association are based ultimately upon nature itself.

491. Civil Laws and Rights. Civil laws bearing upon rights are of two kinds: some establish and determine rights between citizens, as a law declaring that a treasure found in a field belongs to the owner of the field; others refer to *juridic acts*[2] and prescribe certain formalities (beyond those essentially required by nature) for validity. There are five general ways in which *juridic acts* may be affected by civil law.

(1). The law may neither prohibit nor encourage the act, but simply refrain from assisting—as in the case of gambling, when

---

[2] Juridic acts are those by which rights are acquired or quashed.

the civil law refuses to allow its courts to be used for collection of debts so incurred.

(2). The law may prohibit an act and make it illicit, without invalidating it. Thus a man who knowingly sold liquor to a minor where this is forbidden, could not recover the liquor since the transfer is valid though illicit.

(3). The law can make an act rescindable, giving to a court the power of voiding it, as in the case of contracts by minors.

(4). The law can void an act *ipso facto,* but *civilly* only, so that outside of the civil forum the act has natural force. Bankruptcy laws while nullifying the creditor's legal claims may leave the conscientious obligation to pay.

(5). The law can void the act *ipso facto* both civilly and naturally, so that the act has no force in conscience or in a civil court. Some moralists hold that this has been done in the case of outlawed debts, so that one is bound neither legally nor morally.

492. How Far Civil Laws Bind in Justice. Civil laws establishing rights or transferring dominion ordinarily bind from commutative justice even before a judicial sentence has been passed.

493. How Far Civil Laws Release From Conscientious Obligation. In appropriate matter the civil authority can pass laws which make juridic acts, valid in themselves, fully invalid even before a court has ruled upon the matter. But the modern laws invalidating juridic acts probably do not void them *fully* but only *civilly* unless the matter of the law or its wording clearly determines otherwise. For such laws limit the liberty of citizens in contracting and hence are to be interpreted as strictly as possible. Moreover, in these days of separation of Church and State, the legislators may be presumed ordinarily to consider only the civil aspect of such questions.

494. Civil Laws Make Many Rights Actually Inviolable. Civil law bears upon rights in another way. Not only does it define certain rights which reason cannot deduce with sufficient convincingness from the nature of things, but it lends its strong arm to the enforcement of rights which are clearly natural. For though certain rights may be natural, it is not always possible for each individual to protect himself in them. Some physical force, or the knowledge that such force will be exerted if needed, is necessary in order that unscrupulous men may be restrained from violating the rights of others. Usually it is better that the individual should not resort to physical force in the vindication of his rights. Social order will be better preserved if this is done by the State.

495. Definition of Justice. Once we have grasped the meaning of "right" and its ramifications, it is easy to understand the content of justice—the giving to each one what he has a right to have, his complete due, or the moral virtue inclining one to do this. Three things are necessary for justice: (1) that the act be directed towards another person, for no one is, properly speaking, just or unjust to himself; (2) that what is rendered is due by a proper right; (3) that the debt be completely canceled.

496. Division of Justice. Justice is usually divided into *commutative, legal* and *distributive. Distributive justice* concerns the duties which the State owes its citizens, such as protection against unjust aggression; and the rights which it has to certain services from them, as military duty in time of war. *Legal justice* is the other aspect of distributive. It concerns the duties of the citizen to the State and his rights against it. *Commutative justice* concerns the rights and duties of persons, whether physical or moral, in a private and individual capacity, as opposed to their rights and duties as members of the State. Thus a railroad, though the service it renders may be called public, has a duty of commutative justice to render full value to its patrons.

497. Obligations of Justice. It is important to grasp this distinction clearly, inasmuch as commutative justice binds *per se* to restitution while distributive and legal justice do not. The reason for this distinction as regards restitution is evident from the examples given. Clearly the citizen is bound to risk his life for the State in time of a just war. But if he evades his duty, certainly he is not bound to undergo the risk when peace comes so as to make restitution. On the other hand a violation of legal or distributive justice may also offend against commutative. Thus a wealthy man dodging taxes may raise the rate of taxation and so violate the property rights of other citizens. Practically he, a private individual, would be taxing other private individuals. He would be taking from them just as really as if he entered their houses and stole, and would be just as really bound to restitution. However, the fact that legal and distributive justice do not bind to restitution does not lessen the seriousness of the obligation flowing from them. In some cases the duty may be much graver than some obligations arising from commutative justice.

498. Everyone Has a Sense of His Rights. Because there are certain inherent rights in every individual, everyone has an instinctive sense of his rights. Even the most debased slaves probably had some idea of their rights, an invasion of which they would have considered an injustice. At least in this land of democracy and freedom it would be difficult to discover anyone who does not realize that there are some fundamental rights appertaining to him as a human being.

499. This Sense of Rights May Develop. This sense of one's rights though instinctive in everyone has nevertheless undergone development. During the 19th century, "the Rights of Man" were insisted upon to such an extent that there was more danger of exaggeration than of forgetfulness. Our own epoch-making Declaration of Independence brings out into clear relief the fundamental tenet of Christianity and of democracy, that all men are essentially equal and have a con-natural right to life, liberty, and the pursuit of happiness.

500. Importance of a Sense of Rights. It is well that this sense of right and justice should be keenly developed. It is the best safeguard possible of that human liberty which is necessary for the greatest development. Only citizens jealous of their rights can remain free. Men who neglect their rights or freedom will inevitably become the victims of aspiring demagogues and tyrants.

501. Sense of Duty Is More Important Than Sense of Rights.
At the same time, nevertheless, there is a nobler word in the
human language than "right"—and that is "duty." The man
who is continually standing on his rights, who is too jealous of
them, who is always scenting injustice to himself, is a nuisance.
He is the hardest man in the world with whom to get along.
Someone is always offending his sensitive appreciation of himself and his own importance and he surrounds himself with all
sorts of imaginary rights.

502. Sense of Others' Rights Is Natural. Together with this
sense of one's own rights, if it is to be reasonable and well-
rounded, must go also a sense of the rights of others. In un-
sophisticated persons, such as children, this natural correlation
is frequently found. Most boys have a sense of fairness which
leads them to accept ungrudgingly well-merited punishment,
provided it is meted out with impartiality. It is making a distinction where no distinction should exist, rather than strictness,
which offends their sense of justice and right.

503. Sense of Others' Rights Necessary for Order. The moment
we stop to consider, it is apparent that a true sense of right
must embrace others as well as ourselves. For if we have rights,
so have they. It often happens that our own rights cannot be
pushed without conflicting with those of others. Our inalienable
right "to life, liberty, and the pursuit of happiness" must be
regulated so as not to interfere more than necessary with the
like inalienable rights of others. If each one pressed his rights
to their utmost without limitation there would be chaos.

**504. Reconciliation of Rights Is Fundamental Problem of Gov-
ernment.** Hence, the reconciliation of the rights of one with the
rights of others, is one of the fundamental problems of government. A democratic form of government doubtless helps towards
this reconciliation, because it gives the people a chance to voice
their own wishes; but it does not go a great way towards attaining this object. Before a people can rule itself wisely so as to
secure to each the greatest measure of his rights consistent with

the rights of others, it must have developed to a high degree a sense of duty as well as of right.

505. Rights and Duty Are Correlative. If anyone has a right there rests on everyone else the duty of respecting that right. A right implies a duty. They are correlative terms. And of the two, the more important, perhaps, is duty. For if everyone should exercise his rights to the fullest limit of his conception of them there would inevitably be a great deal of injustice done. But if everyone should fulfill his duties perfectly, each one would secure his rights.

506. The Duties of Man. Side by side, therefore, with the rights of man must be put the "duties of man." Important as has been the concept of the rights of man in developing our modern democracies, more important still must be the concept of the duties of man. It is on this point that we in America have failed. Our children have breathed in freedom with the air, as tradition asserts a British officer to have said, but they have not breathed in a deep sense of reverence for the rights of others, of respect for authority, which is an even more necessary foundation for democracy.

507. Exaggeration of One's Rights Interferes with Rights of Others. Too great emphasis upon the inalienable right to life will lead inevitably to living at the expense of weaker men whose same inalienable right is disregarded. An attempt to secure liberty may end in anarchy. A selfish seeking of happiness will lead to an orgy of pleasure seeking. Life, liberty, and the pursuit of happiness are fine-sounding and soul-filling phrases; but they must be balanced by a well-developed sense of *duty*.

508. Dutiful Rather Than "Standing on One's Rights" Man Is Ideal. It is the dutiful child rather than the one aggressively defending his rights who will develop into the best citizen. It is the dutiful parent rather than the selfish right-seeking one who is best filling his place in society. It is the duty-performing official rather than the one who has a high opinion of his rights who serves his country best. And so on throughout the whole catalogue of people and positions, it is the one who does his duty instead of seeking his rights who accomplishes most for himself and for mankind.

509. Scholastic Ethics Is Matchless in Expounding Justice. The treatment of rights, justice, duties as here presented is undoubtedly one of the chief merits of sound Ethics. Justice, as explained by it, is a wonderful and perfect order of rational creation. While it unites all into society for the sake of harmonious co-operation, it guards the freedom of each individual like an impregnable stronghold, and furnishes everyone with the means to unfold his activity. And while thus all-embracing and all-protecting, it is so sacred and sublime that all must revere it, and so firm that nothing can prevail against it. We ought, however, to bear well in mind that justice is so grand, firm and sacred for no other cause than that it rests on a theistic basis. In Scholastic philosophy, man is not looked on as the last offspring of brute creation, but is regarded as a creature of God, shaped after the Creator's likeness and animated with a soul which is the likeness of Divine Reason. Hence, every human being, however frail and feeble in appearance, is rendered inviolable and vested with sacred prerogatives. Nor are rights and laws deduced by Scholastic Ethics from the conditions of earthly existence; they are derived from God's infinite wisdom and holiness and so center in Him who is all order, beauty, and righteousness.

510. Summary. Right is an inviolable moral power independent of physical force. It is important to insist upon the fact that all rights are ultimately based on the *natural law,* and some so closely as to be con-natural and inalienable. Every right implies a duty, and the giving to each one his due is justice. Important as is a sense of rights, a sense of duty is even more important.

SUGGESTED READINGS

1. Ming, *Data of Modern Ethics,* Chs. XIII, XIV.
2. Cath. Encyc., arts. "Justice," "Duty," "Right."
3. Carver, *Essays in Social Justice,* Ch. I.
4. Cronin, *Science of Ethics,* Vol. II, Ch. III.

QUESTIONS

1. Do all rights of citizens depend upon a grant from the State?
2. Give example of a right, and point out *subject, object, title, term.*
3. May all rights be ceded by the subject of the rights?
4. Distinguish between real and personal rights.
5. What is the relation of civil law to rights?
6. Define and divide justice.

FIVE: *Rights to Goods of Soul and of Body*

511. Division of Rights. Rights may be divided, as we said in the previous chapter, into con-natural and acquired, alienable and inalienable, perfect and imperfect, real and personal. But for convenience of discussion they may also be divided according to their object into rights concerning goods of soul, those concerning goods of body, and those concerning goods of fortune. In this chapter we shall consider the first two classes—those of soul and of body.

I. Right to Goods of Soul

512. Right to Means Necessary to Gain Last End. The most fundamental right is the right to whatever is necessary to gain one's last end. This right is con-natural because it belongs to every individual by the very fact of existence. It is inalienable because no one may lawfully cede it in favor of another. Even a parent may not give up to a child what would be necessary for that parent's gaining of his last end. It is limited only by the right of others to the same goods. For if one should happen to have what would be necessary to another for gaining his last end but was not for himself, he would be bound to give it to that other even at the cost of life itself.

513. Right to Goods of Soul. The right to goods of soul in a less intimate way, as meaning merely a reasonable development of intellect and will, is con-natural. It is not, however, inalienable. For sufficient reason one might cede this right and it is not so perfect as to imply a corresponding duty at the cost of the more important rights to goods of body or even of fortune.

514. Definition of Honor. Among the most important of the goods of soul is the right to honor and reputation. It is only less important, indeed, than the right to life. For *honor* in a wide sense is a good opinion of another's perfections, and without this good opinion of others for one's self, life is hardly worth living.

More strictly, *honor* is an external manifestation of that good opinion made to one's face. *Fame* is a common and verbal esteem for the perfections of another.

515. Right to Honor. Everyone has a right to the good esteem that is due a human being, so that the honor which he merits should be given to him. This includes a right to both positive and negative esteem. That is, one must not without reason think evil of another and must also give to him that dignity demanded by the personality in itself.

516. Right to Reputation. *Each one has a right to his reputation,* whether it be true or false. For each has a right to any good he has acquired by his own proper labors, and reputation is such a good. The right to a *true* reputation is absolute and universal. Hence, it is never lawful to destroy such a reputation. The right to *ordinary* fame, whether founded on facts or appearances, is universal. But the right to a *false* reputation is based upon the inconveniences that would result to society if it were lawful indiscriminately to publish the defects of anyone. Hence, this right is limited, and it is superseded whenever the good of another or of the State requires exposure.

517. Rights of the Dead and of Moral Persons. The dead likewise have a right to reputation. Yet inasmuch as they have less need of reputation, it is less of a sin to reveal their defects. Moral persons (for example, religious communities) also have a right to their reputation.

518. Calumny and Detraction. There are two ways in which one may violate another's right to a reputation. One is by *calumny,* which is the false attribution of a crime; the other is by *detraction,* which is the revelation of a true but unknown crime. Both calumny and detraction are of their nature serious sins, though both admit of parvity of matter. Their seriousness is to be judged by (a) the defect revealed, (b) the condition of the person injured, and (c) the injury done.

519. When Crimes Are Secret. Crimes are either *public* or *secret,* according as they are known or not to the community. Public secrets may be public either in *law* or in *fact,* as they happen to have been declared by a judicial sentence or are actually known generally in a neighborhood.

520. When Detraction Is Allowable. Secret crimes may be revealed if the good of one's self, or another, or the common good requires it. But the injury averted should be proportionate to the injury done to the defamed person, and the revelation should be made with the least possible injury. Legally public crimes may be declared anywhere without excuse, unless they have been corrected and forgotten. If they should have been corrected and forgotten the offense of revealing them is against charity, but not against justice, and, therefore, restitution is not obligatory. Crimes actually public may also be revealed without excuse unless they have been corrected and forgotten. Should they have been forgotten, the offense in this case is against both justice and charity and hence restitution would be binding.

521. Newspapers and Calumny. *Editors* may reveal secret defects of occupants of or candidates for public office, when these defects render the persons unfit for the positions. The reasons are both because the public good requires such publicity and because anyone who enters a political campaign may be assumed to cede his right to a false reputation. But editors should be careful as to the truth of what they divulge and as to its actually rendering the person unfit for office. Historians may be allowed greater liberty in revealing the crimes of the past, because the dead have not the same need of a reputation and cannot be hurt by any revelation.[1] However, they should be careful lest the revelation injure persons now living.

522. Responsibility of Listeners. Whoever hears the detraction or calumny and does not stop it when he easily could sins doubly against charity: first, because he does not correct the person detracting; and secondly, because he listens to the defamation

---

[1] That this applies to Church dignitaries we have on good authority. Cardinal Manning wrote in his journal Dec. 9, 1883: "I [Manning] said [to Leo XIII]: 'Se l'Evangelista non ha celato il peccato e la caduta del Guida, perche dobbiamo noi celare il peccato vescovi ed altri personnage?' The Holy Father took this up as a text and spoke long and fully in the same sense." (Purcell's *Life of Cardinal Manning*, II, p. 581.)

of his neighbor. If the detraction is unjust, one voluntarily listening sins *affectively* against justice; if he directly or indirectly induces unjust defamation by approving or questioning, he sins *effectively* against justice.

523. Restitution on Account of Defamation. An unjust defamer (slanderer or detractor) is bound in justice (a) to restore the reputation as soon as possible; and (b) to repair all such injury to goods of fortune as he foresaw at least vaguely. The first obligation is *personal* and ceases with the defamer; the second obligation, however, is *real* and passes on to his heirs. One who cannot restore reputation is not bound (before a legal judgment) to restore in money, since these goods belong to different orders. In restoring reputation, a calumniator is bound to use any necessary means that do not inflict upon himself an injury very much greater than he caused to the other person; a *detractor* may use some equivocal speech, such as that he was unjust, but he may not lie. Restitution of fame is excused if it be impossible; expressly or tacitly waived by the injured party; already accomplished by judicial sentence or lapse of time; or if the injured person has similarly injured and refused to restore.

524. How to Avoid Detraction. The best way to avoid defaming others, or becoming party to their defamation, is to keep the conversation away from personalities. If it once takes that turn someone is likely to make a detracting remark. And even complimentary remarks get to be woefully twisted by passing from mouth to mouth. You remark that Edith and John are finally married after several years engagement and praise her constancy. One of your hearers reports the news with the remark: "I never did believe in long engagements." By the time it has gone through another tongue there has been added the innuendo: "Long engagements are always dangerous."

525. Silence Is Golden. There is a more general reason than fear of injuring our neighbor urging silence upon us. No better way can be devised of strengthening one's will and gaining self-control than by bridling the tongue. "As an arrow that sticketh in a man's thigh, so is a word in the heart of a fool." [2] One should not be a fool. Each one should strive to be strong enough to contain himself, instead of running to a telephone or blurting out the gossip (though innocent in itself) to the first acquaintance he meets. St. James says that a man who offends not by his tongue, the same is perfect. Anyone will find that by the time he has conquered his tongue he will have developed so much control of self that everything else will be easy.

526. Immense Harm Done by Gossip. In this, as in other things, "we are not worst at once." One begins by talking innocently but unnecessarily of his neighbors. Then he goes on to tell their faults, excusing himself upon the ground that they are known. Gradually he slips into carelessness about their publicity and finally into disregard for their truth. He may salve his conscience by qualifying phrases such as "they say" or "have you heard," but he is doing the Devil's work just the same. "Saul slew his thousands, and David his ten thousands," but we cannot count the happiness destroyed, the friends separated, the families disrupted, the souls driven to self-destruction by idle rumors.

527. Rash Judgments. *Honor* is violated *internally* by *rash judgment,* that is by a firm assent of the mind to the fact of another's sin without sufficient reason therefor. Rash judgment differs from *rash opinion* which is merely a *probable* assent; and from rash *suspicion* which is a suspension of judgment, with leaning towards assent. Rash suspicion and opinion are usually merely slight sins. Rash judgment is serious only when it proceeds from an insufficient motive, is firm, deliberate, and concerns a serious matter.

528. Insult. Honor is violated *externally* by insult, which is an unjust injury against the good esteem due a person present. It differs from defamation in that it is directed against honor, not fame. And as honor is greater than fame, insult is more serious. Insult may be either *positive* or *negative,* according as it does what should not be done or omits what should be done.

[2] Ecclus. xix, 12.

Insult from its nature is a serious sin against justice though admitting parvity of matter. Anyone who has formally and seriously violated another's honor must repair the injury.

II. The Right to Secrets

529. Definition of Secret. The right to secrets is a right to a quasi good of the soul, inasmuch as it is in itself an immaterial good distinguished from goods of fortune or goods of body and because secrets do frequently concern strict goods of soul. A *secret subjectively* is the obligation of not revealing some hidden thing; *objectively* it is the thing that must not be revealed. Secrets are of three kinds: [3] (a) *Natural,* whose obligation arises without contract from the nature of the thing itself. Thus one learning of the illegitimacy of another is bound not to reveal this fact. (b) *Promise,* when the obligation comes from an agreement to keep silence about something previously known. (c) *Trust,* when one accepts the knowledge of something before unknown with the understanding that it will not be revealed. There is always this understanding, for instance, in consulting physicians.

530. Rights Regarding Secrets. Everyone has a right to his own secrets, hence, it is not lawful (a) unjustly to *explore* a secret; as by stealing the figures of a bid; (b) to *manifest* a secret; (c) to *use* a secret *unjustly* learned, not a secret of trust; except as we proceed to state.

531. When Secrets May Be Revealed. A *natural* secret may be revealed when it cannot be concealed without serious inconvenience in the case of charity; or inconvenience greater than that resulting to the other party in case of justice. A *promised* secret ordinarily binds from fidelity and under slight obligation. Secrets of *trust* bind from justice and seriously in a grave matter. It is lawful to reveal a *secret of trust* (a) when its disclosure is necessary to avert serious injury from the Church or State, for since the obligation is based upon the common good it ceases when that good requires manifestation; (b) when it is necessary to

[3] Prescinding from the sacramental secret.

avert serious injury to be done to a third party by the person entrusting the secret; (c) to avert serious injury to the person entrusting, since he cannot be reasonably unwilling; (d) to avoid serious injury to one's self, as this is tacitly understood upon accepting the secret.

532. The Medical Secret. A serious situation arises in the case of a physician consulted by a man with a grave, contagious disease who contemplates marriage. If the man persists in his determination to marry before a cure has been effected, may the doctor disclose his condition? Noldin says he may.[4] But ought he? That will depend upon whether or not more good than harm will come from such disclosures. For if reputable physicians were known to make a practice in such cases of informing the other party to the marriage, they would soon be effectively prevented from making such revelations by the fact of men so afflicted going to quacks. There would be no chance of the innocent party's learning the truth and considerably less chance of a cure.[5]

533. When Letters May Be Read. *Letters* form a sort of natural secret and it is in itself a serious sin to read those belonging to other people. However, it is permissible for parents to read the letters of children still under their authority. Moreover, it is evidently allowable by consent; and consent may sometimes be reasonably presumed from the circumstances. Again, public authority may open letters as for purposes of military censorship, when such measures are deemed necessary to avert calamity from the State. This may be done even by private authority if one has good reasons to suspect that so he can avoid serious injury.

III. THE RIGHT TO LIFE

534. The Right to Life. Next in importance to the strictly inalienable right to what is necessary to attain one's last end comes the right to life. It is con-natural and comes to a human being with the very first moment of existence, even before birth; and

---

[4] *Theologia Moralis,* II, p. 664.
[5] Cf. Morrow, *Social Diseases and Marriage,* Ch. III.

it comes by the very fact of being human. It is permanently and universally inalienable, in the sense that no human authority may lawfully and directly take the life of an innocent man. This right is perfect because those who violate it are bound to restitution.

535. Implications of the Right to Life. Implied in this right to life, are all rights necessary to the due safeguarding and development of life. These include the right to a living wage and the opportunity for getting it, and in general whatever is regarded as necessary for the reasonable development of one's personality. At present, however, we shall consider merely licit defense and the killing of innocent persons.

536. Definition of Homicide. *Homicide,* in a wide sense, is the taking of the life of a human being by another man. More strictly, it is understood to be the killing of an innocent man who has not committed and would not commit any crime worthy of death. Man is here taken in a broad sense as meaning any human being, even a human foetus not yet born.[6]

537. Division of Homicide. Homicide is divided into *voluntary* and *involuntary,* according as it is or is not intended; *direct* and *indirect,* according as it is intended in itself or in its cause; *simple* or *mixed,* according as it is merely homicide or includes another crime, as parricide.

538. General Principles Concerning Homicide. It is never lawful *directly to kill a formally* and *materially innocent person.* This applies even to the supreme civil or ecclesiastical authority. Hence, it is not lawful to kill wounded or sick persons in order to put them out of pain; nor a madman lest he kill others; nor persons suffering with a contagious disease in order to prevent its spread.

539. When It is Lawful to Kill an Innocent Person. For a proportionately serious reason, it is lawful to do or omit something in itself indifferent, from which action or omission (beside the

---

[6] For abortion, craniotomy, and similar questions, cf. Coppens, *Moral Principles and Medical Practice;* Eschbach, *Dissertationes Physiologicae Theologicae;* Klarmann, *The Crux of Pastoral Medicine.*

intention of the agent) will follow the death of some innocent man.

540. Special Cases Concerning Homicide: 1. Puncturing the Heart. It sometimes happens that physicians puncture the heart or open a vein of a cadaver either because the deceased made this request, or his relatives wish it. If this is done for the purpose of preventing the burial of a person who may be only apparently dead, it is certainly wrong, even though the person be really dead. But if they have indubitable signs that the person is dead, they may puncture his heart to ease those who desire it. For as it is lawful to bury him it is lawful to pierce his heart, since the same effect comes from either act.[7]

541. Special Cases Concerning Homicide: 2. When May One Lawfully Defend Himself Against an Aggressor? It is lawful for anyone to defend himself or another against an aggressor, even at the expense of the life of the aggressor, provided these conditions are fulfilled:

542. 1. When the Aggression Is Taking Place. The person must be actually an aggressor, that is, he must be really attacking or performing an act from which he can be judged already morally to have attacked—as loading or drawing a revolver. But it is not lawful to kill an aggressor *after* an attack, as this would be vengeance, not defense.

543. 2. The Aggression Must Be Unlawful. The aggressor must be unjust either *materially* or *formally* in his attack. Hence, it is lawful to defend one's self against a madman or a drunkard. But it would not be lawful for a robber to kill the owner of goods he was about to take, although he would lose his own life, because the owner in attacking him to defend very valuable goods is not an unjust aggressor.

544. 3. Defense Must Not Be Greater Than Necessary. Proper moderation must be preserved in the defense. Nothing more must be done against the aggressor than is necessary to repel the attack. This requires three things: (a) Life must not be assailed unless the aggression is (morally) at hand by some act;

[7] Noldin, II, 339.

(b) the life of the aggressor must not be attacked if the danger can be avoided in some other way, as by shouting or fleeing; (c) the aggressor must not be killed if his wounding suffices for defense. But one is not obligated to flee if one will suffer serious injury by so doing, as incurring a reputation for cowardice.

545. Defense of Life. There is little question of the right to defend one's life against an unjust aggressor, even at the sacrifice of the life of the aggressor. The laws of all States acknowledge justifiable homicide, and admit this reason of unjust aggression as justifying it. They likewise admit that the defense of another's life is sufficient reason for killing. If each one did not have this right, serious injury would result to the State.

546. One Is Not Obliged to Defend His Life. But one is, ordinarily, not obliged to defend his own life at the expense of another's existence. For while each one has a right to preserve his life, the duty of preserving it ceases when such hard and abhorrent means are necessary. In certain cases, however, defense would be obligatory. These cases would be: (a) when the attacked person's life is very necessary to the State, or the fulfillment of very serious duties, such as those of a parent to a child; (b) when the attacked person is in the state of mortal sin.

547. One Is Not Obliged to Defend Another's Life. If one is not obliged to defend his own life, much less is he obliged to defend the life of another. But this also admits of exceptions: (a) as when the life of the attacked person is very useful to the State; (b) or stands in some special relation to him, as father, or child, or wife; (c) or when one is by his office (as a policeman) obliged to defend others. And these exceptions bind even under risk of one's own life.

548. Special Cases: Defense of Goods. It is lawful to defend not only one's life, but also one's goods of great value though of a lower order, and that at the expense of killing the unjust aggressor, if these goods can be protected in no other way. This is because such goods are morally necessary for the proper safeguarding and development of life. The goods that may be defended lawfully in this way, proper moderation being preserved, are (a) *Goods of fortune* of great value. This means not only such an amount as to leave one's self or those dependent upon one without sustenance, but also whatever lack of which, considering one's circumstances, would cause serious injury. (b) *Modesty.* For since it is lawful to defend goods of fortune, much more is it lawful to defend modesty, a good far outranking riches. But one is not obliged to kill an aggressor against chastity, but can remain passive, since chastity cannot be lost without the consent of the will. It is said that during the revolution in Mexico many Sisters were actually confronted with this situation. Had it been possible they might have killed their aggressors lawfully, but of course could not commit suicide lawfully. (c) *Integrity of members.* For serious mutilation is a graver loss than would come by loss of goods of fortune.

549. Special Cases Concerning Homicide: 3. Destruction of Foetus. The unborn child, no matter what its stage of development, is a human being, or at least a potential human being, and hence has all the rights of a human being. Its right to life is on a par with its mother's right to life. Therefore, it is no more lawful directly to take the life of an embryo than it is lawful directly to take the life of a mature human being. However, there have been Scholastic ethicians in the past who held that the life of the child might be directly taken when both mother and child would surely die if nature were allowed to take its course. The reasons they gave were that in such a case the child might be looked upon as materially an unjust aggressor, since it would cause its mother's death; there was a conflict of rights in which the mother's right prevailed; the operation merely hastened the death of the child, as it was bound to die very shortly anyhow. Noldin admits the difficulties of the situation and says: "Since the proof from natural principles [the only ones with which we are concerned in Ethics] of the unlawfulness of craniotomy is not entirely plain and evident; it can easily happen that doctors can perform the operation in good faith." [8]

[8] Noldin, *Theol. Mor.,* II, p. 365.

550. Special Cases Concerning Homicide: 4. Premature Delivery. If it is not lawful directly to cause the death of the foetus in order to save the life of the mother, still less would it be lawful to destroy the foetus to save her honor or merely to prevent an increase in the family. But a premature delivery may be brought about for a sufficient cause when there is at least a faint hope of the child living, even though it be weak or defective. Sometimes, too, the principle of two effects following from one cause can be applied, as when treating the mother for some sickness will result in miscarriage, for in that case the abortion is not direct.[9]

551. Special Cases Concerning Homicide: 5. Abortion. Abortion is the ejection of a foetus that is not old enough to live apart from the mother. It is never lawful directly to procure an abortion. However, a premature delivery may be brought about for a sufficient cause when there is at least a faint hope of the child living, even though it be weak or defective. Sometimes, too, the principle of two effects following from one cause can be applied, as when treating the mother for some sickness will result in abortion. In that case, the abortion is not direct.[10]

SUGGESTED READINGS

1. Scaramelli, Treatise II, Art. IV, Ch. II.
2. Rodriguez, *Christian Perfection,* Vol. II, Treat. II, Chs. III to X.
3. Morrow, *Social Diseases and Marriage,* Ch. III.
4. Slater, *Moral Theology,* I, pp. 308-319.
5. Rickaby, *Aquinas Ethicus,* Quest. LXIV, Vol. II.
6. Rickaby, *Moral Philosophy,* Ch. V.
7. O'Malley, *Ethics of Medical Homicide,* N. Y., 1919.
8. Clement, *Thou Shalt Not Kill.*

QUESTIONS

1. What is the most fundamental right?
2. Has one a right to a false reputation?

[9] Noldin, *loc. cit.,* p. 367 ff.
[10] Noldin, p. 367 ff.

3. Have moral persons or groups (*e.g.,* Communists, Jews, Catholics) a right that careless charges should not be circulated?
4. What obligation has one who has been guilty of calumny or detraction?
5. Give example from your own experience or reading of the harmfulness of gossip.
6. What is the obligation of one possessing another's secret:
      (a) natural;   (c) of trust?
      (b) of promise;
7. What conditions must be observed in defense against aggression?

SIX: *Ownership*

I. Meaning and Division of Ownership

552. State of Question. We have thus far under the head of rights discussed rights to goods of soul, as honor and reputation; to quasi goods of soul, such as secrets; and to goods of body. We shall now take up rights to goods of fortune. In this connection we shall first of all consider ownership. This question has been put off until this point because it is an acquired right and hence not as fundamental as the con-natural rights, and because it applies principally to goods of fortune.

553. Importance of Ownership. Dominion or ownership is one of the most important questions in social Ethics. For under our present social system, ownership is necessary to the individual if he is to secure his natural rights to life and honor. Without ownership he would starve and in the process of starvation would have about as much honor as a tramp. It is important, also, in the extent of the relations it affects. Hardly any other relationship covers such a multiplicity of acts as does ownership.

554. Definition of Ownership. Ownership is a legitimate power of disposing of something as one's own, unless otherwise prohibited. *Thing* here is taken generically to apply to immaterial objects as fame and honor, as well as to material objects. Dominion differs from *jus ad rem* [1] which does not give the power of disposing of a thing, and from *mere possession* (as an almoner) which may give the power of disposing of a thing, but not as one's own. The disposition of a thing may be prohibited to the owner in various ways: (a) by *civil law,* as when heirs are prohibited from selling their patrimony; (b) by *agreement,* as when one sells his house to another upon condition that it will not be used as a saloon; (c) by *testament,* as when

[1] Cf. No. 488.

one leaves property to another provided it be used for a special purpose.

555. Principles. Several phrases became common in Roman law as expressing the consequences of ownership and they have been taken over by ethical science: (a) *A thing cries to its owner: res clamant ad dominum*—that is, the owner retains his right over an article even though it should have passed into the possession of another. One who buys a stolen object must restore it to the rightful owner. (b) *A thing fructifies to its owner: res fructificat domino.* For as the whole substance of a thing belongs to its owner, its fruit will belong to him. (c) *A thing perishes to its owner: res perit domino.* More accurately, anything perishing by chance, or by natural process, perishes for its owner; but what perishes through someone's fault perishes to that person at his expense. (d) *It is not lawful to be enriched by another's property: ex re aliena non licet ditescere.* For whoever is enriched *from* another's goods is appropriating the *fruit* of those goods to himself. And the fruit of an·object belongs to the owner of the object.

556. Division of Ownership. Ownership is divided into *eminent domain* and *private domain.* Private ownership is dominion in a strict sense as already defined. In spite of the implication of the term, the State may and does own property by *private dominion.* In addition, however, the State enjoys *eminent domain,* from which private citizens are always excluded. This eminent domain is not an ownership of property in a strict sense, but a supreme jurisdiction. It will be remembered that ownership was defined as "a legitimate power of disposing of something as one's own *unless otherwise prohibited.*" The italicized clause includes eminent domain. For by this supreme jurisdiction the civil authority restricts private domain in various ways. For instance, the State may "condemn property" and force the private owners to sell; it may practically transfer domain from one private citizen to another, as by outlawing debts; or it may even sometimes confiscate private property. For the lawful exercise of this eminent domain, however, two conditions should be fulfilled: (a) that a great utility of the community should demand its exercise, and (b) that the subjects should be compensated if possible.[2]

557. Private Ownership. Private ownership is divided into (a) *perfect,* the power of disposing as one wishes of a thing's substance and its utility; (b) *imperfect,* the power of disposing either of a thing's substance (direct) or of its utility (indirect) but not of both.

558. Definition of Certain Terms. *Use* is the right of employing another's property without destroying its substance. Examples are the use of a house, or of a horse, or the pasturing of one's cattle in another's field.

559. Usufruct. As the name implies, usufruct is the right to use and enjoy the fruit of another's property. Fruits are divided by *reason of origin* into: (a) *spontaneous,* those produced without any special human care; (b) *industrial,* those acquired only by human toil; (c) *mixed,* those which come partly from labor and partly spontaneously, as cheese.

560. The Object of Dominion. Whatever a man can own is the object of dominion. But not every object is capable of the same kind of ownership. Over *internal* goods not distinct from himself (as life), one has not *direct* dominion; over other internal goods one may have full dominion, as also over mixed goods, such as honor and reputation.

561. Division of External Goods. External goods are divided into *movable* and *immovable; interchangeable* and *not interchangeable* so that respectively the same individual article need not or must be returned, as a gallon of oil or a horse; into those *consumable in first use,* as bread, and those not, as a horse; into *corporeal,* as houses, and *incorporeal,* as the right to fish in a certain stream.

II. The Origin of Ownership

562. The Subject of Dominion. By the subject of ownership is understood the person in whom dominion is or may be

2 Noldin, *Theol. Mor.,* II, 359.

vested. This may be a *physical* or a *moral* person. By natural law
every living man is a subject of dominion, even though perpetu-
ally insane, or not yet born. The basis of dominion is the rational
nature. In this sense the right to private property is natural.
Whether or not this right is natural in the sense that the natural
law requires a *system* of private ownership is controverted.

563. The Origin of Dominion. The more common opinion
among Scholastic moralists seems to be that in the beginning God
granted domain over temporal goods in such a way that they
were *common to all* and did not belong more to one than to
another.[3] But the division among individuals of ownership in
both land and movables is licit; and considering all the circumstances, private ownership in at least some things is necessary
for human welfare. As to how division first came about, whether
by force, or paternal authority, or contract, or human law, authorities differ.[4] Most Scholastic ethicians say that it was made by
natural law, though it would seem that they mean [5] with Roncaglia rather *jus gentium*. "Ownership of things," says Roncaglia, "was introduced by the law of nations. This is proven
by the fact that nowhere is ownership found to have been introduced by divine law, but rather God constituted man lord over
all things, and only from Holy Scripture have we the land of
Chanaan assigned to the Israelites by special indulgence. Nor
were division and dominion of things introduced by natural law;
for that rather determined that all things should be common
and only favored (propendit) such division because of the inconveniences which would have arisen from the malice of men
were all things common. I do not, therefore, deny that, the
division being made, a thing belongs to him who has appropriated it, but I assert that the division was not made by the
primeval inclination of nature." [6]

564. Jus Gentium and the Origin of Dominion. Roncaglia defines *jus gentium* as "the first right that was derived from human

[3] Noldin, *Theol. Mor.*, II, 368.
[4] Noldin, *Theol. Mor.*, II, 368.
[5] Kelleher, *Private Ownership*, p. 149.
[6] Roncaglia, *Universalis Moralis Theologia*, Tract. XIII, Cap. II, Q. I, p. 402.

authority and was accepted by God. Often that term was used to signify natural law and thence it is usually called the primary law of nations. But in the present treatise, by the law of nations is understood that right which all or nearly all races have established as necessary, or as very useful for conserving among men the common social life. This right, however, does not embrace what is directly known by the law of nature and is known congenitally, but consists of those conclusions which are deduced by discursive reasoning from practical principles known by the law of nature and which all nations by mutual consent and usage have established as laws necessary and very useful." And among examples of institutions referable to the *jus gentium* he mentions the prohibition of marriage between the different races.[7]

565. Form of Ownership Is Historical. Reverend Dr. Rovelli, speaking before the Giornate Sociale, a Catholic Sociological Congress, held in Milan in 1907, put the same idea in a more modern manner: "Property is an historical form. . . . Hence I ask," he says, "that property be studied without preoccupation with its individual form, and only with the intention of making it more effective in securing social welfare. . . . I have tried to speak of property in the concrete, or rather of the various forms under which property has existed, striving to make clear that none of these forms has a preference over the others, deriving from a natural right innate in man, but that each is determined by social convenience and can vary in the course of history. The reason for the existence of any particular form of property does not come from a pre-existing natural right, but from the fact that it preserves order in the use of riches and that the society in which it is constituted—either by gradual transformation, or, as can happen, and has happened, by a violent change—accepts it peacefully. . . . I believe that it (private property) is simply a form determined by historical reasons, as I have said, and not derived from a natural right pre-existing in the individual. In so far, then, as natural tendencies are concerned, I admit that the tendency for a man to use economic goods to satisfy his

[7] *Op. cit.,* Tract. III, Q. VII, p. 37.

needs is natural, and that when these goods are limited the use for one's self of the same goods is spontaneous and natural; but the way in which a man uses economic goods (for example, whether as private or collective property) is simply an historical result, upon which the right of private property has been formed.[8]

566. Private Ownership Not Necessary. Father Kelleher,[9] pointing out that the classical theologians almost unanimously taught that the division of property does not depend directly upon the natural law, but is derived from *jus gentium,* goes on to say: "Neither can there be any doubt that their belief that division of property was prescribed thus universally . . . was due to a mistaken notion about its necessity for human society. . . . The important point is that these theologians taught that division of property depends immediately on human law. Had they understood that its necessity was not absolute for social peace and stability as appears to have been established since their time, they would not have insisted that it is universally prescribed by the natural law."

567. Form of Ownership Only Justified by Results. "It cannot be too often repeated," says Father John Ryan, "that no rule or principle of ownership has intrinsic or metaphysical value. They all derive their moral validity from their effects, from their conduciveness to human welfare in the complete sense of that phrase." [10] Father F. W. Grafton, a Jesuit, is equally clear in declaring expediency to be the real ground for any form of ownership. "We Catholics must, I think, allow that the extent to which the State may monopolize the means of production, distribution, and exchange is limited only by the extent to which this would be economically for the public good, provided, of course, that no injustice was committed in taking over the various concerns." [11]

[8] Resoconto delle Giornate Sociale di Milano, 7, 8, 9 Feb., 1907 (Milano, Libreria Boggio).

[9] *Private Ownership,* p. 149. This is probably to date the best treatise by a Catholic on this subject.

[10] "Methods of Reforming Our Land System," in *The Catholic World,* Oct., 1912, p. 15.

[11] "A Catholic Social Platform," in *The Catholic World,* Sept., 1911, p. 801.

568. Arguments Justifying Ownership. St. Thomas seems to take the same position. For, after admitting that in the beginning all things were common, he feels constrained to justify private ownership; and he does so by three political or economic arguments. St. Thomas says that private dominion is better [12] than common because (a) each one is more solicitous to procure what belongs to himself than what belongs to the community; (b) affairs will be better ordered if each one has the obligation of looking after himself; (c) a peaceful state will be better preserved if each one is content with his own. [13]

569. These Arguments May Become Antiquated. These would seem still to be sound reasons. Conditions have not changed sufficiently to antiquate them. But the important point is to remember that Scholastic justification of private property rests upon an appeal to the actual effects upon society. If these should be no longer as favorable as those produced by some other form, then Scholastic moralists would have no objection to a change.

570. How State Transfers Ownership. As a matter of fact, as we have seen, the State may by right of eminent domain transfer dominion from one to another. And while compensation is ordinarily to be made to the owner, this might justly be foregone if it would occasion too great inconvenience to the community. In reality, the State is continually, through its bankruptcy laws, thus transferring title without compensation. For if A who owes B $1,000 for goods bought of him should be declared bankrupt, B no longer—according to some moralists—has a legal or moral claim against A, no matter how well able to pay A may become later. [14]

571. Private Ownership Today Not the Same as Medieval. In this connection, it should be observed that there has been

[12] It should be noted that this does not condemn social ownership as unjust. Because private ownership is *better* than common does not necessarily prove that men should adopt that form of holding property.

[13] II, II, Q. LXVI, A. 2.

[14] Cf. Slater, *Moral Theology,* I, p. 438 ff.

going on a gradual transformation of dominion until today we are living under a very different system from that contemplated by the classic theologians under the name of private property. For there is as much difference between feudalism—or direct and absolute ownership and *control* by small proprietors—and capitalism, as between capitalism and the social ownership of capital.

572. Effect of Industrial Revolution on Ownership. St. Thomas and the great classic theologians lived at a time when feudalism had been somewhat softened and was being replaced by a system of small owners. Already in the free towns tradesmen and artisans were banded into powerful guilds and business was conducted from the standpoint of the producer rather than on a competitive basis. Such a condition of affairs lasted until the extensive introduction of steam towards the end of the eighteenth century. But the phenomenon known as the Industrial Revolution marks just as real an abyss between the former system and our own of today as may occur between our own and Socialism at some future date. The transition excited no religious storm, partly because it was brought about by the powers that were already in possession, partly because it was not allied with any well-defined political philosophy. Yet those who know the industrial history of the period cannot fail to realize that it was really a very serious danger to religion. Much of the non-conformity and infidelity in England and in this country can be traced largely to the industrial conditions.

573. How Stock Companies Affect Ownership. Theoretically we may be living under a system of privately owned property, but practically we are not. No matter how much allowance we make for the personal equation, there is much significance in the estimate that ten per cent of the people in the United States own ninety per cent of the property. Such an estimate looms larger if we understand how corporations are today conducted. Fifty-one per cent of the stock can exercise one hundred per cent control; and the owners of the forty-nine per cent, no matter how numerous and well-intentioned, will have no more to say about the employment of their property than the penniless laborer. Moreover, it is possible, if one be on the inside, to gather in fifty-one per cent of the stock by depositing ten per cent of its value, through what is known as buying on margin. A man who has done this is in control of the corporation and its policies. He can declare dividends or pass them, depreciate the value of the stock as a whole or raise it, absolutely without consulting the "owners" of the rest.[15]

574. Holding Companies. The control of property worth 10, 20, 50 times more than they really own can be achieved by the big financiers through holding companies. If, for instance, companies A, B, C, D be each capitalized at one million dollars, then anyone owning or controlling 51 per cent of the stock in each of them can control all of them. The direct and obvious way of doing this is by buying such stock outright. But this would require $2,000,000, and the same object can be accomplished for less. A new corporation, which we shall call Ah, can be organized to hold 51 per cent of the stock of A and B. This would require about $1,000,000. But the man who controls 51 per cent of this stock, or about half a million, will control the $2,000,000 worth of stock of the subsidiary companies. Therefore, he needs only 26 per cent of the combined capitalization of $2,000,000, instead of 51 per cent. If another company, Bh, be organized to hold 51 per cent of the stock of C and of D, it makes possible still another company, Ah^2, to hold 51 per cent of the stock of both Ah and of Bh at a capitalization of about $1,000,000. To control 51 per cent of the stock of this new company would require about half a million, and it would through these holding companies control the $4,000,000 of the original companies. Half a million, therefore, would be controlling $4,-000,000 or 8 times itself. And the process can be carried even

---

[15] For an elaboration of this point, consult "Private Property as It Is," by Wm. J. Kerby, in *The Catholic World*, Feb., 1911.

further. We can represent this graphically by the following figures:

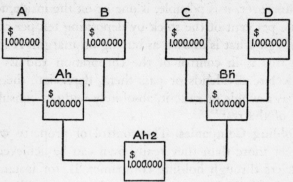

575. Evils of the Present System. The evils resulting from the present system of ownership are many and serious. Whether or not it makes possible a money or credit trust (as Socialists claim), it does allow unscrupulous men to *control* what they do not "own" to the detriment of the legal and moral owners. Also, this absentee ownership of industrial securities produces just as grave evils as the notorious absentee landlordism in Ireland. As Professor E. A. Ross put it, "Distance disinfects dividends," and some of the most kind-hearted, strait-laced people do not scruple to accept interest that was made possible by underpaying and overworking women and children two thousand miles away.

576. Duties of Investors. Persons contemplating investments should consider the use to which their money will be put. If they foresee that it will be used to oppress work people, they cannot escape the responsibility of co-operation. And if they discover after investing that their capital is so employed, they must use what influence they can to change the conduct of the business. Should that be impossible, they should sell their stock. It would seem lawful to sell the stock, because the buyer may be able to exert more pressure than they could. What is sold is not a share in the injustice, but a right to a certain proportionate vote in the company.

577. Remedies for the Evils of Private Ownership. To prevent these evils of absentee ownership, it has been seriously proposed still further to divorce ownership and control. Ownership as being the right to a certain share in any profits, would remain, as also the privilege of disposing of this right as one might wish; but the actual control of the company's policies would be vested in resident directors, elected by a meeting of stockholders held in the factory itself—or, in the case of a railroad, at some point along the line of the road—no proxies being allowed. By bringing the workers and the capitalists together in this way, it is thought that the natural human instincts of charity and fair play will secure just treatment for the laborers.[16]

III. LIMITATIONS OF OWNERSHIP

578. Private Ownership Not Absolute. But whether private ownership flows from the natural law or merely from the *jus gentium,* it is not absolute over external goods. For private ownership, being a secondary right, cannot supersede a primary right. The primary purpose for which corporeal goods were created is that they might be a means to conserve those goods which nature wishes to be common to all. Hence: (a) whoever can work has a strict right to work—*i.e.,* to gain for himself by labor the necessaries of life;[17] (b) whoever cannot work has a moral and a legal right to receive the necessaries of life from the superfluous goods of the rich; (c) anyone in extreme necessity has a strict right to take what is necessary to preserve his life. The dominion of various classes of people is further limited by civil or natural law.

579. Children and Property. Though children may own property, they may not always have the administration of what they own. In relation to children goods are divided into *free,* those

---

[16] Cf. hearings of the Industrial Commission in New York City as reported in *The Survey,* Jan. 30, 1915. Roger W. Babson, president of Babson's Statistical Bureau, Wellesley Hills, Mass., was the one to make the suggestion.

[17] Cf. Noldin, *op. cit.,* II, 69.

acquired by a child by separate industry (outside of the home) or by gift or in some similar way; and *not free,* those the child has acquired by joint labor with a parent. The dominion over free goods resides in the child, but their administration and sometimes their usufruct pertains to the parents. Hence a child who refuses to give his parents such goods over and above the expense of his support does not sin against justice though he may sin against other virtues. When the child works outside but lives with his parents, he should pay for his board; and this may take his whole wage. Should there be anything over and above, the child may secretly keep this back when the parents would spend it on superfluous things or not allow sufficient for reasonable recreation.

580. Wages and Gifts to Children. When working in the family business, a child may not exact pay. One of age may not claim wages for work that was *due* by the fact of his parents having given him life and nourishment; he may exact pay for any work over and above what was so due. Children have dominion over what has been given them absolutely.

581. Married Women and Property. The dominion of married persons is determined by civil law. This varies from country to country and from State to State. The ideal would seem to be that a married woman's rights in her own property and in that of her husband should be just the same as those of her husband in his own and in hers. Whatever motives of policy may have justified a distinction in the past, would seem no longer valid. Yet in some States the property relations between husband and wife are a virtual realization of the old joke, "What's yours is mine, and what's mine is my own." The wife has no control over her husband's property, real or personal. He may dispose of it without her consent and in any way, whereas, the management of her estate is entirely in his hands. Her personal property becomes his property; her real estate is managed by him. He can eject tenants (even his mother-in-law), collect rents, and use the income in any way he pleases. He may give his wife a part of the income from her own property, but he is not bound to do so.[18]

582. Inequalities Between Men and Women. Formerly in Maryland [19] the surviving husband of an intestate woman took a life estate in all his wife's realty. This arrangement sometimes worked extreme hardships to the children. For instance, a wealthy widow with one child—a daughter—remarries and dies without a will. The child, if her mother had only real property, becomes dependent upon the generosity of her step-father. She owns her mother's estate, but can get none of the income until her step-father's death. Until that happens she may be a veritable Cinderella, scrubbing floors and washing dishes while her step-father's children enjoy her mother's money.

583. Husband's Right to Wife's Wages. In many States a man has a legal right to his own wages and they cannot be seized for any debt contracted by his wife without his consent. Yet his wife's wages can be seized for his debts, though she may have had nothing to do with making them and may have been seriously injured by such expenditures. A mistress was once about to pay her cook when she was handed a perfectly legal document requiring her instead to pay the money to a certain saloonkeeper, because the cook's husband had run a bill there. So this woman, besides taking abuse and violence from her husband in his "cups," actually had to pay by her hard work for the liquor that made a beast of him.[20]

584. The Ideal Property Arrangements for Married Persons. The property relations of man and wife should at least be recognized as an equal partnership, though even then most women

[18] S. W. Rep. 63, p. 867; Rev. Statutes 1895, Art. 2967. The Supreme Court of Texas held that during marriage the husband has control of his wife's estate. The Tenn. Rep. 86, p. 333, state that the husband may eject a tenant of lease made by his wife without his consent. As head of the family he controls the wife's realty. According to the same reports (101, p. 347), the husband upon marriage is entitled to his wife's personalty in possession, and at her death to choses in action. A husband recovered land which his wife (who had no issue) had willed to half-brothers and sisters.

[19] Cf. Md. Code 1904, Art. 45, Sec. 7.

[20] This happened in Illinois. The law has since been changed to protect a wife's wages from her husband's creditors. Cf. Ill. Rev. Statutes 1912, p. 1284, Sec. 7.

would probably not be getting the equivalent of what they really contribute. Anything made and saved after marriage (if the source cannot be determined accurately) should be shared half and half; and the wife should have the power of disposing of her portion by will. Comparatively few women are supported by their husbands. The economic contribution of the woman is usually fairly equal to that of the man, as is found out when the mother dies. The husband's wages are then seldom sufficient to buy in the market the same services his wife gave gratis. Her contribution in cooking, washing, sewing, caring for the children, in forcing the income to go as far as possible, in making all that is meant by the word "home," is in most cases worth more than the man's contribution of daily wages.

585. Copyrights and Patents. The dominion of authors brings in some special principles. Author is here taken in a broad sense to mean anyone who by his own talents invents something, as a book, a musical score, a scientific theory, a medical remedy, a new instrument. Before making a work public, an author has, by natural law, perfect dominion over it. Hence anyone who divulges a manuscript or a trade secret against the will of the author is guilty of injustice and must make restitution. After publication an author's rights are determined by civil laws. These laws bind in conscience.

IV. The Acquisition of Dominion

586. Definition. By the mode of acquiring dominion is meant the title or cause of itself suitable to confer ownership. Five different ways are distinguished: *occupation* or *finding, accession, labor, prescription, contract*. Of these, occupation, accession, and labor receive their force from the natural law; prescription from human law; and contract from the private will of men. The acquisition may be *original,* as in the case of occupation, accession and labor; or *derived,* as in prescription and contract.

587. Some Terms. *Vacant objects* are those which never had an owner, as wild animals in a forest or pearls in the sea; *derelict* *objects* are those which had an owner, but actually have not now, as treasures buried centuries ago; *lost objects* are those having an unknown owner. Things lost become derelict when the article is of such trifling value that the owner is presumed to be indifferent about regaining it; when from certain circumstances their owner no longer has any hope of recovering them; or when the owner neglects to recover though he might do so.

588. Occupation. Occupation is the taking possession of something which has no owner, with the intention of acquiring it for one's self. The conditions for acquiring property in this way are: (a) that the object should either be vacant or derelict; (b) that there should be true or real laying hold of it; (c) that there should be the intention of making the article one's own. At present about the only case in which occupation affords a title to property is by hunting, fishing, etc. The civil law usually determines the conditions of occupation and binds in conscience.

589. Finding. Finding is a species of occupation. By natural law the finder of a vacant or derelict object has a good title, but the conditions for acquiring title are usually specified by the civil law. The finder of a lost article may leave it in its place, though one is ordinarily bound in charity to remove it to safety. Whoever takes possession of a lost article is bound in justice to seek the owner (at the owner's expense) and meanwhile to guard it carefully.

590. Accession. Accession is a mode of acquiring dominion whereby something is added to what is already one's own. This may be *natural, industrial,* or *mixed,* according as the increase comes entirely from nature, entirely from human industry, or from both.

591. Natural Accession. Natural accession may be by *fructification,* as in the case of trees; by *birth,* as in animals; by *deposits,* as in changing of a river course. The general principle is *res fructificat domino,* but in each case the civil law usually determines ownership.

592. Industrial Accession. Industrial accession may be: (a) by *specification,* giving a new form, as making bread out of flour;

(b) by *joining,* as when a jewel is set in a ring; (c) by *mixing,* as when two wines are poured into the same vessel; (d) by *building,* as when one erects an edifice upon another's ground. The general law is that the gain should go to the one who contributed most to the combined value, the principal, but the civil law determines this matter.

593. Mixed Accession. Property acquired by *mixed accession*—as by planting in another's field—belongs to him whose property or labor chiefly contributed to the increase, unless otherwise determined by civil law.

594. Labor.[21] By labor is understood human industry, whether spiritual or corporal, suitable for producing goods. Some political philosophers [22] contend that labor is the *only* just title to ownership. This is an evident exaggeration, for all labor deals ultimately with some pre-existing raw material. The pen with which this is written is not due to human labor alone; since a certain ore was necessary for its manufacture, the labor of making the pen cannot by itself give a title to it.

595. Labor as a Just Title. But though labor is not the only, nor even the primary title to ownership, it is a just and legitimate title. For since man is lord of his own actions, both of soul and body, he can exercise his powers either in his own name or in that of another. In the first instance, he is by natural law the owner of the fruits of his labor, whereas in the second case, he has a right to an appropriate wage. What this wage should be will be determined more specifically when we come to treat of wages.

596. Prescription. Prescription is a mode of acquiring ownership by possession in the way and for the time prescribed by the civil or ecclesiastical law.

597. Prescription Is a Just Title. Prescription is a legitimate title to ownership because for serious reasons affecting the common good, human law can, even against the wishes of the owner,

[21] In so far as labor is used in the sense of a wage contract it will be treated under contracts.

[22] Cf. Ryan, *Distributive Justice,* Sec. I, Ch. III.

transfer dominion from one person to another.[23] The reasons in this case are: (a) to prevent ownership being uncertain for a long time; (b) that lawsuits may be easily settled or altogether avoided; (c) that conscientious doubts and fears of losing possessions may be removed; (d) to enforce diligence in the care of one's rights.

598. Conditions for Prescription. There are five conditions required for legitimate prescription:

599. (1) Aptness of Objects. The object must be such as to be apt for dominion by this particular person. Public property may be prescribed by one community against another but not by a private person; stolen articles may not be prescribed by the thief.

600. (2) Good Faith. Good faith is an erroneous judgment by which one prudently judges that an article in his possession is really his. If one has not from the start this erroneous judgment he cannot legitimately begin prescription. And if bad faith takes the place of good faith before the expiration of the time set by law, the prescription is interrupted. Should civil law require good faith in the beginning only, this provision does not avail in conscience. Such a law should be interpreted to mean merely that judicial action is denied, not that it transfers dominion. Whether the bad faith of a predecessor who began prescription invalidates the claim of the successor who himself has in good faith possessed the object for the full time required by law, depends upon the law in that locality. Some codes admit such prescription in the case of a *particular* or *universal mediate successor;* but not of a *universal immediate successor;* other codes allow such prescription even by a universal immediate successor.[24]

601. (3) An Apparent Title. Title is the reason why one thinks a certain article belongs to him, as because he has bought it, or someone has given it to him. A title may be either *apparent* or

[23] Noldin, *Theol. Mor.,* II, 359, 401.

[24] A universal successor is one who succeeds to the whole right of another by some *general* title, whether there be one or many heirs and whether or not the predecessor die intestate. A particular successor is one who succeeds by a particular or *specific* title to some determined thing, as by purchase, gift, or legacy. An immediate successor succeeds directly to the predecessor, a mediate successor follows the immediate.

true. Apparent titles are divided into: (a) *color of title* (titulus coloratus), a cause truly existing but invalidated by some secret defect, as a purchase from a thief; (b) *opined title* is a cause thought to exist, though in reality it does not, as if a person gives money to a servant to buy something and thinks the servant has bought the article when he has stolen it; (c) *presumed title* is a cause capable of transferring dominion which has not taken place, and is not thought to have taken place, but which the law supposes on account of the length of possession. A true title is not required for prescription, for if it were present there would be no need of prescription. At least an apparent title is necessary, else prescription could not begin in good faith. Color of title or opined titles are sufficient unless the other party can clearly prove his own title.

602. (4) Continuous Possession. Possession should be continuous. Prescription once begun can either *sleep* or be *interrupted*. In the one case, the intervening impediment simply suspends prescription, so that prescription may be taken up again later and the two parts added together; in the other, use of bad faith or loss of possession, prescription is lost entirely and must be commenced all over again.

603. (5) Time Determined by Civil Law. Time required for prescription is not determined definitely by natural law. This is left to human law. Prescription of over thirty years avails in conscience; ethicians disagree as to whether prescription over three years holds in conscience or only prohibits legal action, because the mind of the legislators is not clear; moralists are commonly united in asserting that prescription less than three years does not hold in conscience, because the legislators did not intend that it should.[25]

SUGGESTED READINGS

1. Kelleher, *Private Ownership,* Ch. I.
2. Ryan, *Distributive Justice,* Ch. XXI.
3. Grafton, "A Catholic Social Platform," *Catholic World,* Sept., 1911.
4. Kerby, "Private Property as It Is," *Catholic World,* Feb., 1911.

[25] Noldin, *Theol. Mor.,* II, p. 407.

5. Carver, *Essays in Social Justice,* Ch. IX.
6. Cronin, *Science of Ethics,* II, Chs. IV, V, VI, VII, VIII.
7. Finlay, "Socialism and Catholic Teaching," *Studies,* Sept., 1919.
8. O'Rahilly, "St. Thomas's Theory of Property," *Studies,* Sept., 1920.
9. Wallis, *Safeguard Productive Capital.*

QUESTIONS

1. Do Scholastic moralists hold that in the beginning dominion over temporal goods was common to all?
2. When Scholastic moralists say that private ownership is based on natural law, what do they mean?
3. What limit should be placed on the State monopolizing means of production, distribution and exchange?
4. Is private ownership the same today as in the classic days of Scholasticism?
5. Is private ownership absolute?
6. How may ownership be acquired?

SEVEN: *Contracts*

604. Importance of Contracts. In discussing ownership, we said that one of the five ways of acquiring dominion was by contract. Today this is probably the most important way. By far the greater part of all property is owned on account of some contract. Comparatively little property is acquired by prescription, or by labor directly applied, or by finding. Therefore this particular mode of acquiring ownership by contract merits separate and somewhat extensive treatment.

605. Definition of Contract. A contract may be defined as the consent of two or more persons regarding the transfer of a right.

606. Division of Contracts. Contracts are divided: (1) *By reason of their effect* into (a) *unilateral contracts,* those inducing an obligation in only one of the contracting parties, as a gift or promise, and *bilateral contracts,* those inducing an obligation on both sides, as a sale, interest; (b) *naked contracts,* those inducing an obligation only in conscience, and *clothed contracts,* those inducing an obligation also in the external forum; (2) *By reason of the manner* into (a) *consensual contracts,* those essentially performed by the mere consent of parties, and *real* (executed), where an actual delivery of the article is necessary; (b) *solemn contracts,* those entered into with certain formalities; and *simple contracts;* (c) *formal contracts,* those exhibiting the consent expressly by words or signs; and *virtual contracts* where consent is silent; (3) *Contracts of a certain event,* where something is to be done or given independently of chance, as gifts, renting; and *gambling contracts,* those in which the doing or giving depends upon some fortuitous event, as in betting, or in cards; (4) *Pure contracts,* where no condition is mentioned; and *qualified contracts,* where the conditions are stated.

607. Conditions Necessary for Validity. Four conditions are necessary for a valid contract: (a) suitable matter; (b) competent persons; (c) mutual consent; (d) reason for consent.

608. Matter of Contracts. In general whatever can be an object of dominion—whether an article, an action, or the omission of an action—can become matter of contract. Specifically, five elements must combine to make the matter suitable—the object must be *possible, existing, one's own, honorable, and of an estimable price.* The *possibility* must be both *physical* and *moral,* unless one expressly obligates himself to what is very difficult. A contract cannot be made about a thing that *does not exist and is not expected* to exist. Nor can one contract to give what he does not own, except when he reasonably expects to own it. There can be no obligation to perform a dishonorable act. Finally, the object of a contract must have appreciable value. One cannot validly contract about anything already in justice due the other person, as a judge to pass a sentence. If the object be due from some virtue other than justice, the contract is *valid,* though *illicit.*

609. Persons Contracting. By natural law anyone having the use of reason is capable of contracting; and anyone without the use of reason is incapable. Positive human law, however, limits this right to those who have free administration of their property. By this provision *minors,* and to some extent in some places *married women,* are excluded. When such persons have acted without fraud, they may take advantage of the civil law. In some places this law makes their contracts rescindable, or relieves them from the obligation of restoring an accepted article if it no longer exists in itself or its equivalent.

610. Consent. For a contract to be valid in natural law, the consent must be: (1) *true* or *internal,* not merely external or feigned; (2) *free* and *deliberate,* that is, endowed with that advertence, deliberation, and voluntariness necessary for a perfectly human act; (3) *mutual,* that is, given by both parties about the same object; (4) shown by some *sensible sign,* so that it can be perceived and accepted by the other person. Silence, however, gives consent when the contract is favorable to the silent party. But when a contract imposes an obligation on a silent party, his silence must not be construed as consent in onerous contracts, unless he could easily have contradicted the impression created by his silence that he was consenting.

611. Error. *Error* or *deceit, force* or *fear* may invalidate contracts. Error is a mistaken judgment. *Substantial* error is concerned: (a) about the substance of an object, as mistaking brass for gold; (b) or about a substantial quality of the object, on account of which consent is given, as the noble birth of one party to a marriage; (c) or about the substance of a contract, as when one supposes the contract concerns a gift, when it concerns a sale. *Accidental* error is concerned with: (a) an *accidental quality of the object,* as when one buys two-year-old wine thinking it is four years old; (b) or about an *accidental quality of the contract,* as when one thought the price was to be paid in one coin rather than another. *Antecedent* error is such that had it not existed one would not have contracted. *Concomitant* error is such that even if it had not existed one would have contracted.

612. When Error Invalidates a Contract. Any *substantial* error, even though merely concomitant, invalidates a contract because there is a defect in the consent given to the substance of the contract. For anyone who misapprehends the substance of a thing, does not consent to that thing, but to something else. If the substantial error was caused by the deceit of the other party, he is bound to repair the injury resulting from the error.

613. When Error Does Not Invalidate a Contract. No *accidental* error, even though caused by the other party, invalidates a contract. For consent to the substance of a contract is sufficient to make the contract valid. But usually when the error has been caused by one of the contracting parties, the other may at his option rescind the contract.

614. Fear as Affecting Contracts. A contract is made through fear, if fear furnishes the motive for consent in such a way that but for fear it would not have been given. In general, such contracts are valid provided the fear does not take away the use of reason, because the consent is a perfectly human act. Even grave fear, which is not caused unjustly, does not render the contract either invalid or rescindable. But fear, whether grave or slight, unjustly caused for the purpose of extorting consent, though it does not by natural law invalidate the contract, makes it rescindable at the option of the party suffering the fear. The same is true when the fear was not caused to extort consent, provided it was caused by a party to the contract.

615. Contracts to Commit Crime. Contracts entered into for the sake of crime or under conditions of performing a criminal act are invalid in the sense that before they are fulfilled either party may withdraw; and the price, if paid, should be restored. But if the crime has already been committed, the price may justly be demanded, unless the civil law declares otherwise.

616. The Obligation of Contracts. The obligation arising from a contract may be either (a) *natural,* that flowing from the nature of the contract and binding in conscience, but not affording ground for action at law, as the obligation arising from a gratuitous promise; (b) *civil,* that deriving from the civil law and giving action in court, but not binding in conscience, as the obligation of a wife to allow her husband to administer her personal property where the civil law provides for this; and (c) *mixed,* that binding in conscience and furnishing an action in law, as the obligation of an employer to pay wages for work done.

617. Principles Governing Contracts. Every valid contract produces an obligation in conscience, though not necessarily the same obligation as that recognized by civil law. Excepting a gratuitous promise, the natural obligation arising from a contract binds from commutative justice. The gravity of the obligation is *proportionate to the matter of the contract;* serious in serious matter, slight in slight matter. A rescindable contract binds until the one who has the right to rescind does so.

618. Discussion of Contracts. Contracts will be treated under three general classes: (a) *unilateral* contracts; (b) *bilateral* contracts depending upon an event that is certain; (c) *gambling* contracts.

619. Promises. Unilateral contracts separate into *gifts, promises,* and *testaments. A promise is a contract whereby anyone obligates* *himself to another to do or to omit something.* To be valid a promise: (a) must be made with the intention of binding one's self; (b) it must be manifested exteriorly; and (c) must be accepted. The intention of the person promising determines whether the promise binds from fidelity or from justice. There is this difference between the two, that a promise binding from fidelity obliges only under slight inconvenience even in important matters, unless serious damage would occur to the promisee; whereas a promise binding from justice obliges under serious inconvenience when the matter is serious. Also an obligation arising from fidelity gives the promisee no right *in rem*[1] or *ad rem*. But an obligation of justice arising from a promise gives the promisee a right *ad rem*, though not *in rem*.

620. When Promises Cease. A promise, even though binding from justice, ceases: (a) if there should intervene a notable change of circumstances, which if foreseen would have prevented the promise. This is because every promise is made under the implied condition—*if it can be fulfilled without serious inconvenience;* (b) again a promise ceases to bind if before fulfillment the sole or principal motive of the promise ceases; (c) and finally, promises cease to bind if without the fault of the promisor the promise is rendered impossible, illicit, or useless to the promisee.

621. How Far Promises Bind Heirs. Whether an unfulfilled promise should be executed after the death of the promisor depends upon his intention. A *real*[2] promise not fulfilled before the death of the promisor passes to the heirs, unless his intention was otherwise; a *personal* promise does not.

622. Gifts. A gift is a contract through which the ownership of anything is gratuitously transferred by one person to another. It differs from a promise binding in justice in that it gives a right *in rem* and not merely *ad rem*. Naturally, a gift should be made from one's own belongings. Anyone receiving articles of

---

[1] See paragraph 475.
[2] A *real promise* concerns something external to the promisor which can be fulfilled just as well by someone else, as to give alms; a *personal promise* concerns some action of the promisor, as to make a certain journey or to marry.

value knowing that they are really due to creditors, is bound to restitution; if he has not known the indebtedness of the giver and no longer has the article in his possession, he is not so bound.[3]

623. Conditions for Validity of Gifts. By the natural law a gift made and accepted is valid. The civil law, however, may add other conditions, as that there should be some public record of the transaction. But gifts invalid in civil law, may be valid in conscience notwithstanding the decision of a court. If the giver or recipient should die before the handing over of the gift, the same principles hold as for promises.[4]

624. Testaments. *Hereditary succession* is the right of succeeding to the goods and rights of a dead person. The person succeeding to the entire right of the deceased is called an *heir,* and he succeeds by a *universal title,* whether it be to the whole or a part of the deceased's property, whether by will or by law (intestate).

625. When Testaments Are Valid. By a *last will* is understood that disposition by which one determines what shall be done with his goods after his death. From the fact that it is a *last* will it is evident that the testator retains dominion until death and that wills are revocable. All that the natural law requires for validity is that the disposition should be evidently the intention of the deceased; but the civil law may require certain formalities.

626. The Right to Dispose of Property by Testament. Natural law does not determine one's right to dispose of property by testament. So far as the nature of things goes, a man's dominion in material things ceases the moment he can no longer use them —that is, by death. The civil law may or may not concede this right of testament. Civil law may determine that the property of the deceased persons should go to certain heirs, or to the State. As a matter of fact, various nations have limited this power considerably, and the tendency today is to impose heavy inheritance taxes. It is only within recent years that cardinals have been al-

[3] Noldin, II, 548.
[4] See paragraph 609 ff.

lowed by canon law to make wills. Previously their property reverted automatically to the Church. There is no obligation, *per se,* to make a will; there may be *per accidens,* in order to make restitution. But if a will be made, one is obliged by the natural law to leave one's children, if possible, enough to enable them to live according to their station. The determination by the civil law of a legitimate part to be left to a necessary heir, binds in conscience unless the heir be unworthy. Hence, if without just cause, a father deprives his son of what should be his legitimate inheritance, he sins gravely and the recipient is bound to restitution. The same holds true regarding gifts that render a parent incapable of leaving his necessary heirs their legitimate portions.

I. BILATERAL CONTRACTS OF AN EVENT THAT IS CERTAIN

627. Deposits. A *deposit* is a contract by which anything is received for the purpose of being guarded and restored to the owner in its natural condition. The custodian is obliged to use the same diligence in protecting the article as if it were his own. He may not use the article without at least the reasonably presumed permission of its owner. Should damage happen to the article through the custodian's fault he is bound to restore. The depositor ought to pay the fee agreed upon and repair any damage suffered on account of the deposit.

628. Commodates. A *commodate* is a contract by which something is granted to another merely for use for a specific time with the obligation of returning it.

629. Obligation of the Borrower. One who borrows an article for a certain use should not employ it in some other way; he should bear the ordinary expense demanded by the use of the thing, as feed for a horse; he should diligently guard the article from damage and repair any injury happening through his carelessness or by his use in a way not contemplated in the contract; he should restore the object at the time agreed upon.

630. Obligation of the Lender. One who lends is bound to advise the borrower of any serious defects in the object lent. If he omits this in bad faith, he is obliged to restitution. He should meet any ordinary expenses the borrower undergoes to preserve the object borrowed, provided they were not necessitated through the borrower's fault. Also he should not demand the return of the object before the time agreed upon has elapsed unless through some unforeseen cause he should need it immediately.

631. Commissions. *A commission is a contract whereby one person undertakes to do business in the name of another.* The person accepting the commission should use the same diligence in its fulfillment as if it were his own affair. He is bound to observe the terms of the commission, and any loss caused by his failure so to act should be borne by him. All gain coming from the business belongs to the person entrusting it unless otherwise agreed in the contract. The person giving the commission to another should observe all the terms of the contract, should pay all necessary and useful expenses, and should compensate for any loss not due to the fault of the person accepting the commission. If the success of the business depends upon the activity of the commission-merchant or broker, he should not accept a fee from both parties.

632. Loans. *A loan is a contract by which something consumable in first use is transferred to another with the obligation of returning at a given time something else of the same kind and quality.* The borrower becomes the owner of the thing loaned, so that if the thing perishes it perishes to him, if the thing fructifies it fructifies to him. Loans differ from *commodates* or renting, because in loans dominion is transferred over the article consumable in first use, and something similar or of the same species should be returned; loans differ from *exchange* because in exchange the other article is transferred immediately.

633. Is a Loan a Gratuitous Contract? *Per se,* a loan is a gratuitous contract. Hence the lender may not impose any other burden than the return at a given time of another article of the same kind and quality. It has always been held among Scholastic moralists that one sins against justice by exacting a price for the *use* of an article consumable in first use, since the use has no value apart from the thing. If one uses wine, he consumes the wine. The use cannot be separated from the wine. To require payment upon this ground of use, or to require excessive payment upon some other title is usury—a gain unjustly received from a loan. Since usury is appropriating something to which one has not title, it is contrary to natural law, and has frequently been condemned.[5]

634. When a Loan Is Not Gratuitous. *Per accidens,* however, by some external title [6] it may be lawful to demand a price (interest) for a loan.[7] The recognized external titles are: (a) *cessation of gain,* when the lender loses what he would have gained by keeping the article or by using it himself; (b) *damage,* or a positive detriment caused by the loan; (c) *danger of loss* through the possibility of the borrower's being unable to pay back; (d) a *conventional fine* in case the article is not returned at a specified time. In addition some Scholastic moralists admit civil law as a valid title to interest, since the State may transfer dominion in material goods from one to another when grave public considerations demand this.[8]

635. Application to Money Loans. Money is the principal object of loans today. In itself money is sterile, and hence does not justify the charging of interest for its loan. But it is equivalent to fruitful objects, and present economic conditions are such as to justify interest.[9] "Every unit of capital that anyone offers for hire has a productive power; it can call into existence a certain amount of goods. The offer of it to an *entrepreneur* is virtually an offer of a fresh supply of the kinds of goods which he is making for sale. Lending ten thousand dollars to a woolen manufacturer is really selling the amount of cloth that ten thousand dollars, put into his equipment, will bring into existence. Lending a hundred thousand dollars to a manufacturer of steel so as to

[5] Noldin, II, 575.

[6] An external title is a cause apart from the essence of a loan.

[7] For a full discussion of interest, cf. John A. Ryan, *The Church and Interest-Taking;* Cleary, *The Church and Usury.*

[8] Noldin, II, 578.

[9] Cathrein, *Moralphilosophie,* II, 359 ff; Antoine, *Cours d'Economie Sociale.*

enable him in some way to perfect his equipment, is virtually selling him the number of girders or rails that he can make by virtue of this accession to his plant." [10]

636. How Money Is Fruitful.

Hence interest is defined by economists as "what is paid to the owners of capital goods as remuneration for the services these goods render in production." [11] How capital goods affect production is usually explained by positing their increase in any given business while other elements—labor and land—remain the same. The increase in production is said to be due to capital; and capital's share of the total product in the distribution would be this increase in production multiplied by the ratio that the increase of capital bears to the whole capital. [12] Assuming that ten units of capital and ten units of labor produce a given amount, if we increase the capital by one unit, we shall also increase the product. Since the units of labor remain the same, the increase is attributed to the increase in capital, and is said to be the product of one unit of capital. And as eleven units of capital are now at work, it is concluded that the total product of capital would be eleven times the amount produced by one unit.

637. Abuses of Interest.

But this does not justify the charging of exorbitant interest. In spite of the findings of the Russell Sage Foundation and the legally approved rate in some States, $2\frac{1}{2}\%$ or 3% a month would seem to be excessive interest for pawn brokers or those making small chattel loans. In many instances, too, the charges for installment buying are too high. But many of the victims have it in their power to remedy matters by establishing credit unions. [13] From the standpoint of developing character, it would be much better that people should help themselves in some such way, rather than trust to the government curing ills by cumbersome legislation.

[10] Clark, *Essentials of Economic Theory*, p. 149.
[11] Seager, *Introduction to Economics*, 3rd ed., p. 275. The fact that he calls the lender of money the owner of capital goods does not essentially affect the question.
[12] Cf. Carver, *Distribution of Wealth, Essays in Social Justice.*
[13] Ham & Robinson, *Credit Union Primer*, Russell Sage Foundation.

638. Buying and Selling. *Buying and selling is a contract in which two persons agree between themselves about delivering possession of an article for a price.* It is essential that there should be (a) mutual consent, (b) something movable or immovable possession of which is to be delivered, and (c) money as a price. For if there were commercial articles on both sides or money on both sides, it would be respectively barter or exchange, not sale.

639. Obligations of Seller. The article sold should be at least morally what the buyer wants. If it be physically different, but practically as good, the contract is valid; as when a druggist sells a medicine that will serve the purpose just as well. But if it be essentially different, the contract is invalid; as when a merchant substitutes an artificial article for a natural one, *e.g.,* a wine not made from grapes. Also the article sold should belong to the seller, for the seller cannot *per se* transfer dominion that he has not himself. However if the civil law provides that the buyer acting in good faith acquires dominion, this avails in conscience.[14]

640. Distinction Between Defects. *Substantial defects* are those rendering the article harmful, or at least plainly useless for the end of the buyer; *accidental defects* make the object merely less *apt* for the purpose for which it is intended; *obvious defects* are those easily perceived by all; *hidden defects* are those that cannot easily be discovered.

641. When Buying Contracts Are Void or Voidable. If the seller does not manifest substantial defects, even though no enquiries be made, the contract is void; and he is bound to restore the price paid. Enquiry regarding defects, in general or particular, obliges the seller to declare accidental defects, whether obvious or hidden; and if this declaration be not made, the contract is voidable. If no enquiry be made, the seller is not bound to manifest accidental defects; and the contract is valid and licit, provided there was not fraud and the price was lowered in proportion to the defect. But if the buyer be so unskilled that he can-

14 Noldin, II, 589.

not see even obvious defects, the seller should warn him about them all.

642. Delivery. The seller is bound to deliver the article in the same condition in which it was bought and in the place, way, and time agreed upon. In the meantime, he is bound to guard the article as if he were its custodian. Should the article be injured through his formal guilt, he is bound, even prior to a judgment by a civil court, to make good the loss. If he be not formally responsible for the loss, he is not bound to restitution until a civil court determines the matter. Any fruit of a sold article belongs to the buyer, unless there be a different agreement or the civil law provides otherwise.

643. Obligations of the Buyer. A purchaser is bound to warn one who through ignorance intends to sell his goods for less than a just price, or at least a purchaser must give the lowest price consistent with justice. Having agreed upon the price, he must pay it. He must, moreover, accept the goods when delivered according to the terms of the contract. And finally he must use his power as a purchaser for the highest social good.

644. Value and Price. Price is the exchange value [15] of an article expressed in money. *Legal price* is what is determined by public authority. In some American municipalities the weight of a loaf of bread to be sold for five cents is fixed by the city council or commissioners. Legal price binds in conscience from commutative justice.[16] *Common* or *natural* price is the exchange value determined by the common estimate of them. This is not mathematically definite. There may be a variation of considerable extent. However, a merchant dealing in the necessaries of life should not depart more than an approximate 10 per cent from the average price.[17]

[15] Value is one of the most complex of economic and ethical questions. There are few difficulties so long as we confine ourselves to exchange values. But value in use and "essential value" introduce complications. We can only get upon solid ground by going back to our discussion of the end of man. Use and value then acquire ultimate meaning, at least in the abstract. For the time being, however, it is sufficient to restrict the discussion to exchange value. When luxury is considered it will be necessary to go deeper. Cf. Slater, *Questions of Moral Theology.*

[16] Noldin, II, 595.   [17] Noldin, II, 596.

645. When a Price Is Just. Where the law does not determine the price, the *natural* price is just. The common estimate renders this price just, even though it may be imprudent. Hence, moralists hold that a trader may exchange glass beads for gold when the savages of a certain section are willing to accept the bargain.[18] But one who sells above the highest, or buys below the lowest natural price, commits injustice; and he is bound to restitution even before a legal decision. The only circumstances excusing him from restitution before a judicial decision would be the fact that he would suffer peculiar loss by the transaction, or that he has a special affection for the article, or that the article would be bought at the same price by someone else.

646. Conventional Price. Conventional price is the exchange value determined between buyer and seller concerning an article for which there is no open market, as a very rare coin, or a diamond of extraordinary size. This price is just unless it is plainly too large or too small. But, although ordinarily justice is fulfilled if a person pay either the legal or the market price, neither is really based on justice. The price fixed by law will come closer to being a just price. In a self-governing community a legal price will probably not do a great injustice to either seller or buyer for any length of time. In this country, however, outside of war times, the field of legal price is so limited that it may be disregarded in the present discussion.

647. Why Market Price May Not Be Just. The market price, however, makes no pretense of being determined by justice. It is the shrewdness of one man pitted against the shrewdness of another, or even the greed of one against another's need. One wants to sell for as high a price while the other wants to buy for as low a price as he can. When there are numerous buyers and numerous sellers, all knowing their business fairly well, the

---

[18] Cf. DeLugo, *De Just. et Jure,* Disp. 26, n. 42. When you go deeply enough, savages are no more foolish in giving gold for glass than Europeans are in giving it for diamonds. Europeans want diamonds merely because there is a common demand for them among their associates. Ordinarily, the purchaser of a diamond cannot tell the real article from a clever imitation, which proves that he does not want the diamond for itself.

result will be a close approximation to what would be a just price, if the cost to the *entrepreneur* producing the commodities, or the person managing the distributing agency were all that should be taken into consideration. In a society where the actual producer sells directly to the consumer, where there is no production on an enormous scale employing hundreds and thousands of persons who have no voice in fixing the price of the product, then the price reached by the higgling of the market is likely to be just.

648. Medieval Prices Usually Just. Under the medieval system of craftsmen and one or two journeymen or apprentices who formed part of the household, it was possible, as there was no competition, to maintain the rate of reward by limiting the supply. "No serious attempt was made to push trade or develop business, but only to carry on each trade according to the standard on which it was organized and to maintain the habitual rate of reward. According to this policy, the conditions of the producer were allowed to be the first consideration; and the consumer had to pay a price at which these conditions could be maintained." [19]

649. Competition and Prices. But conditions of business have changed immensely since the Middle Ages. The Industrial Revolution has brought big-scale production. This has driven out of existence the small producer ministering directly and immediately to the wants of the community. Department stores have applied the same principle in the distributing end of industry and have largely replaced the small retailer. The ones most concerned, the employees of big manufacturers or distributors, have no voice in fixing the price of the article made or distributed by their labor. As a consequence, competition will often depress the price below the point where it will yield a living wage to them. Not their rights, but what crude, irresistible hunger will force them to accept determines this point. Many times it is only a difference between starving rapidly or slowly. Competition, however, is inexorable.

[19] W. Cunningham, *Christianity and Social Questions*, p. 114.

650. Rent and Interest as Affecting Prices. It is true, that sometimes the actual producers or distributors may not be getting living wages, because the *entrepreneurs,* or the rent-takers, or the interest-takers are absorbing too much. But ordinarily it is probable that stress of competition between capitalists and between managers will keep their shares within fairly moderate bounds. Capital competes with capital for a share in production, just as one firm competes with another to secure a market for its products. Hence in any given case when nothing is known to the contrary, it may reasonably be presumed that where laborers are not sufficiently remunerated it is because the price obtained for their product will not cover just wages. And appearances are not always a safe guide. A man who owns and manages a factory (thus drawing by himself alone wages of management, rent, and interest) may seem able easily to afford higher wages, yet to divide his whole income among all his employees might give only an inappreciable increase to each.

651. The Fundamental Principle for Determining Price. Therefore, it would seem that the principle that the market price is just, cannot be strictly applied today. On the contrary, many persons claim that the market price fixed by competition is usually unjust. A better principle, a more fundamental principle, one that really strikes its roots down into justice itself, would be to say that a just price is one that will yield a just return to all concerned—the actual laborers who produce commodities, the clerks in the stores who distribute them, wages of management to the *entrepreneurs,* and interest to the capitalists.

652. Real "Value." Certainly if this just return be not yielded to all, the equality between the "value" of the article and the price is not preserved. And as Ballerini says: "When the equality is not preserved, so that the seller sells for more than the highest price, or the buyer buys for less than the lowest . . . injustice is committed." [20]

653. Duty of Purchasers. Theoretically a purchaser should pay a price that will allow just wages. But practically it is very diffi-

[20] Cf. Ballerini, *Theol. Mor.,* Tr. VII, No. 380.

cult for him to know what such a price is for each of the multitude of articles offered for sale. Some years ago the National Consumers League undertook to investigate conditions, and issued its label to factories meeting its standard. Also it published a "white list" of retailers. A few articles, as for example shoes and men's hats, bear a union label. But neither unions nor the Consumers League have been able to cover a very large field with their labels, still less have they been able to organize consumers sufficiently to exert much pressure upon manufacturers and retailers to maintain fair conditions.

654. How Best-Intentioned Co-operate in Injustice. Where consumers are organized in a co-operative they can, and usually do, pay just wages to their employees, and the scope of their influence is broadened when the consumer co-operatives conduct wholesale and producer co-operatives. As a general thing, however, the individual consumer has very little opportunity of directing his purchases in such a way that he will not co-operate at least remotely in injustice. The disturbing feature of the situation is that no matter how willing to do the right thing, the purchaser is forced innumerable times into co-operation with what is socially undesirable. He buys grade A milk for which the producers are not getting sufficient remuneration; he buys first class bread, but the wheat farmers are not getting a fair price; he goes to a decent movie and thereby helps a theater to show other pictures that are obscene; he buys a newspaper and in so doing helps the demoralizing spread of lurid descriptions of crime and scandal. The most straitlaced and determined moralist is so enmeshed in the complexities of modern life that he cannot make all his own actions thoroughly good.

655. Definition of Luxuries. Is the purchaser, then, justified in directing labor and capital merely for selfish gratification? May he conscientiously indulge in luxuries? "To give precision to the discussion, luxuries may be defined as all economic goods which are not necessaries. The latter term includes not merely the food, clothing, and shelter necessary to life, but the entire complex of goods which each industrial class finds necessary to its industrial efficiency. The decision as to what these goods are is not to be made by reference to any absolute standard, but through study of each class affected. For example, manual laborers in the United States would certainly include tobacco among the necessaries of life and the economist should include it also in discussing his problems, for the simple reason that the average manual laborer would continue to buy tobacco even though his earnings were too small to allow him to buy in addition goods indispensable to his industrial efficiency. Tobacco is to him a conventional necessary. A formal definition of economic necessaries would be this: The things absolutely necessary to the industrial efficiency of the average family in the class considered, together with the things that are preferred above the absolute necessaries by the member of the family who directs its consumption." [21]

656. Social Returns Should Determine Expenditures. The principle on which we are to judge expenditures is that of social returns. This principle is explained by Seager and was elaborated in the chapter on *Charity*. When no proportionate gain results to society from spending money in a certain way, then that way of spending money is not justified.[22]

657. Auctions. Auctions are sales in which an article is sold to the highest bidder. The sellers are bound to sell to the highest bidder, even though the price be below the smallest price, unless custom warrant withdrawing in such a case. The seller may not advance the price by fictitious bids from persons who do not intend to buy.[23] Buyers may not use force or fraud to persuade others not to bid. Since the seller has no real right that persons

---

[21] Seager, *Introduction to Economics*, 3rd ed., p. 73.

[22] On the question of luxury, consult Bosanquet, *Civilization of Christendom*, pp. 268-303; MacCunn, *Ethics of Citizenship*, pp. 193-225; Sidgwick, in *International Journal of Ethics*, Oct., 1894. The change in the use of the word "luxury" is very interesting. In English it means an article not necessary. In thinking of a luxury it never occurs to anyone to restrict the term to sexual immorality. Yet in Latin this is the meaning of the word. Was this because sexual gratification loomed so large among the Romans that this was the first thing to be secured after the necessaries of life? And does the change in usage indicate a moral change for the better? Let us hope so.

[23] Noldin, *Theol. Mor.*, No. 601.

should attend the auction, buyers will not violate justice in persuading others not to bid. In doing this, however, buyers may offend against charity.[24]

658. Monopolies. A monopoly is the exclusive power of selling certain articles. Monopolies may be either *legal*—that is, due to law—as the postoffice; or they may be *natural,* as following from natural limitation, such as anthracite coal; or of *organization,* due to the possession of facilities on such a scale as to preclude profitable competition, as in the case of telephone companies; or they may be due to the *use of a secret process.*

659. Monopolies and Price Fixing. *Public legal monopolies,* such as the postoffice, are in themselves morally justifiable and may charge almost any price. For what is over and above what would otherwise be a just price may be considered an indirect tax. *Private legal monopolies,* such as water companies in some towns, are also justifiable, but they may not charge more than a reasonable price. *Natural monopolies*—fraud and force excluded—are not unjust, but they must not raise the price above what would be the highest price were there no monopoly.[25] It is evidently within the right of the State to determine this highest price in case of controversy.

660. Definition of Rent.[26] Ethically, rent is a contract by which a certain price is paid to the owner of anything for its use or usufruct. In this sense it is applied to animals and non-commercial buildings as well as to land. Economists, however, prefer to restrict it to land and define it as "the share of income that is assigned or paid to the owners of land, sources of water power, and other gifts of nature which assist production, for the use of these factors." [27] "The amount of rent of a piece of land is the product that can be realized by applying to it labor and capital, minus the product that can be realized by applying the same

[24] Lehmkuhl, *Theol. Mor.,* No. 1121.
[25] Noldin, *Theol. Mor.,* No. 604.
[26] Cf. Antoine, *Cours d'Economie Sociale,* pp. 569 ff; Garriguet, *Régime de la Propriété,* II, Ch. II.
[27] Seager, *Introduction to Economics,* 3rd ed., p. 206.

amount of labor and capital to land of the poorest grade that is in cultivation at all." [28]

661. Determination of Rent. Ordinarily, rent is not determined scientifically. The prospective renter does not actually experiment with the poorest land and the land he expects to rent. There is simply a guess by many different people to establish the market value. [29]

662. Is Rent Morally Justifiable? Scholastic moralists universally sanction rent. And they are more concerned in insisting upon the duties of the tenant to fulfill his contract, to repair damages for which he is ethically guilty, and any damage adjudged against him by a court, than to consider the morality of rent in general. But even though rent be justified in the abstract, it can in the concrete be too high. There are profiteering landlords who drain the life-blood of poor people. They are just as guilty as any pawnbroker charging usurious interest. The general principle regarding rent is that no one has a right to a greater return on such investment than the prevailing or legal rate of interest. Certainly the State has a right to step in to regulate rent, just as well as interest, and the providing of homes at a reasonable rent is a legitimate government activity. It is also a very admirable undertaking for private capitalists.

663. Abuses of Rent System. Anyone who wishes to know how the power to exact rent is abused can profitably read Norman Thomas's chapters in his *Human Exploitation*. Real estate developments, share cropping, tenement houses, are all various phases of the problem of rent. Farmers in the corn belt are not making a fair return partly because the price of agricultural land was too high in prosperous times, and they themselves were somewhat responsible for the price. In addition to being farmers, many of them were speculators in land values. But it should be remembered that side by side with abuses have been many instances of fair relations between landlord and tenant. Some capable

[28] Clark, *Essentials of Economic Theory*, p. 161.
[29] Retail houses will sometimes count the number of persons passing a certain corner to calculate its rental value, but usually the determination is largely guesswork.

farmers find it more satisfactory to work land belonging to someone else, rather than mortgage the land to buy it at a price that includes a speculative value. And many landowners are shrewd enough to realize that they profit more by fair dealings with capable tenants or share croppers, than they would by dealing with shiftless croppers kept constantly in debt for supplies. In last analysis, the plight of some tenants and share croppers is due to their own incompetence. Henry George claims [30] that all ownership in land giving a right to rent is unjust, because labor is the only title to dominion and because rent has been the cause of practically all inequality, poverty, and destitution afflicting mankind.

664. Private Ownership of Land Justified by Results. Labor is one title to ownership, but not the sole, as was pointed out in the chapter on *Ownership*.[31] Nor is private ownership responsible for all our ills. As a matter of fact, the aim of the most advanced social effort today is not to abolish private ownership altogether, but to extend the number of owners. A defense of private ownership does not mean a defense of its abuses, such as *latifundia* and enormous game preserves. Despite its abuses, no system of holding agricultural land has ever surpassed private ownership in social usefulness. If the owners of farms with their personal interest in the matter find it difficult to keep tenant farmers from impoverishing the soil, certainly government inspectors, simply looking out for the community's good, would not do better unless they were much above the present officials in zeal and honesty.

665. World Not Yet Ready for Social Ownership. Accordingly, we maintain that although private ownership is not the highest economic ideal to which we can attain in thought, it is, considering the selfishness of mankind as a whole, the system for today most practical and least liable to incurable abuses. When comes the millennium, when all, or at least a majority of men, shall in practice as well as theory love their neighbors as themselves, giving as much thought to the common good as to their own,

[30] *Progress and Poverty.*
[31] Cf. No. 594, 595.

then the next step, which may or may not be single tax or communistic holding of property, will be taken peacefully and naturally.

666. State Appropriation of Earned Land Values. The fundamental selfishness of man probably makes inadvisable, too, the appropriation by the State of all increment in land values. Unless some distinction is made between the earned and unearned increments, there will be no incentive to use fertilizers, drain the soil, and adopt- the most improved methods of cultivation. For men have not yet become sufficiently altruistic to undertake such labor and expense for the general good.

667. Appropriation of Whole Unearned Increment. Assuming that a distinction between the earned and unearned increment is practicable, there are three courses open to the advocates of social appropriation of the unearned increment. In the first place, all rent could be appropriated. This, practically, would be to confiscate the property outright without compensation to the private owner. Unless the good of the State should urgently demand such a course, it would be gross injustice.

668. Appropriation of Future Unearned Increment. Again, as noted by John Stuart Mill,[32] the State might so regulate the tax as to appropriate all future increase in value. This would be a virtual confiscation of more than the future increase in value; many persons have paid more for land upon the chance of gaining the increase in value than they would have paid had they known that the increment would go to the State. Hence, such a plan must be rejected as unjust unless the greatest social need demands it.

669. Appropriation of a Part of Future Unearned Increment. Finally, a reasonable compensation can be made to the present owners for their chance of acquiring speculative value, and the taxes thereafter adjusted so as to appropriate all future increase in value. The arguments for this course are not conclusive on either side of the question. But it should be kept clearly in mind

[32] *Principles of Political Economy*, Bk. V, Ch. III, Sec. II.

that they concern only the social usefulness of such a policy; if it be for the common good, then it is perfectly justifiable.[33]

SUGGESTED READINGS

1. Clark, John B., *Essentials of Economic Theory,* Chs. VI, VII, IX, X.
2. Seager, *Introduction to Economics,* chs. on "Rent" and "Interest."
3. Ryan, John A., *The Church and Interest-Taking.*
4. Ryan, John A., *Distributive Justice,* Secs. I, II.
5. Cleary, Patrick, *The Church and Usury,* Chs. V, VII, VIII.
6. Ross, J. Elliot, *Consumers and Wage-Earners,* Chs. II, VIII.
7. Slater, *Questions of Moral Theology,* pp. 15-53, 78-98.
8. Wallis, *Safeguard Productive Capital.*

QUESTIONS

1. Define and divide contracts; state conditions for validity.
2. To what extent do promises bind makers? heirs?
3. Define interest. Is it justifiable?
4. On what principle should a just price be determined?
5. Is rent justifiable?
6. Should owner of land receive unearned increment?

[33] John A. Ryan, "Methods of Reforming Our Land System," in *Cath. World,* Oct., 1912; also *Distributive Justice.*

EIGHT: *Labor*

670. Definition and Importance of Labor. *Labor is human exertion applied to the production of wealth.* The ethical bearings of labor as a contract are so important that they more than warrant a separate chapter. For labor is important from the number of persons concerned, the large part questions of labor contracts play in their lives, and the complexity of the problems involved. Practically the whole human race is bound to labor in some way in order to live. Comparatively few, by rent or interest or some other means, manage to escape this universal law. And even those who themselves are persons of leisure are momently brought into relations with those who must labor. They are direct employers, as in the case of their servants; or indirect, by purchasing the product of the labor of others.

671. Labor and Ethics. In the lives of most persons labor questions—that is, the gaining of wealth by exertion—play a dominant part. Karl Marx, indeed, and many of his followers would make the production of wealth the ultimate determinant of ethical thought. "The first instinctive or conscious endeavor of every nation is to provide the means of its material sustenance—to produce wealth; and the manner in which it produces its sustenance ultimately determines its form of organization, division of work or functions, and its notions of right and wrong —its politics, social classes, and ethics." [1] And while this is an exaggeration, economic influences do undoubtedly play an important part in determining ethical opinions. Father Ryan, in his debate with Morris Hillquit, remarked that "even the ethical notions of men vary considerably according to their industrial interests. Consider, for example, the different moral judgments passed respectively by employers and employees upon the strike,

[1] Morris Hillquit, in *Socialism—Promise or Menace?* Ch. IV; cf. also Haney, *History of Economic Thought,* p. 384.

the boycott, the closed shop, judicial injunctions, and the definition of fair wages and fair profits." [2]

672. Complexity of Labor Problems. The complexity of the
problems is evident from the different opinions current upon
many points of them. In some cases even the principles are not
entirely clear; in others the application is exceedingly uncertain
because of the difficulty in getting sufficient data. A fair wage,
for instance, depends first of all upon establishing the principle
that each one is entitled to a living. But we are immediately met
by the further question, should this wage be sufficient for an
individual or for a family? And after settling that point, we have
the task of defining living. Is it to be a Chinaman's living?
Should it be the absolute minimum? If not, how much should
you add? Having determined what is meant by living, there remains the problem of deciding what wage will be required
to achieve this standard. Since the purchasing power of money
varies, the cost of living must vary, too.

673. Ethics and Slave Labor. The ethical principles governing
labor will naturally differ according to the system under consideration. Several such systems can be broadly distinguished.
First of all, we have a labor system based largely on slavery, as
in ancient Greece or the Old South. This system has disappeared from civilized nations, and it is not necessary to discuss
its ethical implications. It is sufficient to say that St. Paul recognized it and that Scholastic moralists have justified slavery under
certain conditions.

674. Ethics and Socialized Labor. Again, we might organize
society co-operatively, or socialize industry as the Socialists demand. But this is still a dream of the future, and probably will
never be actualized. Hence it is not necessary to discuss the
ethics of labor under this hypothetical system.

675. Ethics and Wages. Finally, we may have free men working for themselves or for others. The question of the man work-

[2] An interesting example of economic influence upon ethical opinion is given in
Licht und Schatten (Jos. Spieler, p. 59; cf. also *Kreuz und Charitas,* 1909, p. 143),
where a missionary writes that only those tribes suffering from scarcity of meat
practice cannibalism.

ing for himself is simple. Such a man has a right to the whole product of his labor; and provided he lives up to the principles laid down for buyers and sellers as regards the material with which he works, he commits no injustice. This class of laborers, however, is steadily becoming smaller. Those who are working for wages are increasing rapidly in number and bid fair to increase even proportionately. Their ranks are being recruited daily from men who have failed in business for themselves, as well as from those who never had an opportunity to establish themselves independently. For the amount of skill and capital required for independent industrial activity is getting larger and larger each year. We shall deal principally, therefore, with relations between employers and employees.

676. The Duty to Work. The first consideration in regard to labor is that to work, whether for one's self or another, is a duty.[3] God has placed upon every man the obligation of earning his bread in the sweat of his brow. Of course, the sweat need not be literal. There is an intellectual travail that is as real and as painful as any muscular effort. Physicians, lawyers, clergymen are earning their bread by performing their respective duties, whether or not they do any manual labor involving sweat.[4]

677. The Idle Rich. But it cannot be too strongly insisted upon that everyone who is physically capable of working is morally obliged to work. At every point of the social scale we find the cumberers—men and women who lean and will not lift, take and will not give. The society woman who spends her time in one ceaseless round of inane social "duties," performing no useful

---

[3] Cathrein, *Moralphilosophie*, II, 59.

[4] Shelley spoke of "the agony and bloody sweat of intellectual travail." Cardinal J. H. Newman wrote: "The first book I wrote, my *Arians*, I was almost fainting daily, when I was finishing it; and (except my *Parochial Sermons*) every book I have written, before and since I was a Catholic, has been a sort of operation, the distress has been so great." (Ward's *Life of Newman*, I, p. 296.) And again: "It is one of my sayings (so continually do I feel it) that the composition of a volume is like gestation and child-birth. I do not think that I ever thought out a question, and wrote my thoughts without great pain, pain reaching to the body as well as to the mind. It has made me feel practically, that labor '*in sudore vultus sui*' is the lot of man." (*Id.*, p. 637.)

function in the body politic, often refusing even to reproduce her kind, wherein does she differ from the unwashed vagrant who sponges on the thrifty and preys on the ragged edge of society?

678. Moral Effects of Idleness. Idleness breeds unrest—moral, mental, and spiritual—an unrest that expresses itself in neurotic and erotic craving for sensation. The good common joys of earth—home and love and children—grow flat and stale to over-stimulated nerves and under-stimulated muscles. Natural law is ever a law of compensation: nothing for nothing is its unvarying dictum.

679. The Contagion of Idleness. Unfortunately, however, this law of God is not clearly recognized by many supposedly good Christians. It is the ambition of a large number of people to be able to live without working. They see worthless idlers rolling by in limousines, owning private yachts, spending their lives in a round of meaningless amusements, and instead of despising such conduct, they actually envy it. If they could, they themselves would lead the same sort of life. It is not Christianity or any sense of duty that keeps them from it, but lack of means.

680. Each Must Pay for What He Gets. All such people ought to understand that their desire to get something for nothing, to evade this universal law of work, is the worst thing they could do for themselves. Each pays in one way or another for everything he gets; and the cheapest way to pay is by working for it. Those who, because they have rents or interest, live by the sweat of other people and make no return to society, pay for their violation of this law by a real degradation, a weakening of physical and moral stamina, a failure to see the brotherhood of man and the dignity of labor; and finally they land with Dives, calling out in agony to Lazarus, whom they had spurned on earth.

681. Universality of Duty to Work. Each man, then, has a duty to work. If he is not forced to produce in order to live, because he or his ancestors have stored up capital, he is, nevertheless, bound to make some return to society—to do something to justify his cumbering the earth.

682. Right to Work. But to this duty there corresponds the right to an opportunity to work. Under previous régimes this opportunity was easily furnished. When the earth was being peopled and her children looked out upon virgin resources, all a man had to do was to use the opportunities that were common to all. He could hunt or fish or hew wood as he pleased, and as his skill allowed. There was no one whose permission he need ask if he wanted trout for dinner or fire to warm his hut. The skins of the beasts that he killed furnished him then just as comfortable and satisfactory clothing as does a Fifth Avenue tailor today.

683. Originally No Unemployment. Evidently, there was no question of unemployment here. Of work there was always a superabundance. If a man starved, it was not for lack of work. Employment was the natural and customary thing; unemployment was unnatural and unusual.

684. No Unemployment for Slaves. Again, under a régime of serfdom or slavery there was ordinarily no problem of unemployment. We have had slave uprisings because too much work was placed upon them, because they were required to make bricks without straw, but whoever heard of slaves rebelling because there were no bricks to be made? A slave's work was never done. The amount of labor applicable to a plantation was practically unlimited. It was the easiest thing in the world to find work; and if one did not find it himself, someone else found it for him. An overseer with a black-snake whip, even if he never used it, was always a possibility to stimulate exertion.

685. Unemployment Comparatively Recent. We should be extremely careful not to allow the familiarity of certain phenomena attaching to the régime under which we live to make us think them necessary and inevitable. Indeed, the fact that such unjust and inhuman conditions due to widespread unemployment exist now without being questioned indicates (paradoxical as it may seem) that they did not always exist. For if they had existed when the great Scholastic moralists were writing, assuredly

they would have come in for their share of comment and condemnation.

686. Why Great Moralists Do Not Treat of Unemployment.
But as these men wrote under a régime that was partly one
of serfdom and partly one of self-employers, they did not give
this question of the right to work the consideration that is forced
upon our attention. For them the problem did not exist. Thus
St. Thomas in his epoch-making *Secunda Secundae* makes no
mention of the question. In the society upon which he looked
out, the opportunity to work was almost always present; and
there was no use wasting time talking about such an improbable
hypothesis as that a man should not have the chance to work.

687. Why Unemployment Exists Today. Today, however, the
moralist faces an entirely different situation. A few individuals
have appropriated the natural resources; and as a man needs
natural resources before he can work, he is barred from working unless the owners allow it. If he needs a dinner and is willing to work for it by killing a rabbit (as he might have done
at one time in the world's history), there may be a game-keeper
to arrest him for poaching. Or if he wishes to make something
(as he might have done under a régime of hand work), he dis-
covers that raw materials have all been appropriated or that he
cannot work without the use of tools belonging to someone else.

688. A Man Now Needs Permission to Work. At present the
majority of men can work only by the permission of other men.
In some ways the modern laborer is worse off than slave or serf,
for these were assured at least of clothing and shelter. Over
him, on the contrary, there hangs a nerve-racking uncertainty.
His living depends upon his selling the only commodity he has,
his labor; and in that position he is worse off than the seller
of any other article. For a man who offers oranges, for instance,
can hold them until tomorrow if the price today is not satisfactory; whereas, the laborer cannot sell today's labor tomorrow. It will have disappeared completely; and tomorrow's supply will be inferior if today he does not get sufficient food to
meet his physical needs.

689. Has a Man a Right to Work? What, then, is the answer that moralists give when confronted with this situation? Has a man a right to demand a market for his labor? *Has he a right to work?*

690. Only Modern Writers Treat the Right to Work. It will be only among the modern writers that we shall find any discussion of this subject. St. Thomas and his contemporaries, as we have seen, did not advert to it because it was merely hypothetical in their time. For St. Alphonsus, even, it was hardly a practical question; and we need not be surprised to find him discussing "labor" only in relation to Sunday observance and fasting. Leo XIII, it is true, was *ex professo* and at length treating of the condition of workingmen; but he was living in a country where the effects of the industrial revolution had not proceeded as far as they have in England and in the United States and where the less acute phenomena of unemployment were further tempered by extensive emigration. His failing to mention this phase of the situation was not, therefore, extraordinary. But it seems rather curious that Lehmkuhl with his interest in modern social problems should have insisted strongly in his *Theologia Moralis* upon the duty to work while completely passing over the right to work.[5]

691. Noldin on the Right to Work. Noldin has this short, though very clear, reference: "Every man has a *right to work,* that is, he has a right by just means to seek labor which is lawful for him and to perform that labor, and hence, he has a right to demand that others shall not hinder him in the exercise of this right. The right is founded on another right, that of preserving and perfecting life, to which industrial labor is ordinarily necessary."[6]

692. How Right to Work Is Qualified. Noldin's principle is perfectly plain. And though Noldin goes on to qualify his statement, the qualification really means nothing more than that a

---

[5] Consult the eighth edition of his very complete and thorough *Theologia Moralis* (Freiburg im Breisgau, 1902).

[6] *Theologia Moralis,* II, No. 69.

laborer has not a strict right in commutative justice. Noldin's words are: "No one has a right *to work,* that is to demand that someone else (whether a private individual or the State) should offer or procure him work, even though he be in need of the necessaries of life."

693. Right to Work Is Not Strict. The reason that Noldin gives for this qualification—that "in every case the obligation of supplying lucrative employment is opposed to the right of property"—shows clearly that he means it in the sense in which we have explained it. For in the same way the right of property is opposed to the obligation of actually giving one's possessions to another. Yet all theologians agree that a person in extremest need has a right to take what he needs, and that the possessor has *a duty in charity to give.*

694. Duty of State to Furnish Work. However, to prevent the disorders that would result from asserting these rights there is a duty of distributive justice incumbent upon the State to furnish work to such as cannot otherwise find it. When a government allows such a private appropriation of property as to close all opportunity of employment to any large class, it becomes responsible for affording to each man some reasonable return for the opportunity that would otherwise have been his. The right to private property should never be absolute. The State will not allow a private individual who owns both sides of a navigable river to close it to traffic or to fishing. And as it sometimes compels individual owners of large tracts of land to open roads for the convenience of the public, so it should keep open certain avenues to work that would otherwise be closed by the selfishness of individuals. This is a simple demand of justice.

695. State's Duty Is of Distributive Justice. Each one, then, has a right in legal justice to the opportunity to work. Noldin, indeed, specifically admits this when the number of unemployed is so great as to endanger the good of the community.[7] For all practical purposes this is to acknowledge the right to work, since there can be no question but that this condition is often ful-

[7] *Loc. cit.*

filled. The man out of work is interested in getting a job, and it is all one to him whether the State is obliged in distributive or commutative justice to supply it.

696. Cathrein on the Right to Work. Cathrein, perhaps, brings this right to work out more clearly than Noldin. After speaking of the laborer's insecurity of existence under the present industrial order, he adds: "In order to give the workman a sure basis for his existence, there is ascribed to him *a right to work.* However, this is not a universal strict right. No irrefutable reason for such a [strict] right can be given. . . . But at times society (the municipality or the State) has the duty, according to its ability, to furnish laborers with remunerative employment. For in the extremest need each one has a right to take for himself, wherever he finds it, what is necessary for life. This right belongs also to the laborer. And who will forbid him to unite with others who are in the same condition in the attainment of this object? From such a state of affairs there may easily arise the most serious evils for the community. Hence the authorities are bound to prevent this in some way. The proper way is not the distribution of alms, but the furnishing of lucrative work. This is often to be had, though the laborers do not know of it. Public employment bureaus are, therefore, to be commended. . . . But if work is to be found in no other way, then the municipalities or the State should undertake public improvements (street paving, canals, and the like)." [8]

697. Right to Work Inheres in the Individual. While there is no doubt that unemployment is often so widespread as to cause serious danger to the community, yet as a matter of precision it is well to insist that the right to support himself is inherent in each man, and that even if there were only one citizen who could not find this opportunity to work, the State would be obliged in distributive justice to furnish him the chance. And when he works, he should get a living wage.

698. Leo XIII and the Right to Work. This is a perfectly legitimate conclusion from the words of Leo XIII, and that learned

---

[8] *Moralphilosophie*, II, p. 632.

Pontiff would probably have drawn it himself had his attention been called to it: "The preservation of life," he writes in his Encyclical "The Condition of Labor," "is the bounden duty of each and all, and to fail therein is a crime. It follows that each one has a right to procure what is required in order to live; and the poor can procure it in no other way than by work and wages." The great social reform Pope concluded with inexorable logic that this right to live implies a right to a living wage. Does it not at the same time imply *a right to work for this wage?* If a man has a right to live, and can live only by work, there seems no escape from the conclusion that he has a right to work. For the right to a living wage without the right to work is as profitable to an unemployed laborer as is the water of a mirage to a thirsty traveler.

699. Kelleher and Manning on the Right to Work. We have seen how far Noldin and Lehmkuhl and Cathrein accept this doctrine. They are not alone, however. Father Kelleher, in his excellent book on *Private Ownership,* sees the implications of such a system and asserts that each one has a right to a job or to its equivalent. And Cardinal Manning, though not a theologian nor a scientific social worker, had considerable insight into social conditions and declared emphatically: "Every man has a right to work or to bread." [9]

700. Different Classes of Unemployed. Having determined the abstract right of each man to work, there remains the question of supplying work. In dealing with this problem of unemployment, three distinct classes immediately show themselves. There is the man who is out of work on account of some industrial disturbance. He is capable of working under competitive conditions, but cannot find employment, because there is no opportunity or he has not met it. The remedy is to be found in employment bureaus that will bring the job and the jobless together; in such a readjustment of industry that the periods of seasonal slackness will be balanced, or occupations will be combined so as to insure continuous employment; partly in social

[9] Purcell's *Life of Card. Manning,* II, p. 656.

insurance against unemployment; and partly in the creation of opportunities by the municipality or the State.[10]

701. The Unemployable. Again, there is a class of unemployed who wish to work, but cannot be employed under competitive conditions. They are too old, or infirm, or quarrelsome, or intemperate. In some way, they are more or less defective, ranging from the occasional drinker to the confirmed idiot. No man who is obliged to meet the competition of his fellows can afford to employ them. Hence the State should establish appropriate institutions where they will be given suitable employment and the necessary discipline. Something has been done in Holland and Germany along these lines.[11] But every county and town of any size should be looking after its defectives in a more thorough way than has been done even in Germany, the land of efficiency and thoroughness.

702. Vagrants. Finally, we have professional loafers who do not want to work, no matter what their statements to the contrary. Strict vagrancy laws should take them off the streets and roads, and they should be compelled to work. "He that will not work," said St. Paul, "neither let him eat." We have not yet outgrown this dictum. If an able-bodied man will not work when the State or private persons give him the chance, starve him until he changes his mind. But it is cruel and unwise to put every unemployed person in an institution with a stigma of crime or pauperism attached to it. Provision should first be made for the other two classes, and only such persons as are certainly known to be vagrants sent to compulsory labor.

703. Causes Producing Unemployableness. The different classes of unemployables are recruited from various sources. Some of the defectives are born so, without anyone being to blame. Others are born so through the fault of the parents, but in such a way that society probably could not prevent the situation without producing conditions that would be even worse. And still

---

[10] For an account of what has been done in this direction, consult the Unemployment Survey of the *Am. Lab. Leg. Rev.*, Nov., 1915.

[11] Peter Bonn, *Das Arbeitshaus ohne Zwang.*

others are unemployable through their own abuse of opportunities. The best laws and the most conscientious administration of them can never entirely remove the chance of human beings misusing the gift of free-will.

704. Unemployment. After all is said, however, much unemployment is due to causes beyond the control of individuals. The installation of machines sometimes throws thousands out of work, and it is months or years before these displaced men can find other employment. There is, too, the fundamental problem of so distributing the costs and profits of production that there will be enough purchasing power to buy the products of industry and so give continuous work to everyone. Waddell and Catchings [12] maintain that the real cause of economic depressions such as we have had periodically since the Industrial Revolution, is that profits interfere with distributing this sufficiency of purchasing power. And Edward Bellamy [13] has a persuasive chapter to the same effect.

705. Can Production and Consumption Be Balanced? Some observers think that production and consumption can be balanced while at the same time retaining capitalism. Advocates of a "planned economy" contend that the government can by various schemes prevent overproduction and underconsumption. But whether it can be done without losing more than we gain remains problematical. No proposed measures would so far seem to have solved the problem and provided any ground to believe that there will be no more depressions—that is, that there will always be enough purchasing power to buy the goods offered.

706. Bellamy's Utopia. In *Looking Backward* and *Equality*, Bellamy has given a delightful picture of how a communistic society might insure plenty for everyone at the same time that each would enjoy more liberty than at present. But that is fiction, and one may reasonably doubt whether, human nature being what it is, such a system would work in the admirable way he imagines.

[12] *Business Without a Buyer.*
[13] *Equality*, Ch. XXIII.

707. "Social Credit" Theory. Major Douglas thinks that this purchasing power could be created by what he calls "social credit." [14] Each citizen by the very fact of citizenship would be entitled to an annual credit which Major Douglas believes would be at least $1,500. It is an attractive theory, but the Major's exposition of its practicability is far from convincing.

708. Ethically Minded Should Be Made to Find Solution. Finding flaws in proposed schemes, however, does not solve the problem of distribution. It is an economic problem, but it is also an ethical problem. And certainly if we have the ethical good will, we ought to have the economic intelligence to devise a system of distribution that in this age of plenty would give each one the opportunity of earning a decent living.

709. Essence of the Wage Contract. *Hiring* is a contract by which one party binds himself to perform a certain work, and the other to pay a certain wage. It will avoid some socialistic confusions to get clearly at the start that *the object of the contract* is not what the labor produces, nor the price obtained for it, but the industrial force which one hires or rents to another. Such a contract is honorable and lawful, and sometimes even necessary. Man has full dominion over his own powers and can contract to give their exercise to another. And even though each worker had a right to the full product of his own labor and could not lawfully alienate any portion of it by a wage contract, one would not therefore, have to condemn the wage system.

710. Productivity Theory of Wages. For as a matter of fact, as was pointed out in the chapter on ownership, there is no way of determining just what is the product of labor and what of capital and land. There is a great deal of talk among economists about the productivity theory of distribution, but it fails when the practical application is attempted. In any given case of industrial life we do not know, and probably never will know, just how much should be attributed to any one element. Hence, a laborer

[14] C. H. Douglas, *Social Credit;* Hattersley, *This Age of Plenty.*

by a wage contract may really be getting more than the whole product of his labor.

711. A Living Wage. The amount of the wage, therefore, must be determined by some principle other than actual production. This principle is drawn from the natural end of labor. As a man works in order to support himself and family, a wage for an able-bodied, capable man must be sufficient for such support.[15]

712. Absolute and Relative Necessaries. Here we are met by a distinction between *absolute* and *relative necessaries*. Must the wage be sufficient to obtain what is just barely needed to keep body and soul together, or must it be enough to secure what has become part of the standard of living of the wage earning class?

713. The Standard of Absolute Necessaries Is Elusive. Let us begin by taking the first horn of the dilemma. For such an absolute standard could only be determined by individual experimentation. What is one man's meat is another man's poison, and some men need more meat than others. Besides there are the racial and climatic differences that affect such a calculation. A New Englander might starve on what would support a Mexican in Texas; his mince pie stomach might rebel against chili. In the North more fuel, thicker clothing, more substantial houses are needed than in the South. Where climate allows, is the employer paying a living wage if it be sufficient to provide a loin cloth or hog and hominy?

714. Relative Standard Continually Changing. If we discard the absolute for a relative standard we find that the standard continually varies. The advance of such a standard is shown clearly if we go back a century or two and find what laborers were content with.[16] And in our own frontier days, the food, clothing, and shelter usual for all was far below what workmen demand today.[17] Before America was discovered, the standard of living of European workers did not embrace tea or coffee or sugar or potatoes.

---

[15] Noldin, II, No. 610, 611; cf. John A. Ryan, *A Living Wage.*
[16] Cf. Bosanquet, *Standard of Life.*
[17] Cf. Hollander, *Abolition of Poverty.*

715. How Relative Standard Should Be Determined. The only answer seems to be by some sort of local commission composed of employers and employees. This commission should be empowered by the legislative body to determine the content of a living wage as authorized by law. In this way the cumbersome machinery of legislation would not have to be set in motion every time an increase in wages was necessary.

716. A Living Family Wage. There is a further question regarding the just wage. It must be not simply a wage sufficient to enable the individual to meet the standard at present achieved by the working classes, but it must be a family wage. That is to say, it must be enough to maintain a family of reasonable size in the condition of comfort consistent with the class to which the employee (as an employee) belongs. Such a wage must then be paid to single as well as to married men, because each man is to be looked upon as an actual or prospective head of a household.

717. Hence, No Child Labor. This principle has important implications. For if the head of a family receive a sufficient wage, children will not be forced to work. They should not be robbed of their childhood for the sake of a few pennies a day. The State has a right and a duty to protect its future citizens, to forbid child labor.

718. Equal Pay for Equal Work. If men and women do the same work with equal efficiency, their wages should be the same. For there should be a correspondence between the value of the work and the wage. Women and single men, unless under compulsion justified by unusual circumstances, should hold out for what has been defined as a just wage. For injustice is done those wholly dependent upon wages, if those receiving their support in whole or in part from another source accept less than this amount. It means that wages will drop, that the standard of living will be lowered, and that large classes will be deprived of what they have a right to expect. Such a depreciation is particularly noticeable in the case of shop girls and those doing sewing at home. Some department stores are even said to make a practice of employing girls partly supported in some other way; and many fairly well-to-do women take sewing at starvation pay because they simply want to make pin money.

719. Occult Compensation. May an employee who is receiving less than the lowest just wage secretly compensate himself? If he has freely entered into the contract with his employer, he may not. But if he was compelled by fear or necessity (except when the employer accepts him merely out of charity) he may so compensate himself provided that there is no other way of obtaining compensation and that care be taken to avoid injuring innocent third parties. However, as the one provision is only against legal justice and the other against charity, he is not bound to restitution if he violates them. The same principle of occult compensation may be used to recover for extra work, whether in difficulty or time, that was not provided for in the contract and is done by the will of the employer.

720. Limitations Upon Occult Compensation. Where there is no legislation to establish the content of a just wage, it will frequently be difficult to determine just what it should be, as has been brought out at some length above. Hence occult compensation should be used very cautiously. And ordinarily, the common good demands that a creditor should try first to recover his debt through legal channels.

721. Other Relations Between Employers and Employees. The relations between employer and employee embrace not only the question of wages, but also the hours of work, sanitary conditions in the factory, protection of the machinery, and responsibility in case of sickness. Even where the State does not compel sanitation and the guarding against accidents, employers are bound to make provision for such things if at all within a reasonable expense. Should accident or sickness come, however, even apart from any neglect of duty, employers are bound in charity to succor their employees. For they stand in a special relationship to them, a bond has been made that gives the employees a certain claim upon their employers before other persons standing in no such relationship. It should hardly be necessary to say that employers are solemnly bound to protect their employees so far as possible in their morals and religion. To this end proper facilities for the different sexes should be provided and some supervision exercised. What has been said regarding employees in general applies with even greater force in regard to domestic servants. The relationship here is much closer and the responsibilities much greater.

722. How Can We Compel a Recognition of Duties? Unfortunately some employers will not live up to these duties. As a consequence, inexorable competition frequently forces the best-intentioned employers also to neglect these duties else the additional expense would drive them out of business. The employees, therefore, and those interested in social justice are confronted with the problem of securing these rights in some way other than through the mere good will of employers.

723. Legislation to Protect Laborers. Two broad means of protecting laborers may be distinguished—legislation and organization. Our own more advanced States have child labor laws, regulate the hours of work for women, provide certain requirements in the way of sanitation, fire protection and the guarding of machinery. In a few States accident insurance is compulsory—the State, the employee, and the employer sharing in the expense. To extend such insurance to cover old age, unemployment, and sickness does not differ in principle.

724. Right of State to Legislate. That the State has the right to make such regulations can hardly be doubted. She has the right to use the necessary means to attain her end. Her end is the material welfare of her citizens; and if such provisions be prudently deemed necessary to attain that end, they are perfectly justified.[18]

725. The Eight-Hour Day. It is also well within the State's authority to limit the hours of work and to determine holidays. Excessive hours are not good for the commonwealth. As Hawthorne wrote after his experience at Brook Farm, a man's soul can be very effectively buried under a furrow or a manure pile.

18 Cf. Lehmkuhl, *Die Soziale Frage und die staatliche Gewalt* (Freiburg, 1911).

While work in moderation and under fair conditions is a great blessing, too much work is a curse. To labor all day, to eat, to sleep, to rise again, to work with never a chance for recreation or for spiritual or intellectual cultivation will brutalize men more surely, perhaps, than any other process. On the other hand, however, it is not well that the hours of labor should be too short, nor the holidays too numerous. In such a case there is apt to be rapid demoralization, as the vast majority of men do not know how to use leisure wisely. Eight hours would seem to be a fair average for most occupations, and sentiment in this country is crystallizing around that amount.[19]

726. Trade Unions. Another way in which to gain the saner ends of labor, or most of them, is through organization of the workers. In so far as the conditions of labor striven for and the means used to attain them are just, trade unions are perfectly lawful from an ethical standpoint. That this is usually true can hardly be questioned. "If anyone doubt that the evils resulting from the unions are less important morally, economically, and politically than the benefits they have produced, let him calmly survey the conditions that would exist in England today if the unions were still prohibited by law as they were during the period of English 'wage slavery' in the early decades of the nineteenth century."[20]

727. Trade Union Methods. The justice of the concrete ends aimed at by trades unions must be judged in the individual cases by the principles heretofore set down in this chapter. It will now be necessary to consider some of the means used to attain their ends.

728. Strikes. First in importance come strikes. These may be either direct or sympathetic. A direct strike is a quitting of work by the laborers who have the grievance; a sympathetic strike is a quitting of work by employees who have no direct grievance, whether they be of the same or different employments. The sym-

---

[19] Cf. Florence Kelly, *Some Ethical Gains Through Legislation;* John A. Ryan, "Labor," Cath. Encyc.

[20] Cf. John A. Ryan, "Moral Aspects of Labor Unions," in Cath. Encyc.

pathetic strike is a direct and practical application of the usually elusive principle of human brotherhood.

729. Lawfulness of Strikes. A direct strike is just (a) if the claim is just; (b) if there is no peaceful way of obtaining what is claimed; (c) if the importance of the claim outweighs the evil of the strike; (d) and if there is reasonable hope of success. Sympathetic strikes by other laborers of the same employer, as the brakemen of a railroad where the locomotive engineers have a just grievance, are justified under the conditions just enumerated. For otherwise they would co-operate in the injustice of the employer. In extreme cases this will be true even if such strikes are against another employer, for he might be bound in charity to assist the original strikers by refusing to co-operate in any way with the unjust employer.

730. Strike-Breaking. Strike-breakers are justified when the strike is unjust by lack of one of the conditions enumerated, or when their own need outweighs the need of the strikers and cannot be better served by remaining idle. Otherwise they are helping to perpetuate unjust conditions and so are themselves guilty of injustice.

731. Strikes and Violence. In the case of a just strike, is violence justified either against the employer or against strike-breakers? Only if the good effects obtained are greater than the social disorder resulting from the use of force. This, practically, will never be so, and the loss in public good-will, frequently the determining factor in the success of strikes, usually offsets any gain by violence.

732. Boycotts. A boycott, as used in industrial warfare, is an agreement among a group of laborers to refuse patronage to a particular merchant or manufacturer. Like the strike, it may be either *primary*, directed towards the seller against whom lies the original grievance; or *secondary*, when directed against men who continue to deal with him. The principles for determining the liceity of boycotts are the same as for strikes; since a right of the same nature is concerned. For just as a laborer has a right to his job because he has a right to seek and obtain material goods without undue interference, so a merchant has a right to his patronage upon the same ground. What was said regarding sympathetic strikes applies with equal force to secondary boycotts.

733. Closed Shops. The policy of the closed shop is justified in so far as it is a necessary means to obtain justice, and the unions admit members on reasonable terms. For the right of a non-union man to work beside a union man is no stronger than that of the union man's right *not* to work beside him. It is unreasonable, too, that a man should expect to get all the benefits of organization and to bear none of its burdens.

734. Limitation of Output. Output may be limited when no restriction would mean an undue speeding of the average worker in order to meet the pace of the exceptional man. But it is unjust when it is done merely to make a job last longer.

735. Limiting Apprentices. The number of apprentices may be fixed in such a way as to keep wages at a reasonable level. What is such a level must be determined by the principles enunciated in considering a living wage.

736. Unions Only Effective for Skilled Labor. Trades unions do not ordinarily reach the unskilled laborer or woman worker. To obtain justice for these large classes recourse must usually be had to legislation.

737. Summary of Chapter. Thus we have seen that labor as a contract has very important ethical bearings. Among these implications are the right to work and the right to a living wage. The means used to attain these rights may be either organization or legislation. Under certain restrictions, organized laborers are justified in using the strike, boycott, and closed shop.

SUGGESTED READINGS

1. Ryan, *Distributive Justice,* Sec. IV.
2. Ross, *The Right to Work.*
3. *American Labor Legislation Review,* Nov., 1915.
4. Hollander, *The Abolition of Poverty.*
5. Florence Kelly, *Some Ethical Gains Through Legislation.*

6. Ryan, "Moral Aspects of Labor Unions," in Cath. Encyc.
7. McLean, *Morality of the Strike* (N. Y., 1921).

QUESTIONS

1. Do you think it honorable for those capable of working to live on the labor of others?
2. Is there any way of really getting something for nothing?
3. Has each one a right to the opportunity of working?
4. Can you suggest how the problem of unemployment might be met?
5. What is a just wage?
6. What do you think of the morality of:

        (a) strikes   (c) the closed shop?

        (b) boycotts

(Answer any one.)

7. Can you point out similarities in methods between trade unions and physicians?

NINE: *Contracts with an Element of Chance*

738. Distinction Between Contracts of Certain and Uncertain Events. The contracts so far considered have this in common: they have depended upon events which were certain, in the sense that what was to be done or not to be done by either party did not depend primarily upon chance; and that where they were bilateral there was a real equality between what was to be done by each party to the contract. When a man wants to buy an automobile he does not throw dice with a dealer to determine the price. When a man wants to hire a laborer he does not cut a pack of cards and pay him two dollars should red turn up or five dollars should black come. These contracts were contingent in a way, but not as contracts directly depending upon chance are contingent. A man paid by the piece may get more for one day's labor than for another, and this may depend upon chance in the sense that his efficiency depends upon events over which he has no control. One day he may have a headache, another day indigestion, and so on. But the chance is remote, and the man's average is fairly certain. Besides, there is a real equality between what he does and what he gets; whereas in contracts depending upon chance, it is the chance which determines all. There is no reason in the nature of things why a man holding higher cards than another should receive money from him. He has done no service for which he should be paid. It is all pure chance. That is a very essential distinction to keep in mind, because it has important bearings upon the morality of such contracts. This fact that such contracts offer a reward without a corresponding service having been performed renders them peculiarly attractive for those who wish to get something for nothing.

739. Distinction Between Contracts of Chance and Conditional Agreements. We come now to consider contracts wherein what is done by both parties depends frankly and directly upon chance and in which there is no equality between the service rendered and the object of the contract. Hence, these contracts do not give absolute right to the object of the contract, but only hope of obtaining it. If you buy a ticket to New York, you have an absolute right to the service contracted for by the railroad. If you buy a ticket in a lottery, you have a right only to the *hope* of drawing a winning number. It is the object of the contract and not the consent which depends upon chance. Hence, such contracts differ from conditional agreements.

740. Division of Contracts of Chance. Human ingenuity has devised an almost unlimited number of contracts depending upon chance, and their influence has been very considerable in shaping the destinies of peoples and nations. Various nations have shown a preference for one form rather than another. But the instinct leading to such contracts seems to be almost as fundamental as that of play. Here we shall consider five kinds of contracts of chance, under one or other of which heads all the multiple devices can be grouped. These are *betting, gaming, lotteries, speculation on the exchanges,* and *insurance.*

741. Betting. *Betting, technically, is defined as a contract whereby two or more persons disputing among themselves as to the truth of something agree that some consideration shall go to the one who is correct.* It is perfectly familiar to everyone. Probably no American ever yet reached maturity without having indulged in some harmless betting. "I betcha" can be heard daily in almost any street of our cities, from the lips of urchins and of city fathers. If the contract be merely unilateral, the resulting obligation is one of fidelity or justice according as the bettor intended to bind himself. Should the contract be bilateral, the resulting obligation is of justice, provided the bettor intended to contract validly. The distinction is important, because the obligation of justice binds one's heirs to payment (provided they receive a legacy sufficient to meet the debt); the obligation from fidelity does not. It should be further noted that if a man does not really intend to bind himself he incurs no obligation of paying should he lose; but likewise he may not retain the object of the bet should he win. The conditions necessary that a bet be just may be summed up in two words: (1) there must be a reasonable equality of risk; (2) duties owed elsewhere must not be violated.

742. There Should Be Equality of Risks in Bets. Thus a man may not bet on an absolutely sure thing. If he has truly certain knowledge, the contract is vitiated, because he has not really transferred a hope of gain, and there was no equality of risk. He risked nothing because he actually knew. So in like manner, each party must be able to make good the object of the bet should he lose. If one cannot, then he has really risked nothing, while the other man has risked something. He has not actually transferred a hope of recompense.

743. Duties Owed Elsewhere Must Not Be Violated. But not only must justice be considered between the contracting parties; in addition, no injustice must be done to others. Hence, duties which are owed elsewhere must not be violated by the bettors. Thus a man has no right to risk what is necessary for the support of his family. If he should risk what is so due and lose, the other party to the bet may not lawfully retain it.

744. When Bets Are Illicit. If a bet be just, it is valid, and the object of the bet may be retained. But a valid bet may be unlawful, and other considerations than those of justice affect its liceity. First of all, the bet must be about something honorable or indifferent. Thus a bet that one will fight a duel is unlawful. Again, the motive for betting must be honorable, such as legitimate recreation, a stimulus to do something, and so on. Further, the amount wagered must not be too large. To bet $50,000 on a yacht race, as has been reported done, is entirely beyond reason and cannot be too strongly condemned. Such an accumulation of wealth and power over human beings should not be risked for mere recreation or excitement.

745. Even Technically Lawful Bets Should Be Discouraged. It cannot be denied that all these conditions are sometimes fulfilled in individual bets. Yet even such bets should be discouraged because of the effect upon the individuals concerned and upon others. There is a certain excitement[1] connected with risking one's possessions in this way that gets into the blood and urges one to the taking of greater and greater risks. And even though a particular person may not feel very strongly the craving for this insidious form of sensation, or he may be able to resist it, yet his action in indulging in, or giving countenance to, any form of gambling is giving a certain sanction to the practice, and may entrap weaker persons into what may become a ruinous habit. This is especially true of church fairs employing gambling devices.

746. Hence Betting Is Frequently Forbidden by Law. Again, betting is almost sure to be associated with certain abuses. Racetrack betting, book-making, bucket-shops, are all merely cleverly disguised devices for separating the fool from his money. If it were only the fool who suffered, it would be serious enough, though perhaps salutary for the fool. But the evil radiates in all directions. This is so clearly recognized that all betting on horse-races is in many places forbidden by law. Elsewhere the State contents itself with declaring such contracts invalid and refusing to allow her courts to be used for the collection of any betting or gambling debts. In some places, where the State has not forbidden such betting, public-spirited officials of the telegraph and telephone companies have done what they could to limit the evil by refusing to transmit the news of the races.

747. Underlying Desire of Betting Is Decadent. Prohibition of betting by the State is amply justified, for nothing will weaken the stamina of a people more quickly and surely than the desire to get something for nothing. This desire is the essence of the betting and gambling spirit. People imagine that by betting one to a hundred they can get in a minute what they would have to work years to secure in honorable occupation. They *can* get it —sometimes do—but it is fool's gold that seldom, if ever, is turned to any honorable use and melts through their fingers, leaving

[1] A professional gambler writes: "Gambling fever is very real—as real as intoxication from liquor or drugs, and with much the same symptoms." (*Sat. Eve. Post.*, Oct. 24, 1936, p. 90.)

scars behind. Betting usually denotes a base desire to evade the law of God, "In the sweat of thy brow thou shalt eat thy bread." No nation avoids all gambling, but those nations are strongest and worthiest whose citizens come closest to the ideal of refraining altogether from such practices.

748. Gaming. *Playing or gaming is a contract in which persons engaged in a certain game agree that a reward shall go to the winner.* It differs from a *bet,* in that it is success which wins and not the truth. A bet always concerns the truth of a statement—Maud S. can run first in a field, John Smith will marry Betsy Jones—whereas playing has to do purely with chance, as in craps or *rouge et noir,* or partly with skill, as in bridge.

749. When Gaming Is Just. That such contests be just it is necessary: (1) That there should be no fraud. One who wins by fraud is bound not simply to restore what he has won, but also to compensate the others for the hope of victory that they would have had if there had been no cheating. (2) There should be a moral equality between the players. For if one is certain of winning there is no object for the contract—hope of winning and danger of losing. Hence, a person, who, knowing he will win, deceives another regarding his skill, is bound to restitution. (3) The contract should be entered into freely. Hence, one who plays with a half-intoxicated man, or who compels another by fear or otherwise to play, is bound to restitution. This is a very important point, as will be seen when we come to treat of the exchanges. (4) The players should be morally able to alienate the thing staked, as was said regarding bets. If one should win something that does not belong to the man who risked it, he is bound to restore it to its rightful owner.

750. When Gaming Is Lawful. What has been said about the *liceity* of bets applies equally to playing.

751. Lotteries. A *lottery* is a contract by which one buys the right of obtaining a certain article if the chance should be favorable. It differs from a bet, which supposes a disagreement between the contracting parties; and from playing, which supposes the playing of a certain game.

752. When Lotteries Are Just. Unless there is at least a tacit agreement to the contrary, justice requires equality between what is given and what is received; that is, the price of the chance must not exceed the hope of success. This hope varies inversely with the number of chances. As a matter of fact, however, it is usually understood (especially in the case of charitable organizations) that the amount obtained from the sale of all the chances will exceed the value of the prizes given; hence buyers tacitly accept this condition.

753. Evils of Lotteries. Lotteries lead to so much misdirected energy which consumes itself in unproductive calculations and expectations that most governments have either prohibited them entirely or have enacted strict regulations concerning their conduct.

754. The Exchanges. We Americans sometimes pride ourselves upon the fact of having abolished lotteries, regulated horse-racing, and so frowned upon various other forms of gambling that they are held within reasonable bounds. But this pride is hardly justified while at the same time the most important form of gambling —speculation on the exchanges—flourishes so luxuriantly and with so few regulations.

755. Extent of Exchange Gambling. Operating on the exchanges is probably the most important form of gambling in the world. Poker, and horse-racing, and Monte Carlo are picayune compared with the exchanges of various sorts. This is so because such speculation affects an immensely larger number of people and to a greater extent than any other form of gambling. When a man plays a game of poker, he and his companions and a comparatively few persons intimately connected with them are the only ones affected, except in so far as example counts and every social action affects all society. But speculation upon an exchange is another matter. In the first place, the transactions are liable to be on a much larger scale. Men frequently risk thousands and hundreds of thousands of dollars upon the turn of the market. A speculator is often next door to bankruptcy, and it has been said that none escapes that fate for many years.

756. Ramifications of Exchange Gambling. Besides the operators themselves, however, every stock exchange operation affects thousands of people who would no more think of gambling than of marrying the devil. Many, if not most, of the exchange operations are artificial. They are not real sales at all, but manipulations intended to raise or lower the price of certain stocks or commodities. Hence, every legitimate purchaser or seller of such stocks or articles is affected for good or evil as the case may be. The widow with a few thousand dollars in railroad stock may see her store dwindle because a few big financiers are playing a game she cannot in the least influence. An orphan not yet in his teens may be beggared by manipulations that produce nothing. Every workingman in the country may see his cost of living soar still higher by operations in New York or Chicago that advance the price of wheat.

757. Buying on Margin. Speculation on the exchanges takes many forms; and though they can all be reduced to betting or playing, it will be well to mention some specifically. Perhaps the most widespread operation is buying on margin. For one does not need to be a member of an exchange to do this, and perfectly innocent lambs are daily sheared in this way. A man buys on margin when he pays a broker a certain percentage (usually from ten to fifty per cent) of the market value of a stock and leaves the certificate as security for the rest. In a purely speculative transaction the buyer does not contemplate actual delivery. If the stock goes up, he sells and receives his deposit and the difference between the present market value and that at which he bought. Should the stock go down, he sells or puts up more margin.

758. Puts and Calls. Another form of gambling is by *puts* and *calls*. A put is the privilege of compelling someone to buy goods on a certain date. Obviously, the man who buys the put cannot lose more than its price, though he can gain indefinitely. Calls are just the reverse of puts.

759. "Futures." Dealing in futures on the produce exchanges is practically the same as buying puts and calls. The future price of the commodity is made the object of a bet. One man agrees to buy a hundred bushels of wheat or fifty bales of cotton on a certain date at a certain price. If the price drops, he pays the difference; if it rises, he receives the difference. No delivery was contemplated.

760. Exchange Operations Are Often Fraudulent. All these transactions are really forms of betting or playing a game. If they fulfill the conditions laid down for such contracts they are not wrong in themselves. But the temptation is very strong when one is operating on a big scale to inject an element of fraud or deceit into the game. By buying and selling the same commodity on the same day, by unloading, and in various other ways, big operators attempt to fix the prices to their own advantage. And when as directors they have the power to determine dividends, they may pay them when conditions do not warrant it in order that the market may be maintained while they dispose of what is undesirable at a good figure. Or they may pass a dividend that might be paid in order that stockholders who do not know the situation may sell to them at a lower price.

761. The Immorality of Exchange Operations. All such transactions are as immoral and unjustifiable as playing poker with marked cards. But even though certain of these operations on 'change tending to fix the market price, such as selling short, might in themselves be defended morally, there is one element lacking that is necessary to justify gambling by games—that *the players should engage freely*. In this case it is not merely the actual speculators who engage in the game; real investors and buyers are made parties, whether they wish it or not. They cannot escape from the consequences of this exchange gambling.

762. Exchanges Do Not Steady Prices. Speculation upon the exchange has been frequently defended upon the ground that it subserves a useful purpose by steadying prices.[2] The argument is that experienced operators have special information regarding conditions and "discount" the future in such a way as to prevent

[2] For a thorough discussion very favorable to the exchanges, cf. H. H. Brace, *The Value of Organized Speculation*.

sudden fluctuations in prices. A. A. Osborne has made an inductive study of the New York Stock Exchange to determine the validity of this claim.[3] He concludes: "Our study of speculative activity in 1906 and 1907 has not led us to admit that speculators in those years, incidentally to the pursuit of their selfish individual interests, either guided the flow of capital into investment or 'discounted' the October panic of 1907 and the depression of 1908. . . . The slight degree of dependence shown between the extent of the declines in individual stocks and their subsequent value to investors makes us loath to accept the 'discounting' faculty as an attribute, either of speculators or of stock exchange prices."

763. Exchanges Not Necessary. That exchanges perform no necessary social function[4] seems to be shown by the fact that the United States probably got along as well without them in 1914 as would have been the case had they remained open. There seems to be a growing sentiment against exchanges, and several European countries, such as Austria, Germany, and Norway, have enacted special laws against gambling in futures. There are strong parties for and against exchanges in Germany, and each side claims the same points of advantage and disadvantage. The question is so complicated and one on which we have so little real information as to results, that it is impossible to arrive at a scientific conclusion.

764. Conclusion as to Exchanges. The whole question may be summed up in the words of Father Slater: "If gambling becomes a passion, if the gambler seeks to make it a substitute for honest toil and strives to make it support him or bring him wealth, serious harm has already been done. The gambler produces nothing; he adds nothing to the wealth of the community; he soon learns to shun honest work; he becomes a parasite who preys on society, and eventually brings ruin on others as well as on himself. So that dealing in differences, even if regarded merely as a form of gambling and speculation, must fall under the cen-

---

[3] *Speculation on the New York Stock Exchange* (N. Y., 1913), pp. 145, 146.
[4] Slater, *Questions of Moral Theology,* pp. 145 ff.

sure of the moralist. . . . On many grounds, therefore, the verdict of the moral theologian on the question of the lawfulness of dealing in futures must be that in practice the transaction is immoral and wrong." [5]

765. Is Insurance a Bet? [6] Insurance has often been considered a form of betting. Essentially, it has been said, fire insurance is a case of one man betting that a house will burn and another betting that it will not. It is true that insurance and betting have something in common. They are both contracts depending upon an uncertain event. In each case one pays out a comparatively small sum upon condition that if a certain event happens he shall receive a comparatively large one.

766. Differences Between Insurance and Betting. But the differences between betting and insurance are more important than their similarities. In the first place, the relation between the event which may take place and the insurer is very different. If I bet on a certain horse, my interest in his winning depends entirely on the bet. If I had not bet, his winning or losing would not affect me in the least. But whether I insure a house or not, I am interested in its burning.

767. Whole Spirit of Insurance and Betting Is Different. Secondly, the whole spirit dominating betting and insurance are essentially unlike. In betting I risk the loss of a small sum for the chance of getting a large one. I am dominated by a desire to get something for nothing. When I insure, on the other hand, I am influenced by a conservative spirit. I want to *avoid* the risk, instead of assuming it; by actually suffering a small loss, I want to make sure of not suffering a large loss.

768. Social Consequences of Betting and Insurance Different. Futhermore, the social consequences of betting and insurance are poles apart. Betting merely makes money change hands. It is not in the least to the advantage of society that one man should win rather than another. Nothing is produced by betting,

[5] *Op. cit.,* pp. 156, 158.
[6] Cf. A. J. Dorward, "Betting and Insurance," *Int. Jour. Ethics,* July, 1915.

either from the individual or social standpoint. Indeed, society would be distinctly better off without the whole crew of professional bettors. May their tribe decrease. On the other hand, it is a social advantage to have risks distributed in such a way that a sudden loss will not pauperize anyone. For instance, an important factory employing a thousand men in a small town burns. Unless it is rebuilt, these men will be out of work and they and their families will suffer acute want. Should the owner have practically his whole capital invested in this plant and be uninsured, this distinct *social* calamity would be the result to that community. Hence, it is clear that it is socially advantageous to have insurance losses distributed in such a way as not to bear heavily upon any one person or group of persons.

769. Definition of Insurance. *Insurance, then, may be defined as a contract whereby upon the payment of a comparatively small sum by one party, another agrees to pay a comparatively large sum should some untoward event happen to him.*

770. Conditions for Just Insurance. In order to be just, there must be equality between the risk and the premium. Hence, a thorough study of the field should precede the establishment of rates. Only an extensive knowledge of mortuary statistics can form a reasonable basis for life insurance, for instance. And insurance companies are guilty of gross injustice if, in order to pay excessive salaries to some people, they charge higher rates than are necessary. Such was done as revealed in the famous investigation of New York companies under Justice Hughes.

771. Fraud Makes Insurance Unjust. Again, there must be no fraud on the part of the person taking the policy. The same conditions must govern the transaction as in the case of buying and selling. Substantial defects, such as disease rendering one ineligible, must be revealed. If they have been concealed, the contract is void, unless the civil law provides otherwise. In general, one may in this regard follow the civil law with a good conscience; and he is obliged to follow it when it imposes an obligation upon him.

772. Scope of Insurance. Within recent years the scope of insurance has been greatly broadened.[7] It now embraces not simply life and fire, but almost every risk to which man and his property may be exposed—health, accident, old age, unemployment, cyclone, and dozens of others. Attempts have been made to insure crops and the renting of houses. The term social insurance indicates that we are beginning to see the social value of insurance, and there are some careful students who look to insurance as affording the best means of ameliorating conditions.

SUGGESTED READINGS

1. Cath. Encyc., art. "Gambling."
2. A. A. Osborne, *Speculation on the New York Exchange.*
3. H. H. Brace, *The Value of Organized Speculation.*
4. Slater, *Questions of Moral Theology.*
5. Dorward, "Betting and Insurance," *Int. Journal of Ethics,* July, 1915.
6. *Saturday Evening Post,* "Odds Against You," October 24, 1936. A professional gambler's analysis of games of chance.
7. Present Legislation Governing Stock Exchanges.

QUESTIONS

1. What are the ethics of gambling?
2. Do the exchanges serve a useful social purpose?
3. Is insurance a form of gambling?
4. What are the conditions for just insurance?

---

[7] An Irishman once appeared at an insurance agent's office with the announcement that he wanted to take out a policy. "Fire, marine, life, or accident?" said the too smart clerk. "All four," said the Irishman, "I am a stoker in the Navy."

TEN: *The Family*

773. Importance of the Family. The most important social relations, probably, are those developing out of the family. This is not only because nobody escapes them; it is also because the family was the original school and church and state, and to a large extent the efficiency of these institutions depends upon the family. Originally, the head of the family was the teacher, priest, law-giver, judge and executioner. He united in himself the functions later taken over by other classes. But though shorn of much of its pristine power and influence, the home still remains supremely important. Within the family the average child must learn the duties which will govern every phase of his life, individual and social. Here he should be trained in the fundamental religion and citizenship on which society ultimately rests. The prosperity of Church and State intimately depends upon a sound family life.

774. Sociologists and the Family. There is little wonder, then, that the family has received great attention from philosopher and statesman. There is little wonder, too, that the dominant philosophy of today, evolution, has been applied to the family. It has been customary with certain evolutionists to trace all human institutions back to somewhat analogous conditions among brute animals. Professor Giddings, for instance, asserts there is no reason to doubt the continuity of animal and human society and then proceeds with several pages of *a priori* arguments and unproved assertions.[1] In no field, indeed, is this apriorism more strikingly evident than in that of marriage. Most sociological assumptions in this regard, however, are mere unscientific speculations without proof, and even if proven would serve as little toward solving present day ethical and sociological problems as the famous example of Scholastic hair-splitting relative to how many angels could stand upon the point of a needle.

[1] *Principles of Sociology* (N. Y., 1896), pp. 208, 219 ff.

775. Definition of Family. For us it will be sufficient to say that as among the lower animals, so with man, there is a certain attraction between the sexes that leads in individual cases to a union resulting in the birth of children. When this union is somewhat permanent it is called a "family." This union may be between one man and one woman, when it is called monogamous; between one man and several women, polygamous; or between one woman and several men, polyandrous. Each form of union has been practiced to some extent and recognized by the laws and customs of various peoples.

776. Monogamy Always the Most Prevalent. In no field, perhaps, has prejudice played so large a part in distorting evidence as in the history of marriage and the family. Certain prominent anthropologists have maintained that the original form of the family was a promiscuity between the men and women of a particular tribe or group.[2] But authors equally authoritative, as Letourneau[3] and Westermarck, maintain that the facts alleged in support of such a theory can be explained as consistent with rigid restrictions laid upon promiscuity. Thus Westermarck writes: "The hypothesis of promiscuity, instead of belonging, as Professor Giraud-Teulon thinks, to the class of hypotheses which are scientifically permissible has no real foundation and is essentially unscientific."[4] Professor Howard tells us that probably "one marriage and the pairing of one man and one woman, though the union was often transitory and the rule frequently violated, is the typical form of sexual union from the infancy of the race."[5]

777. Modern Sociological Thought on Monogamy. The whole trend of present sociological thought is well summed up by Dr. Edward C. Hayes in his *Introduction to the Study of Sociology*. Dr. Hayes was professor of Sociology at the University of Illinois,

---

[2] Bachhofer, *Das Mutterrecht;* Morgan, *Ancient Society;* McLennan, *The Patriarchal Theory;* Lang, *Custom and Myth;* Lubbock, *The Origin of Civilization and the Primitive Condition of Man.*

[3] Letourneau, *The Evolution of Marriage;* Westermarck, *The History of Human Marriage.*

[4] *The History of Human Marriage,* p. 133.

[5] *History of Matrimonial Institutions,* Vol. I, pp. 90, 91.

has been president of the American Sociological Society, and his book is praised by Franklin Giddings, E. A. Ross, and Albion Small—all eminent sociologists, and all former presidents of the Society. In the preface to this text-book, Dr. Hayes professes to eschew originality and to give rather, in a systematic way, a summary of sociological thought. We may, therefore, accept his statements as really representing the current attitude of sociologists on this important point.

778. Incomparable Superiority of Monogamy. Professor Hayes says: "Mankind has experimented on a great scale and through long periods with every possible form of domestic organization, and among all highly advanced peoples, monogamy increasingly survives and prevails. Its predominance has been assisted by social and religious sanctions, due to the approval of the influential, but this predominance has been essentially due to the natural selection of the survival of the fittest. Nothing human is perfect, no domestic arrangement makes ideals automatically fulfill themselves; but it would seem that if anything can be said to have been demonstrated by experience, the incomparable superiority of monogamy over other forms of the family seems removed beyond argument." [6]

779. However, Polygamy Was Recognized Among the Jews. But if some non-Scholastic writers have allowed their prejudices to run away with their judgment, some Scholastic writers have allowed their desire to support a preconceived theory to blind them to certain indisputable facts. Only the most unjustifiable apriorism, for instance, can explain Cilleuls' statement: "You will seek in vain in the Old Testament for texts that insinuate the liceity of polygamy among the Chosen People." [7] Polygamy was practiced and recognized as lawful among the Chosen People, and among most semi-civilized races. [8]

780. Why Polygamy Was Limited. For while it is probable that promiscuity was never particularly prevalent nor looked upon as lawful, it is undoubtedly true that both polygamy and

[6] P. 536.
[7] Alfred des Cilleuls, *La Population*, p. 36.
[8] Cath. Encyc., art. "Concubinage."

polyandry were largely sanctioned and to some extent practiced. Apparently the limitations upon the practice arose more from certain physical and economic facts than from moral scruples. It is evident, however, that where the sexes are equally divided, polygamy can exist only upon a very limited scale. There would not be enough women to supply on the average more than one mate to each man. Again, it would be only the wealthy and powerful who could obtain or support more than one wife. Others would be limited necessarily to one.

781. Other Limitations on Polygamy. Nature has arranged other ways to discourage promiscuity and these lower forms of marriage. Polyandry and promiscuity tend to produce sterility, and the offspring of any of these unions will, on the whole, have less chance for successful living than the offspring of a monogamous marriage. Where the children have the same parents there will be greater affection and interest on the part of the parents, and the children are apt to enjoy better and more consistent care. In polyandry or promiscuity no man could know his own children; and for the children polygamy would be somewhat akin to having several stepmothers.

782. Monogamous Ideal Is Natural. Having better parental care, the offspring of monogamous unions will do more than hold their own against the children of other unions. They will live and perpetuate themselves to a relatively greater degree than the others. Hence, there will be a gradual approximation by purely natural causes to the Christian ideal of union between one man and one woman. Such an ideal had been largely attained in Greece and Rome, whatever may have been the practical failure to live up to it.

783. Hence, Unity Is Essential to Christian Marriage. The unity of marriage, therefore, is the first essential of ideal marriage. All lower forms of union are abolished. There are no longer any dispensations from the natural ideal on account of the weakness of human nature. A stiff-necked race must bow beneath this yoke. In thus legislating, Christianity has followed the highest dictates of nature. Apart from any divine institution of monogamous marriage as a sacrament this insistence upon the unity of marriage is in accordance with the progress of the human race. With our historical perspective we can now see that this attainment was inevitable although Christianity by stringent laws has unquestionably hastened a process which must otherwise have been of slower natural growth.

784. National Strength Depends on Right Marriage Ideals. No one thing, perhaps, has contributed so much to the strength and progress of the so-called Christian countries as the high ideal of marriage that has been given them by the Christian Church. For as the individual families that adopt this ideal tend to be perpetuated in greater purity and integrity, forming worthy and valuable units of society, so do the nations that adopt it. In the weeding process of nature the fit survive and flourish, and those who have the highest sexual ideals are fittest. Not material possessions nor commercial supremacy nor a "far flung battle line" shall save any nation's soul alive. Sodom, Babylon, Rome, down through the centuries echo their leper cry: "Unclean, unclean." The race is not to the swift nor the battle to the strong, but to the clean-bodied and clean-souled. Blessed are the pure of heart for they shall not only see God, but they shall also possess the land.

785. Lack of Formal Guilt Does Not Prevent Consequences of Low Sexual Ideals. And this is true even where there is no formal guilt attaching to the lower and racially outgrown forms of marriage. When polygamy was sanctioned under the Old Law it was not sinful, but it was not in accord with nature's highest ideals and a nation practicing it would inevitably go down to oblivion before a clean-hearted people. For invincible ignorance in the practice of polygamy or polyandry does not prevent the natural degeneration consequent to such customs any more than mistake in drinking carbolic acid prevents death. Nature's laws work impartial justice upon the ignorant and the knowing, the guilty and the innocent.

786. Polyandry Lowers Woman. Another reason why monogamous nations surpass polygamous or polyandrous nations is because monogamy raises the status of woman. Where polyandry is lawful, a woman is the mere tool of passion for men. She is not the consort and the companion of one man, the mother of those who are bone of his bone and flesh of his flesh, but the instrument for sexual gratification.

787. Polygamy Lowers Woman. The same is very largely true of polygamy. Women are lowered and degraded, because the union that exists between man and wife cannot be thus divided and extended without destroying the complete unity of interests, of affection, and of flesh which is the essence and being of marriage and which unity alone raises the conjunction of the sexes to a true sacramental dignity. One man and many women, or one woman and several men can no more make a marriage of the highest type than three straight lines can make a sphere.

788. Hence, Polygamy and Polyandry Are Anti-Social. It is a law of nature, however, that no large number of a nation can be degraded without the whole level of a nation being lowered. The object of or reason for the degradation does not matter. There is a sweet revenge that works itself out in time, a poetic justice that will ultimately give a nation its just dues.

789. Successive Polygamy. Various Christian sects have at different times carried this doctrine of the unity of marriage to the extent of forbidding second marriages even after the death of the first spouse. As to a polygamous or polyandrous nation the monogamous ideal is still in advance, a thing to grow toward, so we may consider the absolute finality of the union of one man with one woman as a step in advance of our present standing.

790. Indissolubility of Marriage. Closely allied with the unity of marriage is its indissolubility. The strictest view, which is not held by any Christian church at the present time, is that nothing can dissolve the bond of matrimony. Under such a view remarriage would not be lawful even after the death of one's spouse. The Protestant churches generally allow divorce and remarriage for various reasons, from infidelity to incompatibility of temperament. All the oriental churches allow divorce from the bond at least for infidelity.

791. When Divorce Is Allowable. It is sometimes said that the Catholic Church *never* grants divorce with right to marry during the lifetime of the other party. Rickaby's language, however, is probably more accurate: "In the present arrangement," he writes. "a divorce *a vinculo* [that is, with the right to marry while the other party to the contract is still alive] is obtainable in three cases. First, when of two unbaptized persons, man and wife, the one is converted and the unconverted person refuses to live peaceably in wedlock, the convert may marry again. So the Church understands St. Paul, I Cor. vii, 13, 15. Again, the Pope can grant a divorce *a vinculo* in the marriage of baptized persons before cohabitation. Such a marriage in that stage is also dissolved by the profession of one of the parties in a religious order." [9]

792. The Catholic Doctrine of Indissolubility. The better way, then, in which to put the Catholic doctrine is that a valid Christian consummated marriage can be dissolved only by death. That is the present universal teaching of the Church. Tanquerey, however, tells us that in "France, Ireland, and England there were a few particular councils which, more favorable than they should have been to the authority of kings and civil laws, admitted certain causes for divorce, as incestuous adultery, incurable leprosy, the entrance of one party into religion." [10]

793. Oriental Catholics and Indissolubility. And while the indissolubility of valid Christian consummated marriage is the universally received doctrine, Tanquerey says that "even today some Oriental Christians, who profess the Catholic faith, although they speculatively admit our doctrine, in practice tolerate divorce on account of adultery." [11]

794. Decrees of Nullity. The sphere in which the Catholic Church admits divorce, therefore, is so limited as to be practically negligible. This is true, also, of what is called a decree of nullity, a declaration that no marriage existed. If it can be proven that

---

[9] *Moral Philosophy*, p. 274.
[10] *Theol. Dog., Tr. de Matrimonio*, No. 55.
[11] *Loc. cit.*

there was no true consent, or that some other invalidating impediment (for which no dispensation was granted) existed at the time of the supposed marriage, the Church will decide that there was no real contract and hence either party is free to marry someone else. What percentage of Catholic marriages are declared null in this way, no one knows, but it is probably very small.

795. Impediments to Marriage. Among the reasons for declaring a marriage null is a substantial error regarding the nature or an essential property of marriage, such as the giving of what are known technically as "marital rights." The same is true of serious fear unjustly aroused for the purpose of forcing marriage which invalidates the contract. This applies even to filial fear, provided it be unjustly aroused to compel marriage. Antecedent and perpetual impotency also invalidates marriage. Consanguinity in the first degree, either direct or collateral, is a diriment impediment of the natural law. And finally, what was said about consent in connection with the other contracts applies also to matrimony.[12]

796. Marriage Is Good in Itself. When none of the above-mentioned impediments are present, the marriage contract (according to the natural law) is valid and lawful.[13] Not only so, but the Church looks upon this state as good in itself and as commendable for many persons. It was instituted by God as the means of propagating the human race and satisfying certain desires which He implanted in human nature. As St. Paul says: "It is better to marry than be burnt." And so sacred is the contract that valid Christian consummated marriage is dissolved only by death.

797. The Divorce Evil. Outside of the Church, however, divorces are becoming more and more numerous. But most of the discussion of the question seems to miss the real point, for divorce itself is not the evil. That is merely a symptom or consequence of the genuine evils, such as hasty and unconsidered marriages,

---

[12] Cf. chapter on "Contracts."

[13] The Church has established other impediments that need not be treated in a textbook on Ethics. They may be found in Slater's *Moral Theology*.

infidelity, drunkenness, brutality. If we eliminate these causes, there will be fewer divorces. And hence it would be wiser to direct the energy that is being spent in deploring divorce to eradicating these crying outrages. We hear too much condemnation of people who separate because their mate was absolutely worthless and not enough of the worthless spouse.

798. Separation From Bed and Board. But though the Church will allow remarriage only in the very limited sphere already indicated, she has not the same antipathy to a separation, or a divorce from bed and board. Any serious reason, such as infidelity, confirmed drunkenness, physical violence, will justify such a separation. For the contract to take another for better or for worse until death part, is always conditional. One who persistently violates his or her part of the contract cannot reasonably expect the other to be bound. And hence, though persons who marry should not for any inconsiderable whim subject the other to danger of incontinence they may lawfully separate when there is a serious reason or mutual consent. This is particularly true where there are no children, or where they are grown.

799. Temporary Separation. What has been said of perpetual separation, applies even more widely to a temporary separation. Business or sentimental considerations will frequently justify this. The reason need be only in proportion to the danger of incontinence and the neglect of the children. Long separations, however, are unwise. People tend to grow apart, and both parties expose themselves to the risk of contracting entangling alliances.

800. The Civil Consequences of Marriage. But so far as the civil consequences of the legal contract are concerned the State has a perfect right to legislate. She may establish certain conditions for civil legitimacy, the obtaining of a license, registration, property rights of wife and children, and so on. All should know the civil consequences of marriage before they enter into any such contract. These may vary with each State, and it is advisable to know the local law.

801. May State Forbid Certain Individuals to Marry? The inherent right of a man to marry does not imply a right to marry

a particular woman. Hence the State may in certain circumstances and with due consideration for the moral welfare and
fundamental rights of her subjects, forbid marriages from which
serious social evils would probably follow. This prohibition need
not establish an invalidating impediment. Nevertheless it may
oblige to obedience, just as any other law does. On the other
hand, if persons married in the eyes of the Church but not in
the eyes of the State cohabit, they do not sin against purity, no
matter what disobedience they may commit.

802. State's Right Admitted in Certain Cases. The State's right
indirectly to prohibit certain persons from marrying seems to
be admitted without question in a limited field. Criminals sen-
tenced to life imprisonment are virtually condemned to a life of
celibacy. The State forbids private soldiers to marry without
special permission even in times of peace, and in case of war
temporary celibacy is forced upon vast numbers.

803. Does Common Good Demand Eugenics? This lands us
squarely in the question of eugenics, and whether or not the
State is justified in adopting such theories. The answer is that
she may use such measures as are necessary for her self-protection and self-development. *If* the elimination of the irreclaim-
able criminal and the otherwise unfit can be accomplished
through eugenic legislation, then such legislation is justified. All
depends upon that *if*. For whatever the future may bring forth,
the question is still debatable.

804. Definition of Eugenics. The term "eugenics" [14] is defined
by the Standard Dictionary as "the science and art of improving
the human race by applying the ascertained laws of inheritance
of characteristics to the selection of marriage mates, with the aim
of securing to the offspring a desirable combination of traits, including resistance to outward conditions." This is the generally

[14] Cf. *Heredity and Eugenics,* lectures by W. E. Castle, J. W. Coulter, C. B.
Davenport, E. M. East, W. L. Tower; Karl Pearson, *Scope and Importance to the
State of the Science of National Eugenics; The Groundwork of Eugenics; The Social
Direction of Human Evolution; Publications of the Eugenics Record Office,* Cold
Spring, N. Y.

accepted meaning of the word and the principal emphasis has been upon this feature of the science.

805. Eugenics Sometimes Made to Embrace Environment. It is true that Francis Galton, in establishing a laboratory for the study of national eugenics in the University of London, has defined this new science as "the study of agencies under social control that may improve or impair the racial qualities of future generations, either physically or mentally." And Karl Pearson, one of the leading exponents of eugenics, tells us that "this science does not propose to confine its attention to the problem of inheritance only, but to deal also with problems of environment and nature." [15]

806. Case for Eugenics Has Not Been Proven. But whether we call this science of improving the human race by better breeding eugenics or merely a part of eugenics, there is a very determined group of social reformers bent upon putting such theories in practice. Are they justified? At present, no. For they have not proven their case. Scientific knowledge concerning the inheritance of characteristics is too uncertain at present to warrant such drastic interference with the rights of individuals. About as many facts can be adduced on one side as on the other. Eugenists have made out a case largely by ignoring part of the field through a process of selection that really cannot prove anything.

807. Facts Against Eugenics. In how many instances do twins, for example, turn out differently. They have the same ancestors, yet one will be truthful, industrious, honest, brave; and the other lying, lazy, dishonest, cowardly. Until eugenists are able to explain such facts, they should not tamper with the basic relations between the sexes.[16]

808. Dr. Foerster and Eugenics. Dr. Foerster, who is a very well-balanced writer upon any subject he handles, deals unspar-

[15] Karl Pearson, *The Scope and Importance to the State of the Science of National Eugenics,* p. 10.

[16] Sir Walter Besant has several very interesting novels whose unobtrusive moral is the superior influence of environment to heredity. The general theme, differently treated in each case, is that of a low-born child raised by aristocratic persons as their own and being in all essentials as if to the manner born. Cf. *All Sorts and Conditions of Men, Children of Gideon.*

ingly with the fanatic eugenists. "With regard to the whole problem of heredity," he writes, "it should be always borne in mind that dangerous tendencies on the part of one parent may be balanced by the healthy influence derived from the other. . . . My desire is to protest against the brutal and superficial heredity terrorism with which certain modern eugenic enthusiasts advocate a regulation of human breeding borrowed from the stables and totally foreign to the human race, where the problem of right and duty of propagation is so infinitely more difficult and complicated. . . . Moreover, it is only in the rarest cases that we find two parents who are both of them, physically and psychically, so equally and heavily tainted and defective, that anything could be safely predicted with regard to their children." [17]

809. Dangers of Eugenics. But even supposing that the inheritance of characteristics had been proven, a complete case would not thereby have been made out for legislation to forbid certain persons to marry. The advocates of such legislation should prove further that this course would result in greater social good than at present. It is not at all certain that such would be the case. For the sexual instinct is very deeply rooted and its demands for satisfaction insistent and imperious. To forbid its exercise through marriage might be to make it break forth in anti-social ways bringing in its train indefinitely greater harm to society than comes by the birth of some children with an undesirable heredity. It is one thing to pass a law, another to enforce it. But even if enforced so far as marriage is concerned, our last state might well be worse than our first. "Whom God hath joined together let no man put asunder" might well be matched with: "Whom God hath not forbidden to be joined let no man keep asunder."

810. Nature Is Wiser Than Eugenists. At present nature takes care of such things, and perhaps it is better to trust nature than a few short-sighted pedagogues or venal "statesmen." In balancing the sexes, nature has undoubtedly worked for human betterment. Probably had the statesmen of polygamous times been able to interfere in this regard, civilization might never have advanced

[17] *Marriage and the Sex Problem*, p. 97.

to the idea of monogamy. And the fact that the great majority of the human race seem endowed with fairly desirable bodily and mental characteristics would point to some divinity shaping our inheritance despite the rough-hewing of our ancestors.

811. Dr. Meyer on Eugenics. Anyone but a confirmed eugenist can recognize the wisdom of these words of a real authority upon the question: "A careful student of the literature and of the facts of eugenics realizes the complexity of this problem and the reason why we should be cautious about pushing everything to the point of legislative regulation. It is in the interest of civilization to provide principles and customs rather than laws, and to give the plain sense of the individual a chance to develop and to become effective." [18]

812. Marriage and a Health Certificate. Insistence upon freedom from communicable disease before a marriage license will be issued stands upon a different basis. The fact of certain diseases being communicated to others has been established beyond a doubt, and the State has a right to protect those who could be protected in no other way.

I. Duties of Parents and Children

813. Wifely Obedience. While in the marriage service the wife makes no promise to obey, it is understood that the husband is ordinarily the head of the family. But whatever obedience his wife owes to him is not blind and unlimited. The same principles which govern obedience in other situations apply here. For instance, a wife is not obliged to obedience under a proportionately serious inconvenience. If the man should wish unnecessarily to separate her from her children, to change the domicile, and so on, she has a perfect right to refuse obedience, and her refusal would probably be sustained by a civil court.

814. State's Authority to Define Marital Obedience. The natural and the divine law not being entirely clear upon the limits

[18] Adolf Meyer, M.D., "The Right to Marry," in *The Survey*, June 3, 1916, p. 244. Dr. Meyer is in charge of the Henry Phipps Psychiatric Clinic at Johns Hopkins University.

of marital obedience, the State has a right to determine these limits more definitely. This it has done in some regards and civil courts may decide individual cases brought before them. Thus most States have abolished the supposed right of a husband to inflict corporal punishment upon his wife, and have defined her rights to separate property.

815. Limitations Upon Husband's Authority. No husband, therefore, need be obeyed if he commands the relinquishment of a right guaranteed by the State. Should the wife have property in her own name, the husband may not demand this for his personal expenses. Or if the State gives a wife homestead rights, let us say, the husband's authority does not extend to commanding her to sell to suit his convenience. For she is not obliged to yield a right secured to her by an authority having the determination of such matters left obscure by the natural law. And, indeed, most wives will do well to hold carefully to whatever rights and privileges the State grants them. They should not in the first enthusiasm of the honeymoon give up what they may sorely need within a few years.

816. Husband Does Not "Support" Family. Where monetary relations between husband and wife as regards his earnings and property have not been accurately determined by the State, the wife is entitled to such a share of his income as will enable her to meet reasonable personal and household expenses. The mere fact that the man receives the income in dollars and cents should not make him think that he is "supporting" his wife, that she is a burden upon him, and that he freely "gives" her what she needs. Much undignified bickering over money matters will be avoided if the man will only appreciate the fact that the woman really bears more than he of the family burdens. The prevalent idea that the man entirely "supports" the family "is as absurd a conception as it would be to consider the receiving teller as supporting the bank, or the manager of a factory as supporting all the workmen. The end of the family is not economic profit, but mutual aid, and the continuance and progress of the race. A division of labor does not create superiority and inferiority.

When one considers which party incurs the greater risks, and which works with greater singleness and sincerity for the family, it must pass as one of the extraordinary superstitions that the theory of economic dependence should have gained vogue."

817. Wages of Married Women. Where the woman goes out into the industrial world, because the man's economic earnings are not sufficient to meet the family needs, or for any other reason, the State sometimes secures to her whatever she may make, and sometimes leaves the question undecided. If the State has not spoken, then some amicable arrangement must be made regarding the disposition of her earnings. But the husband certainly has less right over them than he has over his own.

818. All Rights Not on One Side. In general, husbands should remember that if St. Paul says, "Wives, obey your husbands," he also says, "Husbands, love your wives." Where there is love there will be no danger of the man commanding what the wife will not do; without love, the man will almost inevitably become a petty tyrant. He should remember that all rights are not on one side.

819. Parents and Children. Complex as is the relationship of man and wife by themselves, the situation is further complicated by children. In the relationship between parents and children we have a perfect network of rights and duties. In the first place, the children owe their parents love, honor, and obedience.

820. Children Owe Love to Their Parents. This love should be internal and external. A certain exterior reverence is due to parents, but is not sufficient. It must be accompanied by a real affection. This love implies the support of parents when necessary and possible. In case of death, a child who is heir to his parent's property should pay the parent's debts up to the amount of the inheritance; but otherwise he is not bound, except in so far as debts are a result of a duty neglected by children. The obligation to love and reverence never ceases merely on account of age; but of course it cannot be demanded in the same way where parents are grossly unworthy.

821. Children Bound to Obey. Children have a serious obligation to obey their parents in all that is right and lawful and pertains to their care. This obligation lasts until they are emancipated by leaving the parental roof or attaining their majority. In other matters, particularly in choosing a state in life, children are bound to consult their parents, but not necessarily to follow their advice. This applies especially in choosing a religious life, or in marrying a certain person. It is the children who have to live the life selected, and a deep-rooted right gives them the privilege of deciding for themselves. Parents should be very careful about trying to force their children in such sacred matters, and while a child may give up marrying a particular person, he should seldom if ever marry simply to gratify his parents. Serious social and personal evils may very easily result from parents going beyond their rights. On the other hand, however, children should try to realize that a certain wisdom comes from the experience of age and from actually having been married, and they should give the wishes of their parents due weight. However, our own custom of allowing children to choose their own spouses has not worked so satisfactorily that we should condemn too absolutely the practice of other races. But if the children have certain duties, so have parents. They must have, and show their children affection and according to their station in life afford them bodily and spiritual education.

822. Duty to Support Children. Bodily education implies nourishment and station. By the fact of bringing children into the world, parents are bound to nourish them. Ordinarily, the mother should herself nourish the infants, but may be excused by necessity, convenience, or custom. The obligation of support lasts until the children are, according to their station, able to take care of themselves. Should the children be defective in such a way as to be incapable of self-support, the obligation of bodily education would last their whole life.

823. Duty to Educate Children. Parents are likewise bound to procure a social position for their children corresponding to their state in life. And hence, the secular education due the children depends upon the station of the family. When a profession is customary, then the children have a right to this, and the parents should use reasonable diligence to secure it for them. Hence, parents sin gravely if they waste their substance to such an extent that their children cannot attain the station in life to which they have a right.

824. Duty to Educate Children Spiritually. Spiritual education implies instruction in the duties of religion and morality, setting a good example, and employing vigilance in guarding against vices. To most parents the injunction to love their children seems entirely superfluous. Here nature for her own purposes has implanted the strongest and most unselfish instinct in the heart of man. So long, however, as it remains a mere instinct similar in kind to the affection of the tiger for its cub, so long is parental love blind and unreasoning, refusing to see any fault in the child and consequently failing to guard against the formation of vicious and immoral habits. Close observation, patient and prayerful study, reasonable recognition of the right of the child to its own individuality are necessary for successful parenthood.

825. Parents Should Not Shift Their Responsibility. There is great need to insist upon this duty of parents to train their children spiritually. Unfortunately many parents manifest a tendency to shift this responsibility to other shoulders. They seem to think that if their children go to a religious school all will be well. But the school cannot take the place of the home. A teacher with fifty children in a class and having them five hours a day for five days a week cannot possibly exercise over them the influence which parents might. Parents must come back to a sense of their duties.

826. Discordant Elements in the Family. Unfortunately for the peace and harmony of family life, there are certain elements that frequently introduce a strain. Men and women are seldom perfectly congenial even when they first marry. The honeymoon is scarcely over before they realize that each one is an individual with a certain ineradicable selfishness. Differences of opinion develop upon important points, and there is sometimes a complete *impasse*. If the man and woman are of different religions, particularly Catholic and Protestant, or if one has no religion, there will be a gulf between them that can only be bridged by the most sincere affection and by careful respect for each other's convictions.

827. Difference of Age Between Parents and Children a Source of Discord. And while children are a bond of union, they are apt to be also a source of discord. Parents are likely to differ as to the proper way of bringing them up, and the children and mother will sometimes find themselves arrayed against the father. Or if the parents are agreed, the inevitable difference in age between parents and children tends to produce a different outlook on life. Few persons take in new ideas after they are forty. As a consequence the parents attempt to govern the children according to ideals without appeal to the current generation. The children are with the new generation, the parents with the old, and conflicts result. Only the greatest tact on the part of the parents, the frank acceptance of some modification of their views, and a sincere respect for the personality of their children can avoid such a contingency.

828. Children and Heredity. Frequently, even the wisest parents cannot prevent clashes. Indeed, the more one sees of children, the more they seem to be a lottery. The most radical eugenist is forced to stop and think before the spectacle of good, prudent parents with worthless children, and worldly, selfish, exacting parents with exemplary offspring. They who marry, said St. Paul, shall have tribulation of the flesh. That tribulation frequently comes from selfish, ungrateful, willful, wicked children. Those who should be a support and honor in old age are a cross and disgrace. One who begets children needs hope and confidence in God, and the result of all his efforts will frequently be but to make him bow his head in sorrow and say, "Thy will be done."

829. Seriousness of Marriage. Marriage is a serious step and it is fraught with such far-reaching consequences to the individuals and to society at large that it should not be entered upon hastily. Nor should it be recommended as a panacea for all sorts of moral failings. It is a dangerous mistake to assume that the mere fact of marrying will change the frivolous or the debauched into paragons of virtue.

830. As Men Are Before Marriage They Are Likely to Be After. There can be no sounder advice given to a woman than not to marry a man in order to reform him. A Jesuit who had been rector of their scholasticate once remarked that his thirty-five years in the Society had taught him that as a man entered the novitiate, so he died. If that be true of men who go through the wonderful training of St. Ignatius of Loyola, much more true is it of those who marry. The chances are that a man who is a drunkard or impure before marriage will be a drunkard or impure afterwards.

831. Informing Children on Sexual Questions. In this connection the question of giving infomation to children on sexual matters naturally arises. It is a difficult subject. There are dangers either way. But there are two good reasons why children should be informed upon such topics by their parents or by some superior standing in the place of parents when these are incompetent. The first is that the average child will learn them anyhow. Suggestive pictures, advertisements, art galleries, vicious companions will arouse a curiosity that will sooner or later be satisfied. And it is better that pure, truth-telling lips should make the revelation.

832. Why Children Should Be Informed. Again, a child has a right to know these things in order to plan his life wisely. It is a crime to allow a young girl to make a marriage contract without knowing that it means the giving of certain rights over her body. And it is equally wrong, and more unwise, to allow a young boy to give up the possibility of married life by entering the priesthood before he understands his body and the possibility of satisfying certain dormant desires. So whether young men or women are going to marry or take a vow of chastity, they should know what they are doing.

833. The Unmarried Should Know the Problems of the Married. In addition to this, young people of marriageable age should know the problems married persons have to face. And they should have the information before they are in love, so that, if they do not wish these problems they may avoid getting in love. In spite of romantic novels, people do not fall in love—they grow into it. Fortunately, the symptoms of approaching love can be observed, and steps taken to prevent its development. Otherwise, persons who are already married and persons in the religious life would be in a very dangerous way. The parents who have gone through these experiences ought to teach their children so that love will not develop in regard to one who would make an unworthy mate. And one of the problems of married life that ought to be known before love comes is that of birth control.[19]

834. Family Limitation. One of the primary ends of marriage is the propagation of the race. Nevertheless, it is generally agreed that marriage is not invalid nor illicit between those who are sterile. And on the other hand, no one maintains that married folk are morally obliged to have as many children as would be physically possible.[20] Strictly speaking, the Scholastics do not condemn birth control or family limitation,[21] but rather the use of artificial means to prevent conception. For this position they usually rely upon the argument that artificial contraception involves the misuse of a faculty. But Cooper, distrusting the validity of this argument, prefers to base the opposition on the social consequences of contraception.[22] Once the lawfulness of contraception is allowed, its practice is likely to be carried to such excess that we are faced with the problem which Theodore Roosevelt characterized by the striking phrase, "race suicide." There is

---

[19] Cf., *Birth Control,* by Rev. John Cooper, N. C. W. C., 1923.

[20] Koch-Preuss, *Handbook of Moral Theology,* V, p. 472: "Broadly speaking, married couples have not the right to bring into the world children whom they are unable to support, for they would thereby inflict a grievous damage upon society." For a more detailed treatment of the relations between husband and wife touched upon in this paragraph consult Koch-Preuss, V, pp. 463-498.

[21] Cf. Latz: *Rhythm of Sterility and Fertility in Women.*

[22] Cf. *Am. Eccles. Rev.,* July, 1929.

much more danger of national decay following from empty cradles than from overpopulation.

835. Social Importance of Marriage. Marriage, however, is not an individual affair. The number of marriages, at what age, how many children, vitally affect society as a whole. For marriage is the institution whereby human society is continued and the species reproduced. It is readily comprehensible, therefore, that there should be various policies advocated regarding marriage.

836. Can There Be Overpopulation? Until the end of the eighteenth century, the generally accepted theory was that the more marriages contracted at an early age and the more children born of them, the better. And today many persons are of the opinion that there cannot be too many people in the world. Socialists quite generally maintain that overpopulation is a phenomenon of a capitalistic society, and Spencer maintained that nature automatically provides a check upon the increase by making civilized people less fecund.

837. Malthus' Theory. However, it is probably true, as Malthus contended, that if men and women married as soon as possible, the world would soon be overpopulated. China furnishes an excellent example of this contention. He also held that the population tends to increase in a geometrical and the food supply in an arithmetical ratio.

838. How Far Malthusianism Is True. This is probably true, as it is true that the earth *tends* to fly off into space from the sun. As a matter of fact, however, the earth does not fly off because the tendency is counteracted by other forces. Neither does the population increase in a geometrical ratio. Marriage is delayed, many persons are sterile, wars, plagues, and other natural phenomena carry off large numbers. Besides, the pressure of population begets improved methods of production and transportation that make the food supply increase in more than an arithmetical ratio.

839. Malthusianism and Statistics. As a consequence, we find that the necessaries of life have outdistanced the population. "In the last fifteen years the population of the civilized world, excluding China, has been increasing at the rate of 1 per cent a

year, whereas the average annual increase in the five great cereals
—wheat, corn, oats, rye, and barley—has been about 2.5 per cent.
In other words, production has increased two and a half times
as much as was necessary to keep *per capita* consumption constant." [23]

840. Further Statistics. Taking some single countries, we find
that: "In Great Britain, for example, the national income increased from £27 per head in 1867 to £40 per head in 1901,
or a gain of nearly 50 per cent. As compared with the increase
in population, the principal industries of the United Kingdom
have similarly outstripped the increase in numbers in the past
fifty years. The production of coal, relative to the population,
has increased from 2.62 tons to 6.07 tons; of pig iron, from 13.5
tons to 22.9 tons; of shipbuilding, from 9.72 tons to 23.52 tons." [24]
Similar facts might be adduced for the United States, France,
and Germany.

841. Conclusion as to Overpopulation. While Malthus is most
likely correct in the abstract, concretely there does not seem to
be any reason for fearing overpopulation in this or the next generation.

842. Summary of the Importance of the Family. Our discussion of the family has shown that it is the most important social
institution in the world. The basis of national and individual
strength is the family. Generally speaking, the healthier the family life, the healthier the individual and the State. Those nations
with the highest ideal of the unity and indissolubility of marriage have won out in the struggle of nations.

843. Past Changes in the Family. During the course of centuries the structure of the family has changed and one function
after another has been abandoned. Some of these changes, as
the break-up of the patriarchal family or the foregoing of capital
punishment by the father, have undoubtedly been advances. In
a certain way they have weakened the family ties. Probably those

[23] J. H. Hollander, *The Abolition of Poverty*, p. 22. Cf. also *Crop Reporter* of the
U. S. Dept. of Agriculture, Apr., 1912.
[24] Hollander, *op. cit.*, p. 25.

who first witnessed them bewailed the fact that the family was disintegrating and parental authority being undermined. But the general result has been good.

844. Contemporary Changes in the Family. But how far can we go upon this road without destroying the basis of national strength? Are there tendencies in family life today which if unchecked will work our ruin? It is difficult to judge dispassionately our own times. We are too close to see events in proper proportion. Nevertheless, we may venture to say that a loss of the ideal of the indissolubility of marriage through divorce is an unmixed evil. And again, that to carry further the processes which are at work to destroy home influences will be a national calamity. Many homes have become mere boarding houses for their members. All the members are seldom together except for dinner, and frequently not then. Parents and children are possessed by a feverishness that drives them out every night in the week. Movies, the legitimate theater, autoing, are all doing their share to disintegrate the family. As a consequence children do not get that careful and minute training which they should. Their parents do not see enough of them to train them.

845. What Should Be Our Aims? What can be done? Try to arouse an appreciation for the old-fashioned family. Have them take their recreation at home with each other. Discountenance the rush and hurry which now possess them. Give them the ideal of their grandparents, and this nation will grow in strength and power till it will be invincible. Loyalty to Church and State urges upon us the duty of restoring the influence of the home. You who read these lines and are married, go back to the outlook of a generation ago. You who are not married, aim in marriage to form a home.

SUGGESTED READINGS

1. Huxley, T. H., *Evolution and Ethics,* Ch. I.
2. Castle, W. E., *Genetics and Eugenics,* Ch. XXVII.
3. Rickaby, *Moral Philosophy,* ch. on "Marriage."
4. Cath. Encyc., art. "Marriage."
5. Cath. Encyc., art. "Concubinage."

6. Foerster, *Marriage and the Sex Problem*, Pt. I, Ch. IX.
7. Adolf Meyer, "The Right to Marry," *The Survey*, June 3, 1916.
8. Hollander, *The Abolition of Poverty*.
9. Cronin, *Science of Ethics*, II, Chs. XIII, XIV.
10. Cooper, *Birth Control*. (N. C. W. C., 1923.)
11. McCann, *Contraception a Common Cause of Disease*, St. Louis, 1936.
12. Koch-Preuss, *Handbook of Moral Theology*, V, pp. 463-547.

QUESTIONS

1. Does nature indicate that monogamy is the ideal?
2. Do all States of the United States allow divorce?
3. Look up latest statistics on ratio between marriages and divorces.
4. What are the dangers of eugenics?
5. What are the duties of parents to children?
6. Is there overpopulation?

ELEVEN: *Political Relations*

846. Summary of the Preceding Chapters. Up to the present we discussed in social Ethics the fact of individuals associating as individuals, and the ethical implications of this association. Chief among the moral questions involved were "the right to life, liberty, and the pursuit of happiness"; property rights as represented by private ownership; contracts of all kinds; and finally family relationships as between man and wife, parents and children.

847. Political Relations Are Now to Be Considered. But all this does not exhaust the social relations of men. There is a further relation that we may call political, which affects more or less directly all the actions of men. Even questions of individuals associating as individuals can be adequately discussed only by acknowledging an authority among men to determine obscure points. This authority resides in the State. For, among all civilized beings, association leads to the formation of another institution —the State—which completes family life in somewhat the same way as family life completes the individual life.

848. Definition of State. A State may be defined as the union of many persons under one supreme authority for the better attainment of their common temporal good. Unity and sovereignty, therefore, are essential to the idea of the State. Without unity there would be mere aggregation; without authority, there would be anarchy; without sovereignty, the State would be subordinated to some other society. The State cannot be subordinated in this way, because there is no other society with a higher temporal end. To secure the common welfare is the highest temporal end possible.

849. The Importance of the Origin of the State. How did the State come into existence? What was its origin? This is an important question in Ethics, for as water cannot rise higher than its source, neither can the authority of the State be greater than its author.[1]

850. How the State Is Natural. The Scholastic conception of the origin of the State is that God gave man a social nature and so constituted the world that a social life was necessary for man's well-being. In this society, from the nature of things, and, therefore, "naturally," there must be authority. And as God is the Author of nature, He is the Author of this authority. It is God-given and divine, not in the sense of God's selecting a particular individual to exercise it, but in the sense that God designed authority to govern society. It is as natural and almost as necessary for a man to be a member of a State as to be a member of a family. A condition of absolute anarchy existing for any long period of time is impossible. Anarchy never has been and never will be. Even during the terrors of the French Revolution, there was not anarchy in a strict sense, for there was always a form of government exercising authority.

[1] Hobbes in his *Leviathan* (Ch. XIII) contended that originally each man's hand was against every other man. Society was a constant warfare. Out of this melee a few emerged more powerful than the others. They subdued certain weaker men by main force and established an ascendancy of fear. The ultimate basis of the State's authority, therefore, is force. Might is right. "It is manifest," he wrote, "that during the time that men live without a power to keep them all in awe, they are in that condition which is called war, and such a war as is of every man against every man. . . . To this war of every man against every man this also is consequent, that nothing can be unjust. The notions of right and wrong, justice and injustice, have there no place. Where there is no common power there is no law; where there is no law, no injustice."

Rousseau, as Hobbes, found nothing natural in society, but his original man is gentle, industrious, care-free—the exact opposite of Hobbes' savage. Rousseau's aim was to evolve some theory of society that will guarantee to the individual the largest measure possible of that sweet freedom he originally enjoyed, "to find a form of association which shall defend and protect with all the strength of the community the person and the goods of each associate, and whereby each one, uniting himself to all, may nevertheless obey none but himself and remain as free as before." Bk. I, Ch. VI.

This, Rousseau believes, is accomplished by what he calls the "social contract." In the beginning of the State each man made a contract with all the others whereby he gave up his freedom and received theirs from them. Where the State is already in existence there is a virtual contract made by residing therein.

No one today takes Hobbes very seriously. Nor do modern sociologists believe in a formal contract between individuals. They look upon society as natural to man, and in so far they are in accord with sound Scholastic Ethics. But they have this in common with Hobbes and Rousseau, that they make the power of the State merely the aggregate of the powers of the individuals.

851. State Probably Developed from the Family. It is probable that the State developed easily and naturally from the family, and that the first political authority resided in the one who already possessed authority in the family. The first State, of course, was very much simpler than those of modern civilization. Only as society became more complex was there a greater division of function and a more developed political life. Even in Roman days, the father exercised functions which we long ago took from him to give to the State—so long ago, indeed, that most people do not realize that he ever possessed them. For his own family the Roman father was law-giver, judge, and executioner. He exercised these three functions of *government* and even had authority to inflict capital punishment.

852. Form of State Not Determined by Nature. But though the State in the abstract is a divine institution drawing its authority from God, He does not determine the particular form its government shall take. The State may be democratic or monarchic, representative or autocratic. The only basic principle that must underlie all States is that all civil government must be for the good of the governed.

853. True Test of State Is the Good of People. The goodness of a particular polity is to be determined by its results for the people. Democracy is not in itself better than autocracy; its virtue depends upon the nation having reached a certain degree of civilization and ability to govern itself. Before a people has reached such a stage, a monarchy is better. And it should not be forgotten that a democracy as well as a monarchy can be tyrannical. The majority in a republic can, and sometimes does, ride roughshod over the inherent rights of the minority.

854. Divine Right of Kings. The divine right of kings, therefore, in the sense that God designated any particular individual to rule and gave him authority, is a myth. Only in the theocracy of the Jews could that be rightly said. At the present day, no sovereign can validly claim a divine right in this sense. It is only in the sense that authority is necessary by God's design and that he happens to possess the power that any individual can be said to rule by divine right. The power of a czar is no more from God than is that of the president.

855. No Sovereign Designated by God. To attribute the authority of a particular sovereign to special selection by God is to confuse *a* polity with *the* polity. By God's dispensation *some* polity is necessary, but not necessarily a monarchy, and still less any individual monarch, whether George V or William II. The form of government might just as well, or perhaps better, be something very different, or its authority exercised by different persons. God does not directly give to a king authority to rule any more than He gives the power to heal diseases by touch. The divine right of kings is as much a fiction as the supposed ability of English sovereigns by virtue of their office to cure sickness.

856. The Sovereignty of the People. It is much nearer the truth, indeed, to say that the people are sovereign.[2] We do not mean in the sense that a pure democracy is the only lawful form of government, but in the sense that government exists for the common good. When that is not attained, the particular polity, no matter what its form, ceases to be legitimate. Interpreted in this way, the American Declaration of Independence is perfectly true. Governments do derive their just powers from the consent of the governed, inasmuch as they exist only for the good of all concerned. However, it is not true that the people may recall for any whim that strikes their fancy the powers delegated to a government. So long as the government, with reasonable success, is meeting the end of every polity—the common good—it should continue, unless in the establishment of this government a peaceful means of making a change has been especially provided.

857. Titles to Authority. Apart from the *grounds* of political authority, however, as giving a basis for the authority in the abstract, is the question as to the *title* by which any particular individual exercises this authority.

---

[2] Cf. Bellarmine, *De Laicis,* Bk. III, Ch. VI; Suarez, *Defensio Fidei Catholicae,* Bk. III, Ch. II, Sec. 5; Ryan, *Cath. World,* Dec., 1918.

858. Popular Election as a Title. The most obvious title is popular election. But this may not have been the oldest title, as a greater unity and organization are necessary for a popular election than was probably possessed by society when the first State came into being.

859. Possession as a Title. Most likely the first title to political authority, and one still applicable, is the fact of possession. If someone was exercising other than political authority in a community, it would be the natural thing for him to continue in authority as the transition was made; and the very fact of possessing power would have been a valid title to it. Even today, actual possession of political authority may be a true title. This can come about either by the consent of the governed or by prescription. That the consent of the governed can give title will not be denied now. For as all governments exist for the good of the governed, the conclusion of the governed that it is better to accept what was once an unjust usurpation, rather than attempt to remove it, makes just the exercise of authority by the possessor. The only thing which could stand in the way would be the claim of the ousted sovereign. But as he could exercise authority legitimately only in so far as it was good for the people, their judgment that their good demands allegiance to the actual possessors of power nullifies his claim. Fortunately we have gotten away from the idea of any State being a sort of personal possession of a sovereign, or that it cannot be alienated from him for the common good.

860. Prescription as Title.[3] Prescription may also be a true title, since it is necessary that there should be some ruler. Without a government the common good cannot be attained, and if any particular government possesses authority more harm than good will probably result from trying to dispossess it. Thus the common good comes to demand the retention of what began as an illegitimate government even in the face of the claims of what

[3] Cf. McDonald, *Some Ethical Questions of Peace and War,* pp. 53-61. (Lond., 1920.)

would have been the legitimate government could it have retained power. Unlike prescription as a title to private property,
it is not necessary in the case of political authority that it should
begin in good faith. William the Conqueror of England, whether
or not he assumed the throne with a good title, after gaining a
firm hold upon the kingly power had a just claim not to be
disturbed.

861. Conquest and Annexation. What has been said of *de facto*
governments in general applies also to conquest and annexation.
Whether Germany was justified or not in taking Alsace-Lor-
raine, her title could become just by prescription.

862. All Political Authority Is Limited. However, no matter
what the title to political authority, or what the form of government, this authority is definitely limited. It is true that it is
spoken of as supreme, but the word supreme here must be understood as meaning simply that it is not subject to any other State.
We must insist that this authority is subject to the moral law,
and that the moral law guarantees certain inalienable rights to
the individual. The State exists for the good of the individual,
and not the individual for the good of the State. Any theory
making the State omnipotent is un-Christian and must ultimately
lead to disaster.[4] In harmonizing the claims of the State and
those of the individual, no philosophy has been more successful
than the Scholastic. This follows the golden mean, defends the
individual against unjust aggression by the State at the same time
that it insists upon the individual's duties to the common good.

---

[4] The idea of the absolute character of State supremacy is not confined to rulers or
subjects of autocracies. Professor Willoughby, of Johns Hopkins, for instance, holds
the State to be "secular, positive, independent, and absolute" (*The Nature of the
State*, pp. 380, 393). Cf. *The Catholic World*, Nov., 1917, article by John A. Ryan,
"A New Theory of Political Sovereignty"; Professor Laski, *Studies in the Problem of
Sovereignty*, p. 208, says of this attitude: "We have been, perhaps, too frankly wor-
shipers of the State. Before it we have prostrated ourselves in speechless admiration, deeming its nature matter, for the most part, beyond our concern. The result has been the acceptance of a certain grim Hegelianism which has swept all
unprotestingly into the vortex of a great all which is more than ourselves. Its goodness we might not deny. We live, so we are told, but for its sake and in its life,
and are otherwise non-existent. It (the State) has become a kind of modern Baal to
which the citizens must bow a heedless knee."

863. How Far Authority of State Extends. It may be asked, indeed, who is to determine the limitations of the State? And in the concrete who is to decide when the State is right or wrong? In general, the authority of the State to command obedience comes from God, and is a genuine moral authority. That is, the State can make laws inducing a real moral obligation. Her laws are in this different from the regulations of a club. And they so bind not because they merely reinforce the natural law, specify obligations already due, but because the State has real legislative power.[5] But the right to make laws in addition to the natural and divine laws does not mean the right to contravene the natural or divine laws. If any State official contravenes these absolutely supreme laws, he is exceeding his authority and merits no obedience. The individual in such a case must follow his conscience, and while ordinarily he can bring his conscience into conformity with the demands of the State upon the principle that authority is usually right, there are times when he must prefer martyrdom to obedience.[6]

864. The State Has Duties. Whatever may be the particular polity established, then, the State is not absolutely supreme. It is limited in its rights and has certain important duties to perform. In the first place, the State must protect the rights of its individual members. As human beings they have certain inalienable rights to life, liberty and the pursuit of happiness. Also they may have certain acquired rights, as to property. These the State may not infringe and it must guarantee them against unjust aggression.

865. Some Philosophers Have Limited the State's Duties to Protection of Individual Rights. So important, indeed, is the protection of rights that some political philosophers have thought it summed up the whole duty of the State. They believed that

[5] Cf. Ryan, "The Moral Obligation of the Civil Law," *Catholic World,* Oct., 1921.
[6] Some of those who have been loudest in condemning a supposed blind obedience to the Church, wished during the European War to insist upon a blind obedience to the State. We were to give unquestioning adherence to anything Mr. Woodrow Wilson said or commanded. There was a virtual assumption of infallibility in a sphere where even the Pope does not claim to be infallible.

prosperity for everyone would automatically result by the government simply preventing some grosser forms of injustice, such as robbery, and allowing each one to compete freely with others. Even in our own day it has been a familiar Democratic slogan, "the less government the better." More advanced conceptions of the State have had to win their way against the cry of paternalism.

866. State Has Positive Duties. But it is recognized quite generally now that this negative office of government will never secure the welfare of its citizens. Life has become so complex that something more positive is needed. All men are not born equal; and a government run on the assumption that they are will inevitably allow much cruelty and injustice. The physically, economically, intellectually, and morally weak must be given special consideration.

867. State's Duties to Industrial Classes. Of course, the classes cannot be rigidly divided in everyday life. Some will be in several classes at the same time. But the essential point of the theory is to recognize inequality and the need for help. Thus competition of itself will not necessarily bring sufficient compensation to all engaged in labor. Experience has shown that the State should step in to fix a minimum wage. Likewise, the State should furnish employment to those who cannot otherwise obtain it. Old-age pensions, insurance against sickness, accident, and unemployment are all functions of the State made necessary by the fundamental principle that the State exists to secure the good of all.

868. State's Duties to Defectives. In the same way, the State should provide for the blind, deaf, dumb, feeble-minded and those in any way defective. They are wards of the nation. While not created the equal of their fellows, they have a right to protection and the opportunity to seek happiness according to their capacities.

869. State's Duties as to Morals. Further than this, the State has an obligation not only towards the physical well-being of its citizens, but also in regard to their morals. Even where the State does not profess any particular religion, it should do everything possible to advance the spiritual welfare of its subjects. This embraces the censoring of the press and of the theater, regulation of amusements, gambling, liquor traffic, and the protection of the .young and weak from temptation. Most modern States err on the side of too much liberty, which is taken advantage of by the vicious and criminal elements. The European war has familiarized us with censorship; free speech and a free press have been variously limited through the exigencies of national necessities. And while peace has brought a return to former customs, the right of government to limit freedom in this direction has been clearly recognized.

870. Connection Between Morals and Prosperity. Even though the end of the State be the temporal prosperity of its citizens, it has the right and the duty to protect their moral life. For temporal prosperity and morality are closely united. All true individual and national prosperity is based on virtue. The virtuous individuals are happy, the virtuous nations are prosperous. However specious may be the promises of vice, the primrose path of dalliance always leads to disaster. The wages of sin is death.

871. State's Duties as to Religion. Closely connected with the question of morals is that of religion. For religion is the strongest force making for morality. Hence for this reason, as well as because religion is a serious obligation on its citizens, the State should do all it can to further religion. It is possible to do a great deal without a State religion. Protection can be accorded against unjust attacks; certain fostering measures can be adopted; and officials can set an example of the spirit of religion.

872. Should Church and State Be United? In the abstract, the State has the obligation of professing the true religion, as each individual member of the State has that obligation. The *ideal* is a union of the true religion and the civil authority, each supplementing the other in its work for the common good. Concretely, however, it seems well-nigh impossible to realize this ideal. Where realization has been attempted by a union of Church and State, both Church and State have suffered. The Church has lost because the civil officials have tried to use the Church for selfish ends. They have assumed an authority over ecclesiastical acts and appointments which did the Church more harm than she got good from the association. On the other hand, the State has lost by having large bodies of her citizens use their civil power simply for the good of another organization. Questions which would be largely political in a State without an official religion and would be settled simply on their merits, come to be considered from the standpoint of their effect on the political influence of the Church. Taken by and large, the lesson of history points to the desirability of separation, such as we have in this country; and we should guard jealously the tradition which draws a clear line between a man's activities as a churchman and as a citizen. The mixing of certain churches and ministers in politics on the ground that some questions (such as prohibition) are moral is an insidious danger which should be frankly recognized.

873. State Has Rights. But if the State has certain duties towards its citizens, it has also certain rights.

874. Right of Taxation. One of the fundamental rights of the State is that of taxation. As the State exists for the common good, it may require the individual citizens to contribute the means necessary to accomplish this end. Here, however, we are met immediately by the difficulty—how are the contributions to be apportioned? Are taxes to be equal, or in proportion to the benefit derived, or according to the power to give? They cannot be equal, as some cannot give anything; nor can they be allotted in proportion to the good derived, as dependents get the most good, yet are utterly incapable of making any return; therefore, the only practicable and just method seems to be to exact taxes in proportion to the citizen's ability to pay. "From each according to his power, to each according to his need" is sound fiscal policy as well as true justice.

875. Obligation to Pay Taxes. Ordinarily fiscal laws bind by legal justice. Unless they are unjust or merely penal there is a grave obligation to pay taxes when demanded. But if it is customary for persons to conceal a certain percentage of their goods, then one may do this with a good conscience. Otherwise he would be paying more than his proportional share, as the levy is regulated by the expected return. A municipality, for example, which needs $500,000 to meet its legitimate expenses, fixes a tax rate which will bring this sum from the assessed property. Should it be customary to render property at one-half its real value, then the rate will be twice as high as if all property were returned at its full value. Hence, any one individual who assessed his property at its full value would be paying twice as much as the taxing authority really expected from him and intended to levy.

876. Taxes and Commutative Justice. Tax collectors who allow themselves to be corrupted, and those who bribe them sin against commutative justice and are bound to restitution.

877. Prohibition as a Right of the State. Another right of the State concerns the prohibition of certain articles. Not only has the State the right to put a prohibitive tax or tariff upon a particular article, but it may, when there is sufficient reason, entirely prohibit its use, manufacture and sale. This refers especially to certain drugs and liquors. The ethician says: *If* it be found that the privilege of using such articles is invariably abused by such a large number of persons that the good of the whole community or a large part of the whole is endangered; and *if* the use can be stopped by prohibition: then the State has a perfect right to prohibit. Whether or not these conditions are fulfilled in regard to cocaine, whiskey, and so on, must be determined by the proper authorities—in a republic by the people. No inalienable right of the individual is violated by compelling him to abstain from certain drugs.

878. The State's Right to Military Service. Again, the State has a right to require not only certain material contributions, but also personal service. This may be either civil or military, though ordinarily the question arises regarding war. As the State has a right to defend itself or to engage in a just war (as we shall see in the following chapter) and it can carry on a war only with soldiers, it may require its own citizens to undertake that service. Of course it may hire mercenaries to fight, or it may depend upon volunteers. But if the State chooses conscription, even when it could employ mercenaries or volunteers, the citizens are bound to obey. Even in time of peace compulsory military training may be necessary as a preparation for war. The advisability is to be determined by each State according to its methods of deciding such questions.

879. The State's Right to Punish. When any of these rights of the State are violated, that is, when its just laws are broken, the State may punish the offender. Punishment may be medicinal, as curing the criminal; deterrent, as tending to keep others from imitating him; and retributive, as vengeance for the outraged order. Probably the State may not punish on pure grounds of retribution, apart from all hope or need of deterring possible imitators of the crime.[7]

880. Capital Punishment. There is no disagreement as to the State's right to punish for medicinal and deterrent purposes. But there is a growing sentiment among many ethicians that the punishment may not include the taking of life. While Scholastic moralists maintain the right of the State to inflict capital punishment when it is necessary to maintain order, they welcome the tendency to limit its use to a few serious crimes, such as murder, and they recognize the authority of the State to forego the exercise of this right. Though the State has the right to mutilate criminals, as was done frequently in the past, it is probably wiser not to do so.

881. Prison Reforms. Undoubtedly, the reformation of the criminal should be kept constantly in view. The milder discipline of our prisons today[8] is a great credit to modern civilization. Advance has been made in looking upon prisons as a sort of hospitals where the socially diseased are cared for and cured, and also in recognizing that many persons previously considered criminals are really defective and should be treated in special institutions apart from the formally guilty.

[7] Cf. Rickaby, *Moral Philosophy*, p. 174.
[8] Cf. Dickens, *American Note Book;* McMaster, *History of the United States,* Vol. I, pp. 92 to 102, for prison conditions in this country previously.

882. Sentimentality in Dealing With Criminals. But while such humane standards are gratifying, there is a danger of sentimentality. There are some vicious criminals who will not respond to kindness and there are also some men who need to be deterred from committing crimes by fear of condign punishment. Such criminals whatever their intellectual status are moral defectives and if found incorrigible and not amenable to teaching or helping should be made *life prisoners*.

883. Lynching. Ordinarily the passing of judgment and the execution of punishment should be in the hands of rightly constituted State officials. Hence what is known as lynching is generally wrong. But it may sometimes happen that the regular procedure of law will be so slow that the real effect—as a deterrent —will be lost. If that be so, and a whole community, including the sober-minded and conservative, feel that swift punishment is necessary to protect society against indefinite repetition of such acts, then it may act directly; for the law derives its authority from the community. This has probably been the case at certain times in some places in the South. Yet it is open to such grave abuses, there is so much danger of acting through passion without sufficient evidence, and the multiplication of lynching in itself constitutes such a serious menace to the peace of the community, that it should be used only as a last resort. Whatever may be the theory by which it can be allowed abstractly, the moralist will be very slow to sanction lynching in the concrete.

884. Inalienable Rights of Citizens. In enforcing its demands, however, and in inflicting punishment for the violation of its laws, there are certain limits beyond which the State may not go. For while reason teaches that the individual must frequently yield his rights for the good of the whole, yet he has some inalienable rights that the State must not infringe.

885. The Citizen's Right to Physical Integrity. One of these inalienable rights in the opinion of many moralists, is the right to the physical integrity necessary that he may reproduce himself. Some States, as Indiana, would mutilate certain criminals in such a way that this would be impossible. For a thorough discussion of this question and a long weighing of pros and cons, the reader is referred to the *American Ecclesiastical Review*.[9]

886. The Right to Liberty of Opinion. Liberty of opinion, so long as it remains a mere opinion, is of course beyond State control. The State cannot tell what a man is thinking unless he gives outward expression to his thoughts. Hence, the State cannot, if it would, infringe a man's liberty of opinion.

887. Freedom of Speech and of the Press. But when a man gives outward expression to his opinions, whether by voice or pen, the State may take cognizance. And if the opinions so expressed be calculated to endanger the welfare of the community, he may be lawfully punished. Freedom of speech and of the press, the liberty of speaking or writing on any and every topic, is not an inherent right of the individual. Too much rather than too little license is allowed in this country.

888. Freedom of Worship. On one particular point, however, a man has a right to freedom so long as the way in which he exercises his right does not endanger the commonweal. That is a right to freedom of worship. Even the Catholic Church, claiming to have the whole unadulterated truth, admits the possibility of invincible ignorance. The individual who is invincibly ignorant must follow his conscience, and it would be unjust to force an external compliance that would be valueless and worse. His interior conviction is the important thing and that cannot be reached by material force.

889. Right to Freedom of Worship Not Unlimited. But such freedom of worship is not unlimited. The moment it endangers the public good, the State may vigorously suppress it. And the most tolerant governments have acted on this principle. Thus England forbade the suttee in India, and the United States prohibited the practice of polygamy among the Mormons. In the same way, certain European governments forbade the outward practice of Protestantism, others of Catholicism, at the time of the Protestant revolution. With our present experience it seems

⁹ Cf. Index.

strange that Catholics and Protestants could not live together peaceably, but at that time it was probably true that to have had any large number of citizens become Protestants in a dominantly Catholic country, or Catholics in a dominantly Protestant country, would have meant civil disorder.[10] Church and State were so united that disloyalty to one was equivalent to disloyalty to the other. In this matter of politics and religion, one could not be a heretic without being a traitor.

890. When Citizens May Rebel. If a State habitually and seriously violates the rights of its subjects to their clear and grievous hurt, or if it consistently and irremediably neglects its duties, then its subjects may, after using all legal and amicable means, at last resort to force, if they do it, not as a mere party, but as what may be considered the moral whole.[11] The reason is that all civil authority comes through the people.

891. No Right to Suffrage. But though all civil authority may come through the people, an individual has no inherent right to take part in the government. The State may limit his participation in almost any way it sees fit. At present, the tendency is to extend the part that it is possible for individuals to play, but it should be kept in mind that this is a political not an ethical question. Suffrage may justly be withheld on the score of age, sex, color, property, and almost any other reason.

892. The Duty to Vote Honestly. But while no one, whether man or woman, has a strict right to vote, once that right is conferred upon one by the State one has a duty to use it, as well as to use it honestly. There can, of course, be no question as to his duty to use his vote honestly, if he use it at all. He should not vote for those who will prostitute their office for their own selfish ends. One is not justified in voting for a bad candidate even when his election is assured, for the effect upon one's self would be too degrading. The only case in which voting for an unworthy nominee is justified is when he is the best of a bad lot.

10 Cf. art. "Toleration," in Cath. Encyc.; T. W. Allies, *Church and State.*

11 Rickaby, *Moral Philosophy,* p. 341. He there discusses a seeming contradiction between this doctrine and the Encyclical of Leo XIII.

893. The Duty Not to Refrain From Voting. Not to vote is equivalent to voting with the forces of corruption, since it is in one's power to kill one vicious vote. One cannot refuse the responsibility, for the election depends upon those who do not vote as well as upon those who do.

894. How Not Voting Affects Elections. Indeed, the effect of a good man's not voting is sometimes equivalent to doubling the corrupt votes. The votes of the vicious may sometimes have twice the power they would have if all the good men had voted. Suppose, for instance, that in a certain city there are a hundred thousand persons having the right to vote. To simplify matters, say that there are only two candidates. If everyone voted, one candidate would need 50,001 votes to be elected, but if half the people refrained from voting, then 25,001 votes would be sufficient to elect, and each vote would have been doubled.

895. The Duty to Vote in Primaries. This duty to vote applies to the primaries as well as to the final election. Indeed, the most important work is done in the primaries. For if all the candidates nominated are bad, then the good voters have no choice. They become agents of corruption in electing corrupt officials.

896. Duty of Public Officials. Those possessing political authority.are bound to exercise it for the common good. There is as much need, perhaps, to insist upon this in democracies as in autocracies, for strong pressure is frequently brought to bear upon elected officials to make them serve the selfish interests of some people. The vicious principle that to the victors belong the spoils, which so long dominated politics, is an instance in point. Men are likely to be Republicans or Democrats (or whatever may be their party affiliation) rather than Americans. Party is put above country, and a congressman who votes against the caucus of his party is visited with the same scorn as if he had betrayed the nation.

897. All Officials Must Act for the Good of the People. An elected official should be brave enough to go against his party if the good of the people demands it. Not the orders of party bosses, not the demands of powerful cliques, not even the clearly expressed will of his party should make an official waver in following his judgment as to what is right. There can be no question as to any case except the last—when he is sure that his constituents wish him to act in a particular way. A certain plausibility attaches to the argument that in a representative democracy an official should have no opinion of his own but should always act as the people wish. However, it is only a plausibility for it is practically impossible (except when a man has been elected upon a platform of one plank) to tell what the people do want. If a referendum be taken, we no longer have a representative democracy in so far as the referendum is effective, but the people taking a direct part. And even an election will get out only a fraction of the voters, who in turn are only a fraction of the people. Usually a very small but aggressive minority by a shower of telegrams, by lobbying, or in some other way succeeds in posing as the people. Hence, the wisest and best thing for a representative to do is to vote according to his own conscience. If he is confident that these convictions are opposed to the will of his constituents, he should either take the consequences of opposing them or resign. He is not justified in co-operating in what he is convinced is evil.

898. Summary. Over and above the family, then, we have the State, a union of many persons united under one supreme authority for the purpose of better securing the common temporal good. This State is natural, in the sense of being a necessary outgrowth of human association. Hence its authority comes from God, though mediately through the people. There is a divine right of kings and presidents only in this sense, that there must be *some* authority in each State. Who should possess it and how is not determined by God; and while each State is supreme, it has a supremacy strictly limited by the natural and eternal laws. These mark out certain duties of the State towards the citizens, as protection of life, property, and morals; and certain duties of citizens to the State, as paying taxes, giving military service, and (in republics) voting honestly.

SUGGESTED READINGS

1. Rickaby, *Moral Philosophy,* Pt. II, Ch. VIII.
2. Cronin, *Science of Ethics,* Vol. II, Chs. XVI, XVII, XVIII.
3. Belloc, *The Servile State,* Sec. IX.
4. Rousseau, *The Social Contract,* Bk. I, Chs. V, VI.
5. Hobbes, *Leviathan,* Pt. II, Chs. XVII, XVIII.
6. Ryan, "A New Theory of Political Sovereignty," *Cath. World,* Nov., 1917.
7. Cath. Encyc., art. "Toleration."
8. Burns, Delisle, *The Morality of Nations.*
9. Burgess, John W., *The Reconciliation of Government with Liberty,* Ch. V.
10. *Extension Magazine,* August, 1910, "Are Our Skirts Clean?"
11. Ross, "Does the Volstead Law Bind in Conscience?" *Homiletic and Pastoral Review,* May-June, 1924.
12. Ryan, "The Proper Functions of the State," "The Moral Obligation of the Civil Law," "The Duties of the Citizen," "The Rights of the Citizen," *Catholic World,* May, Oct., 1921; Jan., March, 1922.
13. McDonald, *Some Ethical Questions of Peace and War,* Pt. I, Chs. IV to VIII.

QUESTIONS

1. How did the State originate?
2. What is meant by the statement: The authority of the State comes from God?
3. Is political authority subject to moral law?
4. Should the duties of the State be limited to protection of the rights of individuals?
5. What do you think of separation of Church and State?
6. Have citizens inalienable rights against the State?
7. What is the American system of freedom of worship?
8. Is there an obligation to vote?

TWELVE: *International Ethics*

899. State of Question. So far we have discussed the rights and duties of States to their subjects and of subjects to their States. Now we take up the rights and duties existing between States. For though a State is the highest civil power, and each State (no matter how small) is supreme within itself,[1] yet they are not emancipated from mutual responsibilities. They are bound by both natural and positive law. The positive law (frequently called "international") is the result of a *contract,* expressed or implied, and its sanction is the same as that of any other contract. In Ethics, we are concerned chiefly with the natural law of nations.

900. The Natural Law Applies to States. The natural law binds nations as it binds individuals. England has no more right to seize the territory of Venezuela than an individual Englishman has to pick the pocket of an individual Venezuelan. Rights that are valid against private citizens are by the natural law valid against States other than that to which the citizen belongs. An individual citizen may sometimes for the sake of the common good be obliged to forego property or other rights at the command of his own State—or of the State in which the property is—but no other State can speak to him with such authority. Should a foreign State usurp the office of his own State, or the State in which the property is, either by attempting to transfer dominion over certain territory, or in any other way, it is violating justice as prescribed by the natural law.

901. States Are Moral Persons. There are several reasons for maintaining that certain natural rights and duties exist between States independently of custom and contract. One is that States are moral persons and just as when individual men come in contact with each other there arise automatically rights and duties, so does this happen between moral persons.

[1] For the exact meaning of the word "supremacy" here see preceding chapter.

902. State Officials Subject to the Moral Law. Again, the moral law is universal. Because each man acts in union with others or as their representative, he is not freed from his obligation to keep this law. It is true that there is a certain very evident tendency for men to act differently as individuals and as officials, whether of a government or of a corporation. The manager of a stock company will mistreat and underpay his employees in a factory as he would not think of mistreating and underpaying servants in his home; and a diplomat will lie and bully as he would never do in private life in looking after his own interests. But this does not justify such conduct. So far as reason goes, it tells us plainly that the same fundamental laws govern men as officials and as private citizens.

903. International Law Presupposes Natural Law. Furthermore, the existence of positive international law presupposes natural law, else there would be no obligation to keep an agreement or treaty. To act upon the theory that solemn treaties are mere "scraps of paper" to be torn up as soon as they cease to serve the interest of one party, is to reduce international relations to the level of a pack of jackals. There can be no permanent peace, no sense of security among nations, as long as any powerful States govern their conduct by this practical negation of the natural law.

904. States Have Duties of Justice and Charity. As in the case of individuals, the original duties of States may be resolved into those of justice and those of charity. Duties of charity are chiefly positive and indetermined. Such duties do not oblige in all cases, do not confer rights upon the other party, and their neglect involves no obligation of restitution. But this is not to say that duties of charity are optional. They oblige as sacredly as do duties of justice though their violation does not involve restitution. However, while States come under the universal law of charity, there are some distinctions between their obligations and those of individuals. The government may not freely give up for the good of others what is needed for its own citizens, since its primary duty is to look after those it represents. Again, since the State has no future life, its actions are limited to this world. The duties of justice are mainly negative and confer upon the other party a right to restitution if they are not fulfilled. They oblige always and in every case. The original rights of justice belonging to every State are: (a) the right of self-preservation and development; (b) the right of independence.

905. The State's Right of Self-Defense. Every person has a right to defend himself against unjust aggression. In the case of a State this includes the protection of its citizens, even when they are beyond its territorial dominion. Under the same head would come the right to a certain external respect for its representatives and symbols.

906. State's Rights to Self-Development. While each State has a right to development, this must always be attained with due regard to the rights of others. Territory may be acquired or markets gained, but only when the rights of one's neighbors are not violated. Over its internal affairs each State is supreme. If it wishes to admit some goods and prohibit the importation of others, to tax some and not others, to show preference to some States, that is its own affair. No other State has an inherent right to object; and of course no other State would be justified in using military force to keep open a port.

907. Intervention. Though each State has a right to independence, *intervention* may sometimes be justified or even compelled. This will be true when it is required in order to defend the rights of its own subjects. Again, it will be required by charity when a neighbor State asks for aid against unjust aggression. Still another ground for intervention would be such oppression as would give the citizens a right to rebel.

908. When Is Intervention Justified? May civilized States intervene, however, to prevent crime or to provide an adequate government where it is lacking? The answer to these questions is, Yes. But the facts in the case should be carefully scrutinized. History gives us few instances where intervention upon these alleged grounds has resulted in anything but evil to both sides. England's occupation of India and Egypt was probably justified.

Perhaps, the United States should have interfered more directly in Mexico to secure order. But for any one State or nation to imagine that it is divinely commissioned to impress its own peculiar concept of civilization upon the world—whether that be Teutonic, or Saxon, or Gallic, or Latin, or what not—is to be drunk with pride. It is simply the case of the divine right of nations instead of the divine right of kings and has just as little foundation. No nation has a right to force another to adopt what it considers a higher way of living, any more than the individual uplifter has a right to compel another individual to live according to his ideals. Only when a nation becomes a public nuisance, as it were, may another interfere.

909. Titles to New Territory. Secondary rights and duties arise from international agreements. One of the most important of these rights concerns the acquirement of new territory. The titles for such dominion are practically the same as in the case of individuals—*occupation, accretion, cession, conquest, prescription.* But the conquest will not be immediately valid, unless it is undertaken to vindicate a violated right. We say *immediately valid* because (as was noted in a previous chapter) the common good may require the continuance of a government which originated in injustice rather than the going through the throes of attempting to restore the government which would have been just had it retained its power.

910. Conditions for Binding Treaties. Treaties are international contracts, and as such follow the same principles as private contracts. The parties must be sovereign States, the matter of the treaty must be physically and morally possible, and the consent of the parties must be free, mutual, and clearly expressed. A treaty derives its binding force from the natural law requiring the keeping of faith.

911. How Vindicate a State's Rights? But what if these rights of a State in its relations with other States be violated? How are the rights to be vindicated? How is the violated order to be restored? When the rights of the individual are infringed, he may appeal to the courts of his State to adjudicate his claims. If necessary the State will use its police force to secure his rights. But there are no such courts to which States can appeal. The individual is subject to the State, and when individuals disagree it is the superior which decides. As between States, however, each is equal. There is no superior to whom they can have recourse. They are in about the same position that individuals would be in were there no stable government, no civil courts. Each must depend upon itself.[2]

912. No Court of Nations. Where individuals are brought into contact with each other without a stable government to maintain order, much violence ensues. Each man goes about armed, and each will draw upon slight provocation for fear that the other may get an advantage over him. Our own frontier communities were examples of this. Nations have done likewise. There has been no authority to maintain order among them, to secure each one's rights, to punish wrong-doing; and each one has gone about, figuratively speaking, with a sixshooter on its hip.

913. Is War Justifiable? This question of the use of force between nations, or of war, has always been a serious one for Ethics. Is war, or a "contention carried on by force of arms between sovereign States," ever justifiable? Can the individual citizen conscientiously engage in such organized slaughter, or must he absolutely refuse, though his refusal mean a blank wall and a firing squad at dawn?

914. Were the Early Christians Pacifists? Some sociologists have claimed that the early Christian Church uncompromisingly opposed war. "It was not only that the primitive church was unpatriotic," writes Dr. Stewart of Dalhousie University, Halifax; "it was violently antipatriotic; the feeling was boldly denounced as unworthy of those who had been baptized. . . . The most obvious sign of their spirit was the fierce resistance against enlistments in the Roman army; ecclesiastical penalties were inflicted upon a soldier who returned from a campaign, and at least one

[2] This is true in spite of the League of Nations and the so-called World Court, as was shown clearly in regard to the imbroglio between Italy and Ethiopia.

of the great persecutions arose from the systematic effort of the
Church to put obstacles in the way of recruiting." [3]

915. St. Martin's Scruples. Undoubtedly, this is an exaggeration, as is shown by St. Sebastian and Torquatus, Roman soldiers,
and the Thundering Legion, composed almost entirely of Christians. Nevertheless, as late as the time of St. Martin of Tours (d.
396) this question was agitating the consciences of Christians.
Soldier and the son of a soldier, St. Martin resigned upon the
eve of battle because he felt that he could not rightfully kill his
fellowman. "Caesar, until today I have served thee," said Martin
to his emperor-commander; "now permit me to serve God. I am
a soldier of Christianity and it is not lawful for me to make war."
For answer he was put in irons, and a scrupulous Christian of
today would probably fare no better at the hands of a modern
Caesar.

916. Distinction Between a Just and an Unjust War. But Martin's question was already becoming an anachronism, for since
St. Ambrose, the great Bishop of Milan (d. 397), who was the
first to write *ex professo* of Christian duties, no moralist of note
has condemned all wars absolutely. To St. Ambrose we owe the
fundamental distinction between a just and an unjust war.

917. When a War Is Just. That a war be just it is necessary that
all the moral elements of an act—object, end and circumstances
—should be good, or at least indifferent. If any one of these
elements of the act be bad, the whole situation is vitiated.

918. When Must a War Be Defensive? The end of a war must
be the protection of rights. Hence, the primary title of a State
to go to war is that the State's rights are menaced or actually
violated, and cannot in any other way be protected or repaired.
A secondary title may come from the call of another State unjustly jeopardized, or by the fact that innocent persons are oppressed and cannot otherwise be assisted.

919. When War Is Unjust. War for the acquisition of territory
which belongs to another State is simple brigandage. It is likewise unjust to wage war for personal ambition, to avert political

[3] "Is Patriotism Immoral?", *American Journal of Sociology,* March, 1917.

disaster at home, or merely to preserve the relative position of nations. A commercial war, or more accurately a war for the spread of commerce, is usually unjust. Only *unfair* exclusion from markets will justify it, and it is difficult to imagine such a case. For no State has an inherent right to trade with another State, in the sense that the other State may not justly prefer to deal elsewhere.

920. Objective Acts of War Must Be Just. Again, the object of the act (that is, the warlike actions taken in themselves) must be good, or justified by the principle of two effects following from one cause. Thus it is unjust to employ more force than necessary. This applies both to combatants and non-combatants. To give no quarter, even after the enemy has been thoroughly conquered and wishes to surrender, is murder on a large scale. To make war on non-combatants, on women and children, is unjustifiable barbarism.

921. The Barbarities of War.[4] Once the dogs of war are let loose, it is difficult to keep them within the bounds of civilized custom. The records of Sherman's march to the sea, of English conduct in the Sepoy rebellion, of our water cure and other tortures in the Philippines, of the international intervention in China during the Boxer rebellion, do not make us very proud of humanity. There is an old saying, "Scratch an Englishman and you find a barbarian," and this is equally true of the Germans, French, Italians, and Americans.

922. Circumstances of a War Must Be Just. Finally, the circumstances concretely connected with any war must be good or indifferent. And the most important circumstances are that war must be a *last* resort and that the good accomplished must outweigh the evil. It cannot be too strongly insisted upon that recourse to arms should be had only when all other measures have failed. When it is possible to settle matters satisfactorily by some other method, no matter what right has been violated, war is unjust. Judged by this standard, many wars will be looked upon as immoral. Our own civil war might have been averted but for

[4] Cf. Irwin, *The Next War.*

the firebrands on either side who kindled the passions of the North and South until they could be quenched only in blood. Probably the difficulty of the *Maine* might have been arranged diplomatically but for certain loud-mouthed "patriots." The many cases in recent history of amicable settlements of disputes prove that many other differences might have been settled so. The Venezuelan trouble, the Canadian boundary, the seal fisheries of the Northwest and many others demonstrate the superiority of peaceful to warlike measures.

923. In War Both Sides Frequently Lose. Most wars are a crude and painful way of cutting off one's nose to spite one's face. The good attained rarely, perhaps, offsets the damage even to the victor, so that few wars are really justified. After some naval maneuvers off the New England coast, Mr. Hennessy once asked Mr. Dooley who won. "I don't know who won," replied the philosopher of Archey Road, "but I know who lost—the United States Treasury lost." That sums up most real wars as well as sham ones.

924. The Fallacy of an Indemnity. Two things may be gained by war which seem to be an advantage—territory or an indemnity. Neither is really a gain, as has been demonstrated by Norman Angell in *The Great Illusion*. He points out there that an indemnity must be paid either in goods or money. If paid in goods it is equivalent to giving a bonus to foreigners to compete with home industries—certainly not a great advantage. If paid in money the nation is no richer, for money in itself is useless. Money simply represents purchasing power, and if the supply of money is increased in proportion to the store of goods, the purchasing power of any unit decreases. Assume, for instance, that there were vast stores of gold coin in the banks of Paris during the siege of 1871. What would have been the result of distributing this among the population? That the price of bread and everything else purchasable with money would have risen. To increase the area affected and transfer this gold to Germany does not change the situation. To spend it within Germany is to raise prices, not to increase purchasing power; to spend it outside is to give employment to competitors of German citizens.

925. The Fallacy of Territory. The acquisition of territory is equally futile. No nation can own territory today in the sense of getting tribute from it. Only in so far as stability of government increases the purchasing power of the inhabitants it is advantageous to acquire territory. And this stabilization results in as much benefit to other industrial nations as to the one said to "own" it. Thus, in spite of the Monroe Doctrine, it would be advantageous for us if England, or any one of the leading civilized nations, exercised a sufficient protectorate over Mexico to insure peaceful development of that country's resources. Our merchants would sell more because the Mexicans would be in a position to buy more. And we would benefit as much by England stabilizing the Mexican government as by doing it ourselves—maybe more. A few decades ago fire-eating patriots were shouting at political rallies: "Fifty-four-forty or fight." It was a catchy alliteration, but had no more political wisdom back of it than "The Old Oaken Bucket" or any other phrase picked at random. We did not get fifty-four-forty and we did not fight. But we are just as well off as if the stars and stripes flew over that strip of territory, and a great deal better off than if we had fought.

926. The Weakness of Power. Bigness of territory is no advantage to the citizens of a State individually or collectively. It is as absurd for a person to take pride in belonging to a big State as for a woman to boast of obesity. In 1912 the individual citizens of Norway, Sweden, and Switzerland were reaching as high a standard of living as those of France or Germany or Great Britain; and the national securities were selling higher than those of any of the so-called great powers.[5] Nor was bigness a protection in the great European war. England, France, Russia, Germany have suffered terribly, while small Switzerland, Holland, Denmark, have been comparatively safe. In fact, bigness would seem to be a disadvantage. The consciousness of power induced

[5] Norman Angell, *The Great Illusion,* p. XI. Read the whole of Ch. V, Pt. I, for a fuller exposition.

a pride which brought on this war, and produced such an alignment of nations that the proudest will probably be eliminated as a factor in European politics. On the other hand, the weaker nations had no such pride and escaped this horrible maelstrom. Indeed, as Professor Carver remarks: "That the meek shall inherit the earth is probably a scientific statement. It means that the unmeek, the proud, the haughty, shall be exterminated." [6]

927. Few Wars Are Just. Merely from the standpoint of the individual and victorious nation, therefore, few wars are justified. The Iron Chancellor himself saw this. "Even victorious wars," he wrote, "can only be justified when they are forced on a nation, and we cannot see the cards held by Providence so closely as to anticipate the historical development by personal calculation." [7] And when we take into consideration the whole of humanity, almost all wars are ruled out.

928. Further Limitations on War-Making. A State should sometimes refrain from making war for what would be in itself a just cause if it sees that this war, though useful in itself, will produce great damage for Christendom, or for the world at large. This is because nations are not entirely independent of each other, but form a natural society which in certain cases obliges one State to sacrifice its individual advantages to the collective and universal interests. This advanced conception of internationalism looking upon humanity as one great brotherhood and subordinating the interests of a single State to the general good of the world, was probably first worked out clearly by the Dominican, Francis Vittoria. He is quoted by Mgr. Battifol [8] as saying: "If a city cannot be retaken except at the cost of more considerable evils to the State, the devastation of many towns, the death of a great number of men, and if the reconquest will result in enmities between princes and provoke new wars, the government ought to renounce its right of going to war."

[6] *Essays in Social Justice,* p. 33.

[7] Bismarck, *Gedanken und Erinnerungen,* Vol. II, p. 93, quoted by Bernhardi, *Germany and the Next War,* p. 18.

[8] *Le Correspondant,* Oct. 25, 1914.

929. The Militarist Position. While all wars are not to be condemned, as we have seen, yet it is devoutly to be wished that their tribe may decrease. With this end in view, it is well to understand the militarist extreme and to oppose it wherever and whenever possible. According to the militarist philosophy, might is right. All life is a struggle for the survival of the fittest, and the nation that survives is right. There is bitter competition between individuals and between States that can be settled only by war. Any one nation, if unhindered, could in a few years people the world, and war is one of the ways to prevent this over-population. Further, war is the highest school of virtue. Without this supreme test, men would degenerate into mollycoddles and pussyfoots.

930. Ethically Fittest Do Not Survive Through War. In answer to such a position, it may be said that survival in such a struggle has nothing to do with fitness in an ethical sense. Wars prove nothing in the moral sphere. They merely demonstrate which side was stronger, not which side was right. Competition that culminates in war is not essential. Almost all the differences between States can be settled in other ways. There is no more reason for one State to fight another for trade, than for one city to fight another city. Military power does not bring commercial success. Every merchant knows that in buying stock he never considers the army or navy of the man trying to sell to him. All he wants to know is the price and quality of the goods. And other things being equal (things which are not affected by military power) the citizens of a non-military State can outsell the citizens of the military or naval one, since they will pay less in taxes.

931. Physically Fittest Do Not Survive Through War. Wars do not make for the survival of the fittest even in a materialistic or physical sense. On the contrary, the warlike nations are ultimately supplanted by the more peaceful ones. For it is the physically fittest who are sent into battle. The defectives of all kinds are kept at home to propagate the race, and war, therefore, becomes the process of killing the best and preserving the worst.

932. Overpopulation Need Not Induce War. Problems of population, in our present condition of civilization, need have no influence in inducing war. Any nation that is overpopulated—a point that is to be proved—can find relief in emigration. And, as has been said, it is not at all essential to its welfare that the emigration should be to its own colonies. It is mere sentiment, not sound political reason, that makes statesmen think colonies necessary. The ordinary Englishman, for instance, is neither better nor worse off because the American colonies won independence.

933. False Assumption Underlying Many Wars. As a matter of fact, most wars come from such false assumptions as that the acquisition of territory or the exacting of an indemnity are advantageous, or from a false sentiment based on still falser social psychology. Advocates of force, when driven to admit the futility of force as a means of material gain, will fall back on high-sounding phrases about national honor. There is less sense, really, in a nation going to war to avenge its violated honor than for a church to make "converts" by the sword, or for two individuals to fight a duel because one impugned the other's honesty. In the cases of the church and the duel you at least reach the offending parties, no matter how little outward conformity may have to do with real beliefs or shooting a man with one's honesty. Perhaps some day wars will be as much out of fashion as duels or religious persecutions.

934. Nations Are Not Homogeneous. War rests upon the false social psychology that nations are homogeneous, and, therefore, that what one of a nation does, or at least what officials of a nation do, the whole nation does. Really it is as absurd to lump all English, or all Germans, or all Mexicans, together as for the Chinese to lump all foreigners under the suggestive appellation of "devils." A Chinese Boxer felt that he had avenged the national honor by killing a Frenchman, though a German had done the deed, let us say, which roused his ire. We are no whit more civilized in killing Bavarians for what Prussians did, though they happen to have the same government. "The disappearance of most international hostility depends upon nothing more intricate than the realization of facts which are little more complex than the geographical knowledge which enables us to see that the anger of the yokel is absurd when he pummels a Frenchman because an Italian swindled him." [9]

935. Carlyle on War. Carlyle has put this fallacy of war very clearly: "What, speaking in quite unofficial language, is the net purpose and upshot of war? To my own knowledge, for example, there dwell and toil in the British village of Dumdrudge usually some five hundred souls. From these, by certain 'natural enemies' of the French, there are successively selected, during the French war, say, thirty able-bodied men. Dumdrudge, at her own expense, has suckled and nursed them; she has, not without difficulty and sorrow, fed them up to manhood, and even trained them to crafts, so that one can weave, another build, another hammer, and the weakest can stand under thirty stone avoirdupois. Nevertheless, amid much weeping and swearing they are selected; all dressed in red; and shipped away, at the public charges, some two thousand miles, or say only to the south of Spain; and fed there till wanted. And now to that same spot in the south of Spain, are thirty similar French artisans, from a French Dumdrudge, in like manner wending; till at length, after infinite effort, the two parties come into actual juxtaposition; and Thirty stand fronting Thirty, each with a gun in his hand. Straightway the word 'Fire' is given; and they blow the souls out of one another; and in place of sixty brisk, useful craftsmen, the world has sixty dead carcasses, which it must bury, and anew shed tears for. Had these men any quarrel? Busy as the devil is, not the smallest. They lived far enough apart; were the entirest strangers; nay, in so wide a universe, there was even, unconsciously, by commerce, some mutual helpfulness between them. How then? Simpleton! their governors had fallen out; and instead of shooting one another had the cunning to make these poor blockheads shoot." [10]

[9] Norman Angell, *The Great Illusion,* p. 317.
[10] *Sartor Resartus,* p. 133.

936. Wars Unite Nations. Nations are not homogeneous, but the way to make them approximate unity is to undertake war against them. Suppose, for instance, that Japan looks upon the exclusion of Asiatics from our States as an insult to her national honor. Does this mean that every American favors exclusion? Not at all. We know that a very large party opposes all limitation of immigration; we know that certain powerful interests want Asiatics admitted. What then is the wise thing for Japan to do? Go to war? Of course not. War will merely unite all Americans in upholding the law. Her wisest policy will be to bide her time while the Japanese in this country and their friends work by parliamentary means to secure the repeal of the law.

937. Wiser Means Than War. Or again, suppose that a high tariff is about to ruin English exporters to the United States. Should England therefore go to war? Of course not. For even supposing that England were successful, she would have destroyed the purchasing power of our citizens. The thing for her to do would be to work quietly to secure the election of the party favoring low tariff.

938. The Foolishness of Most Wars. Nations are never homogeneous, and to kill some citizens for what others did is the height of folly.[11] It would be foolish if the operation could be accomplished without injury to one's own citizens. It is the quintessence of foolishness when one's own citizens will be punished almost as much. One State trying to thrash another might very well say, like the father whipping his boy: "It hurts me more than it does you."

939. War Breeds Vice. Furthermore, war, instead of being a nursery of virtue, is a hotbed of vice. Courage, endurance, sacrifice are all developed just as well, if not better, in times of peace, and with a slighter admixture of the vices particularly prevalent among soldiers. Where did the men who give heroic examples of

11 A few years ago there was a short story called "Helen of Troy" in one of our popular magazines. Therein is related how the son of an Irish bricklayer married a beautiful Greek girl. As soon as the old man heard of it, he went out and beat up the first Greek banana vender he met. Grave and reverend statesmen frequently do about the same thing when they make war.

bravery in time of war acquire their training? Behind some grocer's counter or tending sheep. And women, as a rule, are just as brave as men, and more self-sacrificing than they, though they have not had the doubtful advantage of military experience.[12]

940. The "Interests" Favoring War. In any peace propaganda, however, there are many strong "interests" [13] that must be recognized and opposed. And first of all come the war traders. Those who engage in the sale of materials of war know that it is to their advantage to foster the military spirit. The more one nation spends on preparation, the more the others are forced to spend. It is an endless chain. A few individuals are enriched, but the vast

---

[12] The following letter to the *Manchester Guardian,* which appeared at the time of the Boer War, brought out very clearly the weakness of the "school of virtue" argument:

"Sir: I see that 'The Church's Duty in Regard to War' is to be discussed at the Church Congress. This is right. For a year the heads of our Church have been telling what war is and does—that it is a school of character; that it sobers men, cleans them, strengthens them, knits their hearts; makes them brave, patient, humble, tender, prone to self-sacrifice. Watered by 'war's red rain,' one Bishop tells us, virtue grows; a cannonade, he points out, is an 'oratorio'—almost a form of worship. True; and to the Church men look for help to save their souls from starving for lack of this good school, this kindly rain, this sacred music. Congresses are apt to lose themselves in wastes of words. This one must not, surely cannot, so straight is the way to the goal. It has simply to draft and submit a new Collect for war in our time, and to call for the reverent but firm emendation, in the spirit of the best modern thought, of those passages in Bible and Prayer-Book by which even the truest Christians and the best of men have at times been blinded to the duty of seeking war and ensuring it. Still man's moral nature cannot, I admit, live by war alone; nor do I say with some that peace is wholly bad. Even amid the horrors of peace you will find little shoots of character fed by the gentle and timely rains of plague and famine, tempest and fire; simple lessons of patience and courage conned in the school of typhus, gout, and stone; not oratorios, perhaps, but homely anthems and rude hymns played on knife and probe in the long winter nights. Far from me to 'sin our mercies' or to call mere twilight dark. Yet dark it may become; for remember that even these poor makeshift schools of character, these second-bests, these halting substitutes for war—remember that the efficiency of every one of them, be it hunger, accident, ignorance, sickness, or pain, is menaced by the intolerable strain of its struggles with secular doctors, plumbers, inventors, schoolmasters, and policemen. Every year thousands who would once have been braced and steeled by manly tussles with smallpox or diphtheria are robbed of that blessing by the great changes made in our drains. Every year thousands of women and children must go their way bereft of the rich spiritual experience of the widow and orphan."

[13] During the Spanish-American War a conundrum was current, "Why is the war like brandy?" The answer was, "Because it is good for Cramps." Cramps was a big shipbuilding firm that had large government contracts to construct battleships.

majority suffer from such enormous expenditure in unproductive ways.

941. Government-Owned Munition Plants Only a Partial Solution. Perhaps the problem would be partly solved by the various governments taking over the munition factories. But the solution is problematical and at best would be merely partial. For only a completely socialized State could take over all the industries directly and indirectly depending upon war.

942. Yellow Journalism and War.[14] A hardly less important expression of commercialism versus peace is found in yellow journalism. Newspapers recognize that to sell they must exaggerate. As a consequence they are absolutely conscienceless in dressing up reports of differences between nations. It was probably yellow journals, with their melodramatic tales of Spanish treachery and their cry of "Remember the *Maine*," that brought on the Spanish-American War at that particular time. Had they reported that incident impartially, had they cautioned prudence and urged an investigation, we should most likely not have engaged in the conflict when we did. Again, there is in the popular mind induced by this irresponsible journalism a certain spread-eagleism, an attitude that sees no fault in one's own nation, but faults innumerable in others—a loud-mouthed patriotism that is ready to call every man a traitor who happens to advocate peaceful methods. A few hours in looking over a file of the newspapers of 1861-65 will bring home to anyone the part of these false patriots. Looking back on that struggle from the vantage point of fifty years, we can see that the real patriots were those who tried to settle the difference between the North and South by parliamentary means, and those who resolutely set themselves against unfounded tales of cruelty and oppression. But in those papers we can read how each side accused the other of what neither would now believe. We are proud of the courage and gallantry of those who were our fellow-countrymen, whether they wore the blue or the gray. Yet, under the tutelage of the press, many (perhaps

---

[14] For the way in which each side was fed falsehoods in the European War, cf. Ponsonby, *Falsehoods in Wartime.*

most) persons in each section believed that the other was a military despotism bent on its destruction, murdering prisoners, making special war on women, children, and the sick.

943. Southerners Were Called Assassins. Out of a multiplicity of examples, we shall select one from the North and one from the South. Thus the correspondent of the St. Louis Democrat, writing from Booneville, July 25, 1861, said: "At 3 o'clock in the morning they [Union volunteers under a Captain Cook] were attacked by 100 mounted men and 300 infantry, with two small cannon. The sentinels were shot down, and the guns taken possession of before the sleeping men awoke. Then the butchery commenced. 'No mercy to the Dutch' was the cry (most of the home guards were Germans), and the defenseless men were assassinated without mercy. . . .

944. Southerners Were Called Murderers. "At this moment there appeared suddenly upon the bloody field a company of our own men, led by Captain Elsner, and they gave a most destructive fire upon the thick crowd of murderers. . . .

945. Southerners Accused of Murdering an Aged Judge. "The state of things in Benton, Pettis, and Morgan counties is dreadful. The bands of rebel marauders and thieves steal horses, stock, provisions, and everything they like. The venerable Judge Tirey, 72 years old, a strong Union man and a slaveholder himself, was tied to a tree by Jackson's marauders and shot like a mad dog. His body was literally torn to pieces."

946. No One Now Believes These Tales. Would anyone now speak of Southern troops as murderers, assassins, horse thieves? Would anyone believe that they shot defenseless old men in cold blood and afterwards mutilated their bodies? Today we can see that the men who wrote and published such stories were really not the truest patriots. Rather those who cautioned calmness, who asked for evidence, who gave the enemy credit for sincerity and chivalry, were the real friends of the country.

947. Northerners Were Accused of Intending to Enslave Southerners. Side by side with these Northern charges, place this specimen of Southern journalism. "The Southern press should keep before the people of the South and of the world the astounding and unparalleled fact that the army which invaded Virginia brought with them 30,000 handcuffs which were taken from the spoils of the enemy. This surpasses all that we have heard of Russian and Austrian despotism. It is almost impossible to realize that in the United States, boasting itself as the freest and the most enlightened of all nations, the most deliberate, inhuman and atrocious plan should have been formed to degrade and enslave a free people of which there is any record in this or any other age." This is quoted in *Leslie's* (1861), p. 120, from the *Louisville Courier's* account of the First Manassas. It is put under the caption "Rebel Exaggeration." Yet just below, without any hint that they might be exaggerations, are detailed accounts of "Rebel Barbarities at Bull Run."

948. Yellow Journalism Tends to Grow Worse. This evil of yellow journalism tends to grow worse and worse. New forms of exaggeration, new appeals to this false patriotism must be constantly devised; for as one form grows stale it becomes useless from a journalistic standpoint. And so one fosters the other. The public, weary of the drab dullness of everyday life, demands of the newspaper a certain amount of sensationalism and grows more rampant the more it gets.

949. What Is the Individual to Do When His State Goes to War? But if the properly constituted authorities of any State have engaged in war, what is the individual citizen to do? Is he to institute an investigation to determine which side is right? Ordinarily, the private citizen is to presume that his country is right. Here as much as any place applies the principle that in doubt one stands for authority. International problems are so complicated, and the real facts of any case are so hard to get at, that usually one cannot arrive at practical certainty by any other method.

950. When the Citizen Should Not Support His Country. Yet this is very far from accepting the chauvinistic motto: "My country, right or wrong." "Yet how are we going to escape it unless we boldly say that whether in a particular case a citizen should support his country or not depends entirely upon what his country is doing? To say this means a thorough revision of many of our patriotic mottoes. It means a revision of that motto which so often passes as a truism, the motto so often quoted from Lord Strathcona, that every man's duty is to prepare himself to defend his country. Does not any healthy conscience at once protest that everything turns upon whether his particular country is worthy to be defended? If we think for a moment of countries which are not in the least worthy of defense, countries on whose behalf it were a thousand pities that any honest man's blood should ever flow, do we not realize that the very opposite of our motto may well be the case? It is true, in a sense, that a soldier's first duty is obedience, but if even a Death's Head Hussar had turned his sword on the German lieutenant who shot Edith Cavell, should we not feel that Death's Head Hussars retain some element of nobility? . . .

951. Patriotism Does Not Mean a Total Surrender of Individual Judgment. "But in repudiating the formulas of a pagan patriotism we do not repudiate patriotism itself any more than we repudiate family affection when we say that a dutiful son need not support his father in a course of crime. A man has duties to all the world, but he has special duties to his own flesh and blood, just because the ties of natural feeling enable him to serve his family with an effectiveness which he can show nowhere else. Thus, too, the members of a single nation, united by bonds no less fundamental than the bonds of a household, can do their best work for mankind by developing their nation along its own line of progress, drawing forth its special powers, fulfilling its special function in the world commonwealth. But in the one case as in the other, no duty is more urgent than that of rebuking the faults of those for whom we chiefly care. It was not Lord North when he screamed about loyalty to the flag, it was Lord Chatham when he blessed the American arms and prayed that some great disaster might overtake his country, who was the true British

patriot. And the day is surely coming when Karl Liebknecht will
be revered by the Germans as the Fatherland's most genuine
son."

952. Prospects for a Lasting Peace. It was the dream of the
Middle Ages to reach this system [15] by granting a certain power
of arbitration to the Bishop of Rome. Men's passions proved too
strong for such a check, and nationalism won a far-reaching
victory when the representative of France struck Boniface VIII
in the face with his mailed fist. Whatever influence the papacy
had heretofore exercised as a peacemaker in European politics
vanished almost completely. Nor did the attempt of Benedict
XV to revive it seem to have been successful.[16] May we dare hope,
nevertheless, that as the State developed out of the family, so an
honorable and effective League of Nations may ultimately come
to be?

SUGGESTED READINGS

1. Norman Angell, *The Great Illusion*, preface.
2. Bernhardi, *Germany and the Next War*, Ch. III.
3. Herbert L. Stewart, "Is Patriotism Immoral?" *American Journal of Sociology*, March, 1917.
4. William Hard, "Traitors," *The New Republic*, Nov. 24, 1917.
5. Charles Macksey, "War," in the Cath. Encyc.
6. Cronin, *Science of Ethics*, II, Ch. XIX.
7. Rickaby, *Moral Philosophy*, Pt. II, Ch. VIII.
8. Charles Plater, *A Primer of Peace and War*, the whole book, but especially Pt. IV.
9. McDonald, *Some Ethical Questions of Peace and War*, Pt. II, Chs. I, II, IV, V, VI.
10. Stratmann, *The Church and War*.
11. Eppstein, *The Catholic Tradition of the Law of Nations*.

QUESTIONS

1. Discuss the saying: "My country, right or wrong!"
2. Can a State wage an unjust war?
3. If a State may go to war unjustly, should citizens take a blanket oath to support their country in any war it may declare?

[15] *I.e.,* a system of international responsibility.
[16] Cf. *Atlantic Monthly*, Nov., 1917.

4. Are all acts against an enemy justified in war?
5. From an ethical standpoint, which deserves greater respect from the citizenry, the army or the police force?
6. What real advantages can a nation gain through war?
7. Discuss the statement: "Until human nature changes, wars are inevitable."

THIRTEEN: *Conclusion*

953. Summary of Whole Book. We have now reached the end of our discussion of Ethics. We began with establishing the fact that God was man's ultimate end, and the consequent distinction between good and bad as what leads man to or away from that end respectively; from that we went on to discuss duty, and law as making duty concrete; then came a consideration of individual Ethics as being the relations of man to God and of his duties to himself; finally we discussed social Ethics as embracing all the rights and duties of men in their relations with other men, both as individuals and as groups, either in the family or in the State.

954. Social Ethics Becoming More Important. As we look back over this discussion, there is one fact which stands out with ever increasing clearness as we proceed—the fact that Social Ethics is beginning to play a more and more important part. This is coming about in two ways. Partly it is that the increasing complexity of human relations is constantly producing new duties of one individual to another. Partly, too, it is because we realize that no individual can fulfill all his duties without the assistance of thousands of persons—persons whom he may never have seen.

955. New Social Sins Are Being Recognized. Professor Edward A. Ross has worked out very strikingly how society is always finding new kinds of sin. Even the youngest of us can remember when certain political practices now generally reprobated were widely tolerated. Buying and selling votes was considered almost legitimate in the early part of the nineteenth century. In President Jackson's time the theory that the government belonged to the political party which happened to be elected was so firmly believed that no one objected to the principle. The same thing is true of other relations. Stock watering, for instance, until very recent times was looked upon as entirely lawful. The most sincere Christians had no hesitation in accepting enormous

354

profits in this way. It was not that the wealthy men who sat in the front pews were hypocrites. They were not ashamed that they had made fortunes in this way, because they did not consider it anything to be ashamed of. A few generations ago an employer was thought to fulfill all his duties by giving what the employees were willing to take. If he could get them to work for less than would really support them, he considered himself lucky, not sinful, and the public conscience did not rebuke him.

956. Men Are Their Brothers' Keepers. Instance after instance of this change in public opinion regarding moral questions might be given. Many pages could be filled with illustrations. This increasing tenderness of conscience is one of the bright points of the twentieth century. Men seem to be coming to realize more and more clearly that they are their brothers' keepers. We are beginning to see that there have been many priests and Levites, but few Samaritans.

957. Preventive Philanthropy Coming Into Vogue. But there has been a further awakening of conscience during recent years. Enormous sums have always been given in charity, such as that performed by the Good Samaritan. When a man was seen to be dying from neglect, pious hands could usually be found to give him help. Today, however, we see that this is not enough. Not only must we help men who have been set upon by robbers —we must prevent the robbing. One great achievement of the twentieth century has been the rapid development of preventive philanthropy. Previous generations have been satisfied with helping men when they were in need; today the ideal is to keep them from getting into such a condition.

958. The Modern Good Samaritan. The modern edition of the Good Samaritan, therefore, is not content with taking up the man who has been set upon by robbers and paying his hospital expenses. He wishes also to police the road from Jericho to Jerusalem, in order to keep the robbers from injuring other travelers. The modern philanthropist is not satisfied with helping a poor woman feed her children because her husband's wages are not sufficient to meet the family budget. He wishes to raise the husband's wages to the proper sum. Modern workers realize that it is as much a duty of charity to guard machinery, to maintain sanitary factory conditions, as it is to take care of orphans after the neglect of these precautions has robbed them of their parents.

959. Co-operation Necessary to Fulfill Duties. But there is a still further delicacy of conscience coming into being. We are beginning to see now that no matter how keenly any individual realizes his social duties and no matter how strongly he desires to fulfill them, he cannot do so without the co-operation of others. The manufacturer may wish to pay living wages, but he cannot do so unless his competitors are willing to do likewise. His hands and the hands of all good and conscientious employers in that particular line of industry will be tied by one unscrupulous man. If he is to do his objective duty, he must find some way of coercing all others to do theirs.

960. Consumers Need Help to Live Up to Obligations. Again, the purchaser of goods is bound not to co-operate in injustice by buying goods made under unjust conditions. But he cannot fulfill this obligation unless he can compel the manufacturers and retailers to maintain good conditions.

961. Morality Must Be Social as Well as Individual. Not only is each man his brother's keeper, but he cannot fulfill the obligation of this relation unless all others fulfill theirs. There was a time when the emphasis of the ethician was principally upon the individual. It was assumed that if he wanted to do what was right he could. The main thing, therefore, in the mind of the moralists was to convince the individual that he had a duty. Now we are coming to see that this is really a shallow view of things. No man is sufficient unto himself. Not only must the individual be willing to do his duty, but he must make all others willing to do theirs. We are members one of another. No one member can by itself fulfill its own peculiar functions properly. Co-operation is necessary. It is the old story of the hands and eyes and brain and stomach over again. Each must do its part properly in order that each of the others can perform its function.

962. Legislation and Morality. Now the only way this can be accomplished is through legislation and public opinion. It is not that we can make a man good by act of parliament. Those who advocate social legislation do not believe in its power to change the heart of man. But they do think, and rightly, that even material justice is something. If a man who wants to murder another is kept from doing so by the police, there is that much gained. The object of his attempt or hatred is about as well off as if the fear of God had been put into his would-be murderer's heart.

963. Importance of Legislation. And so the place of legislation in Ethics is coming to be larger and larger. It does not remove the need of the preacher, but it supplements his work. And legislation of the right sort will at least enable those of good will to do what they should. Without legislation, even the right-minded could not fulfill their objective duties.

964. Today's Contribution to Ethics. This, then, is the great contribution of modern times to the science of Ethics. First, an increasing realization of the neighborliness of man—a keener perception of the fact that each one is the keeper of everyone else. And secondly, the further realization that these responsibilities cannot be fulfilled by merely individual effort.

965. Your Duty. I would leave you, therefore, at the end of this study of Ethics with keener consciences as regards both individual and social duties. I would dare hope that you have come to understand the place of man in the universe and in society better than you did, and that you have from this study appreciated more fully certain duties incumbent upon you. And I would dare to hope that you will have come to see that the duty of everyone is to improve the condition of society to such an extent that material wrong-doing will not be forced upon anyone by reason of the social co-operation into which he must enter. Realize your duty to help on with might and main the progress of social regeneration. If God has given you talents, He will require an account of them. Do not sit with idle hands while there is so much work to be done. Do not draw into a narrow selfish circle. Get out into the busy marts of men; go where they congregate; throw yourself into life in its intensest point, and make your impress upon it—the impress of a courageous, right-minded, wise and thoroughly instructed man or woman. Be a doer of the Word, not a hearer only.

QUESTIONS

1. Which do you think is more important, individual or social Ethics?
2. Is legislation necessary to enable individuals to live ethically?
3. Name two ethico-social problems that you think should have been solved after nineteen hundred years of Christianity.

LITERATURE

References on particular points will be found at the end of each chapter. Here are indicated some of the best treatises dealing with the whole, or a large part of the field of ethics. The Catholic Encyclopedia has bibliographies after articles on various ethical subjects. Other lists will be found in Baldwin, *Dictionary of Philosophy and Psychology,* especially under articles "Ethical Theories," "Ethics." Unfortunately, most of the works by Scholastic authors are not available in English.

WORKS NOT IN ENGLISH BY SCHOLASTIC AUTHORS: Meyer, *Institutiones Juris Naturalis* (Freiburg, 2nd ed. 1906); Costa-Rossetti, *Philosophia Moralis* (Innsbruck, 2nd ed. 1886); Castelein, *Institutiones Philosophiae Moralis et Socialis* (Brussels, 1899); Gutberlet, *Ethik und Naturrecht* (Munster, 3rd ed. 1901); Zigliara, *Philosophia Moralis* (Lyons, 3rd ed. 1880); Liberatore, *Institutiones Ethicae et Juris Naturalis* (Prato, 7th ed. 1880); Russo, *Praelectiones Philosophiae Moralis* (1891); Stoeckl, *Lehrbuch der Philosophie* (Mainz, 7th ed. 1892); Cathrein, *Moralphilosophie* (Freiburg, 4th ed. 1904); Ude, *Ethik* (Freiburg im Breisgau, 1912).

The works of the great theologians, though using revelation as well as reason, will be found very helpful: DeLugo, *De Justitia et Jure* and *Responsio Moralis* (Paris, 1868-1891); Liguori, *Theologia Moralis* (Rome, 1905); Ballerini, *Theologia Moralis* (Rome, 1877); Noldin, *Compendium Theologiae Moralis* (n. d.); Lehmkuhl, *Theologia Moralis* (St. Louis, 1902).

WORKS IN ENGLISH BY SCHOLASTIC AUTHORS: Joseph Rickaby, *Moral Philosophy* (N. Y., 1888); Rickaby, *Aquinas Ethicus* (N. Y.); Cronin, *Science of Ethics* (Dublin, 1909); Brosnahan, *Digest of Lectures in Ethics*

(Baltimore, 1912); The Catholic Encyclopedia; Rickaby, *Oxford Conferences* (N. Y.). *The Ecclesiastical Review* and the *Homiletic and Pastoral Review* have numerous invaluable discussions of moral questions scattered through numbers; Koch-Preuss, *Handbook of Moral Theology* (5 vols., 1924); Henry Davis, *Moral and Pastoral Theology* (N. Y., 1935).

WORKS BY NON-SCHOLASTIC AUTHORS: Martineau, *Types of Ethical Theory* (Oxford, 1886); Green, *Prolegomena to Ethics* (Oxford, 1883, 5th ed. Oxford, 1906); Sidgwick, *Methods of Ethics* (London, 1890); Spencer, *Principles of Ethics* (N. Y., 1897); Stephen, *Science of Ethics* (N. Y., 1882); Paulsen, *System der Ethik* (Berlin, 1894); Ladd, *Philosophy of Conduct* (N. Y., 1902); Mezes, *Ethics, Descriptive and Explanatory* (N. Y., 1901); Paley, *Moral Philosophy;* Wundt, *Ethics;* Janet, *Theory of Morals* (N. Y., 1892); *Moral Theology,* Hall & Hallock (N. Y., 1924).

INDEX

Numbers refer to paragraphs

Numbers refer to paragraphs

Numbers refer to paragraphs